MARINE REEF AQUARIUM HANDBOOK

Robert J. Goldstein, Ph.D.

With 170 photographs

Illustrations by Michele Earle-Bridges

BARRON'S

Dedication

This book resulted from the tireless instruction and encouragement of my reef hobby mentor, Jeff Voet of Raleigh, North Carolina. Blame him.

All inquiries should be addressed to:
Barron's Educational Series, Inc.
250 Wireless Boulevard
Hauppauge, New York 11788

International Standard Book No. 0-8120-9598-7

Library of Congress Catalog Card No. 96-38130

Library of Congress Cataloging-in-Publication Data
Goldstein, Robert J. (Robert Jay), 1937–   .
       Marine reef aquarium handbook / Robert J. Goldstein.
           p.   cm.
       Includes bibliographical references (p. 184) and index.
       ISBN 0-8120-9598-7
       1. Marine aquariums. 2. Coral reef animals.
   3. Marine aquarium fishes. 4. Marine invertebrates as pets.
   I. Title.
   SF457.1.G63   1997
   639.34′2—dc21   96-38130
                                                              CIP

Printed in Hong Kong

987

Photo Credits

Zig Leszczynski: inside back cover, back cover (Tailed Sea Slug), (Clown Anemonefish), (Pacific Cleaning Shrimp), pages 13, 65, 67, 82, 90 top, 90 bottom, 92 top, 99 top right, 109, 122, 123 top, 123 bottom, 124 left, 124 right, 125 top left, 125 top right, 125 bottom left, 125 bottom right, 126, 133 top left, 133 top right, 133 center left, 133 bottom left, 133 bottom right, 135 top, 135 bottom, 136 top, 136 center, 136 bottom, 137 top left, 137 top right, 137 bottom left, 137 bottom right, 142, 143 bottom, 144 top, 144 bottom, 146, 149 left, 149 right, 159 bottom, 160 top left, 160 top right, 160 bottom, 162, 164 top, 164 bottom, 165, 166 top, 166 bottom, 168 top, 169, 171 top, 171 bottom; Dr. Lucy Bunkley-Williams: back cover (Large Giant Clam), pages 114 top left, 114 top right, 115, 116, 143 top, 145 top; Sallie Boggs: page 117; Chris Huxley—Courtesy St. Lucia Tourist Board: pages 1, 15, 119; Courtesy of Barbados Tourism Authority: page 2; Courtesy of Singapore Tourist Promotion Board: back cover (Orange Cup Coral), page 3. All other photos by Robert J. Goldstein.

Cover Photos

Front cover: Boulder Coral, *Montastrea*; inside front cover: Tree Soft Coral, *Litophyton arboreum;* inside back cover: Bicolor Dottyback, *Pseudochromis paccagnellae;* back cover from top left to top right: Orange Cup Coral, *Tubastraea* sp.; Tailed Sea Slug, *Philinopsis gardineri;* Clown Anemonefish, *Amphiprion ocellaris;* Pacific Cleaning Shrimp, *Stenopus tenuirostris;* Mushroom Polyp Coral, *Rhodactis* sp.; (Center) Large Giant Clam, *Tridacna maxima.*

Acknowledgments

Many generous people reviewed chapters and good-naturedly offered constructive advice and information. Chapter 1, on natural reefs, was reviewed by Dana Riddle; Chapter 3, on water quality, by John Ferrell Kuhns of Aquascience Research Group; Chapter 5, on the nitrogen and carbon cycles, by Stan Brown; Chapter 9, on UV sterilizers and ozonizers, and Chapter 11, on light and lighting, by Stan Brown and Dana Riddle; Chapter 12, on plants, by Dr. Rick Searles of Duke University and Dr. Steven Miller of the National Undersea Research Center; Chapter 13, on corals, by Stan Brown, Patrick MacMillan, and Dana Riddle; Chapter 14, on coral diseases, by Dr. Ernest H. Williams, Jr. of the University of Puerto Rico and Dr. Esther C. Peters of Tetra Tech, Inc.; Chapter 16 on molluscs by Dr. Ron Shimek; Chapter 22, on care and breeding of fish by John Tullock and J.R. Shute; and Chapter 23, on diseases of fish, by Dr. Ed Noga of North Carolina State University School of Veterinary Medicine.

Contents

Preface

The marine aquarium hobby had its beginning in the 1950s, when, with the introduction of synthetic sea salt mixes, clownfish and their host anemones, damsels, butterfly fish, and angelfish were first widely kept in captivity. It was another twenty years before coral reef aquariums became popular, following the introduction of actinic light, trickle filtration, and finally the development of the Berlin system of light, live rock, and protein skimmer total water quality management. For the origins of successful reef aquariums, we must thank the pioneer Dietrich Steuber, mentor of today's leaders, Alf Jacob Nilson, Peter Wilkins, Charles Delbeek, and Julian Sprung.

The hobby is new. Other equally important and still active pioneers are Walter Adey, Bruce Carlson, Larry Jackson, Martin Moe, Mike Paletta, George Smit, Dana Riddle, Albert Theil, John Tullock, and J.E.N. Veron. References in the back of the book will identify many other contributors to specific areas.

Corals in captivity offer unending surprises, new types of animals that never before could be kept alive and can now be propagated, and new opportunities to understand a few of the myriad interactions on a coral reef.

Merulina *are leafy corals with flaring or concentric plates.*

Chapter One
Natural Reefs

Coral reefs are magical marine islands and submerged cities populated by myriad bizarre invertebrates and almost invisible plants. Coral animals live everywhere, from the Arctic to the Antarctic oceans, but usually build reefs only where the water is crystal clear, warm, nutrient poor, and within a narrow range of oceanic salinity.

Corals are of two ecological types, those that rely on a symbiotic relationship with algae (hermatypic corals) and those that do not (ahermatypic corals). The latter obtain their nutrition the old-fashioned way, by capturing minute animals (zooplankton) and plants (phytoplankton) carried in the water column. These corals need no other food source, and they can live where light does not reach, as inside caves and at great depths.

Hermatypic corals require light for their symbiotic algae, and can live only where adequate light is available. They are most abundant in shallow water and never occur in caves. Hermatypic corals derive a very small proportion of their nutrition by capturing plankton. The bulk of hermatypic coral nutrition is supplied by the waste products of the symbiotic algae contained in their tissues. Using light as an energy source and waste ammonia of the coral as the principal nutrient, these symbiotic algae manufacture and excrete excess amino acids and carbohydrates, which are then taken up by the host coral.

The algae are called zooxanthellae. Their photosynthetic activities also draw dissolved calcium from the surrounding water and the coral subsequently excretes it as calcium carbonate. Hermatypic corals, in concert with their internal zooxanthellae, are among the most important builders of coral reefs, but not the only ones.

Corals contribute only part of the coral reef. Calcareous red, brown, green, and blue-green reef algae are reef builders. These algae produce calcium carbonate that provides stiffening of their tissues,

Red sponges and soft corals bedeck Anse Chastanet coral reef at St. Lucia attracting divers and snorkelers to the coral covered slopes bathed in azure Caribbean waters.

Deepwater sponges and corals, somber gray in the dark blue depths, reveal brilliant reds and golds under stroboscopic light. Coral reef at Barbados, West Indies.

enabling them to withstand surge and predators. In some cases the calcium carbonate outweighs the algal protoplasm. Red algae are responsible for massive structures on reef tops called ridges, and for most of the cementing deposits between stony corals everywhere. While reef algae may go unnoticed by snorkelers and divers, without them there would be no tangs or parrotfish, or coral reefs as we know them.

Early coral reefs date back about 50 million years when the herbivorous surgeonfish or tangs first appeared. Modern reefs are less than five million years old, coinciding with the appearance of the coral grinding parrotfish.

No living reef today is more than 5,000 years old, when the seas rose and temperatures warmed after the last ice age 18,000 years ago. The skeletons of older reefs, uplifted on volcanic islands around the world, are evidence of previous warm periods between ice ages.

Today's coral reefs appear hard as rocks, but are as ephemeral as sandy beaches. Storms batter and destroy branching coral forests unprotected by barriers or depth, while massive corals flourish. No matter the depth or location, the steady erosion of all corals by boring worms, snails, clams, and the peculiar fish that live among them is more subtle and important than the dramatic and temporary destructive power of storms.

Reef Classification

For all their similarities around the world, coral reefs are the product of both the creatures that build reefs and the oceanic forces that mold and erode them. Reefs associated with continents, such as the Florida-Belize-Honduras barrier reef and Australia's Great Barrier Reef, are called *shelf reefs*.

Reefs that grow upon mid-oceanic islands, undersea mountains, and oceanic volcanoes, such as the Hawaiian islands, are called *oceanic reefs*. *Atolls*, such as Johnston and Etawetok, are circular reefs that have continued to grow along the rims of volcanoes or mountains that have slowly been submersed by a falling sea floor or a rising ocean level. Atolls are abundant in the tropical Pacific and are uncommon in the tropical Atlantic.

A *barrier reef* is a massive outer reef that protects a large area from the battering of the open ocean. A barrier reef might be narrow (a hundred feet from one side to the other) or vast (a half mile across). The outer edge might gradually drop off to a shallow plain or suddenly and dramatically drop straight down into deep water. On an outer continental shelf, the drop might be to perhaps 150 feet. Barrier reefs on an oceanic volcanic island might drop off 300 feet to the lowest depth at which hermatypic corals can survive, yet the slope of the mountain continues another 1,000 feet to the abyss. If the coral reef drop-off is almost vertical, the outer edge of this reef is called a wall.

Reefs inshore of the barrier reef and in shallower water are called *fringing reefs*. An atoll surrounding a lagoon can be called both a barrier reef and a fringing reef. Small and scattered fringing reefs of an acre or so protected by a more seaward barrier or fringing reef are called *patch reefs*.

A *bank reef* is a shallow water reef that has grown upon an elevated plain or a shallow part of a continental shelf. Many islands and reefs in the northern Caribbean have developed upon the extensive limestone Bahamas Bank. A deep hole (blue hole) in a bank occurs when the roof of a vast cave collapses to the limestone floor below.

Some southern Caribbean volcanic islands such as Bonaire have oceanic barrier reefs close to shore whose walls drop off rapidly into very deep water.

Reef Habitats

The outer area of a reef may face vast open reaches of ocean. During storms, great swells crash upon and destroy the more fragile corals. This part of the reef fronting on the ocean is the *reef front* or *fore reef*. The top of the reef, most exposed to wind, tides, and intense heat and ultraviolet rays, is the *reef crest*. The shallow, shoreward, quiet area behind the reef crest is the *back reef*. Closer inshore of the back reef there may be continuous fringing reefs or isolated patch reefs.

Because the reef zones are exposed to the elements in different ways, they are colonized by different corals, noncoral invertebrates, and algae.

Corals living near the surface often have pigments that block ultraviolet radiation that might damage their tissues. Their zooxanthellae photosynthesize mostly in the red range.

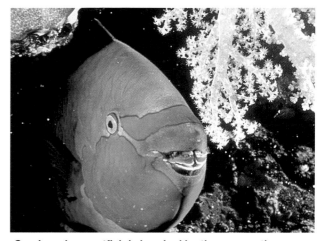

Gaudy male parrotfish is brushed by the spongy tissues of a soft coral at a coral reef in the clear tropical Pacific waters off Singapore.

Deep water corals don't receive much red light, as its energy is largely depleted close to the surface. Some deepwater corals have pigments that shift high energy blue light to lower energy green and yellow wavelengths (see Chapter 11) so that even at these depths their zooxanthellae can photosynthesize. Other deepwater corals are somehow capable of harnessing the extremely weak red light that manages to reach these depths.

Reef areas exposed to moderate sea wave action and bright light are colonized by fast-growing but brittle staghorn and elkhorn *(Acropora)* corals. During violent storms, the *Acropora* forests are battered into fragments that both grow back and also become hard substrata for other corals to colonize. On the fore reef, the pounding oceanic swells do not allow growth of delicate staghorn corals. Instead, surge-tolerant boulder types are abundant. Boulder corals also thrive in the equally violent shore zone.

Calcareous algae also adapt to the different zones. Encrusting coralline red algae

Fossil coral reef on Bonaire, Dutch West Indies, towers above present day sea level.

grow as sheets on exposed rock, while upright reds and greens grow where the surge is moderated.

Stoplight parrotfish (Sparisoma viride) feed on coral rubble near the shore in Bonaire.

Nutrients

Plant nutrients are scarce in tropical ocean water far away from rivers and land runoff. Some nutrients are delivered to well-lighted surface waters (the photic zone) when deep currents are diverted upward by submerged mountains or rock outcrops, or crash into another current of different energy and temperature. These swirling eddies disturb the sediments, releasing accumulated minerals that are swept upward into surface waters.

Coral reef lagoons are often far more richly populated with corals, algae, and other animals, compared with reefs facing open ocean waters. That's because the lagoon inhabitants not only use sparse incoming nutrients, but also retain and recycle the nutrients already there. Fish consume attached algae almost as fast as these plants grow, and because almost all the fish are coral reef residents rather than transients, their wastes remain within the immediate reef vicinity. On an outside reef, those wastes will be partly dispersed, but in a lagoon they are far less diluted by currents. Many of the herbivorous tangs, in particular, are also coprophagous, consuming the droppings of other fish as these wastes fall through the water column, then passing them through the long intestines for further biological degradation. For fish that eat plants and plant debris (detritus), tangs provide another round of digestion of the microbes that live and feed on these plant particles.

The coral rubble from storms grows microalgae. This rubble is consumed, ground up, and used as a food source by parrotfish. Their droppings contribute to reef sand used by sediment-burrowing microinvertebrates and microbes (infauna). Very few nutrients are exported, and reefs grow ever larger with time.

Chapter Two
Basic Equipment

Aquarium

The two options for a home reef tank are glass or acrylic plastic. Advantages of acrylic are its glistening beauty, ease of molding to any shape with polished corners or no corners at all, beautiful matching cabinet stands, frequently built-in fanned lighting fixtures and filtration compartments, and lighter weight. Disadvantages are numerous and important. Acrylic is more expensive. The curved front panel or flat hexagon and octagon shaped acrylic tanks, while pretty in the store, distort or repeat images to distraction. Periodically the inside front wall of the tank must be cleaned with a blade, sponge, or filter floss to rid it of unsightly algae. Plastic is more easily scratched than glass—from a sand particle caught by the sponge or a knocked-over rock or hard coral. Scratches provide thin tracks in which algae grow, leaving an unsightly line that can be removed only by draining the tank and polishing the acrylic. Based on cost and acrylic's ease of scratching, most aquarists select glass tanks. Acrylic stands are no longer unequalled in beauty either; today, cabinet stands with Chinese figures on black or colored enameled panels, and matching hoods, are available for all large tanks.

A well-constructed large tank of glass or plastic should have braces connecting the panels at the top and bottom. The most cost-effective approach is to order your tank factory-drilled for a 1–1.5 inch PVC bulkhead fitting at a bottom corner or an upper side panel for drainage to a sump. If you are converting an undrilled tank to reef use, ask your dealer to drill the tank for you at your own risk. If not (some tanks have tempered glass that shatters, while old glass may become brittle), use a prefilter/surface skimmer that siphons water over the frame to the sump, or ask your dealer for recommendations.

Stand

A reef tank is a beautiful amenity that the owner enjoys showing visitors. Its size and location should be decided early, with the living room or den usually the first choice. The underlying floor support—2 by 4 inch wood frame studs, concrete—limits maximum tank size. A concrete floor in a den is usually risk-free, but watch for cracks in a settling house than can shift the floor into uneven planes. Although the corner of a wooden stud floor should support the weight of a large reef tank, even a slight sag poses the risk of stress on the glass bottom, resulting in sudden panel separation or a cracked glass. The strongest location on a wooden floor is a corner.

The typical reef tank is 70–135 gallons. It is set up with 1–2 pounds of rock (see Chapter 4) per gallon tank size, and often 2–4 inches of sand or gravel. The remaining 75 percent of tank capacity will be filled with water. Let's calculate the weight of any tank fully set up.

Jeff Voet installs lighting above a newly established 135-gallon reef tank in the author's concrete floor basement fish room. Over three inches of aragonite gravel, live rock takes up most of the bottom.

The weight of the average tank and stand is a little more than 1.5 pounds per gallon, more for larger tanks. A 55-gallon tank and stand will weigh about 85 pounds, a 100-gallon setup about 175 pounds, and a 135-gallon capacity setup about 250 pounds. About 75 percent of the tank will be filled with water, weighing 8.25 pounds per gallon. About 25 percent of the tank will be occupied by rock and sand or gravel. Estimate the rock and sand/gravel at 17 pounds per gallon or 17 pounds times 25 percent of the gallon capacity of the tank.

Let's estimate the weight of a 135-gallon setup. We've already estimated tank and stand at 250 pounds. Next, measure the base of the tank. A 135-gallon tank will be 18 inches back to front (wide), and 72 inches side to side (long), equal to 6×1.5 feet or 9 square feet. Using the square foot method to calculate the aragonite gravel needed, estimate 6.5 pounds per inch of gravel depth per square foot of tank bottom. For 3 inches of aragonite gravel you will need $6.5 \times 3 \times 9$, or 175.5 pounds of gravel. It comes in 44-pound sacks, so four sacks will be just right ($4 \times 44 = 176$). The square-inch method to calculate the pounds of aragonite sand needed to fill a tank to a particular depth is to multiply $L \times W \times D$ (where D is depth of sand desired) in inches, divide the product by 1728, and then multiply by 70.

A 135-gallon tank is 24 inches high. After adding 3 inches of gravel, another 3 inches will be displaced by 1–2 pounds per gallon of live rock. At a minimum, the rock will weigh 135 pounds. If the tank is filled 75 percent with water, the water alone will weigh 835 pounds. And so the total weight of a 135-gallon reef tank in pounds = 250 (tank and stand) + 176 (gravel) + 135 (rock) + 835 (water) = 1,396 pounds or almost three quarters of a ton, with the weight distributed to four or six legs of the stand.

The weight of a reef tank precludes using household furniture as ad hoc stands. Commercial stands are well built and reliable. Homemade wooden stands should be constructed of 4×4 or larger pressure-treated lumber and have numerous deeply screwed cross braces to protect against warping.

You cannot overbuild a stand.

Every large tank should be sandwiched on a half-inch styrofoam platform to absorb slight unevenness where the tank bottom meets the top of the stand. Every stand should be shimmed to eliminate the slightest unevenness.

Finally, leave enough distance between the tank and any walls (4–6 inches) for the dissipation of heat. Keeping a reef tank cool is a difficult problem, and open space can be a great aid to its solution.

Power

A reef tank needs too much electricity to share with your home entertainment center. Lighting, which consumes most of the electricity to a reef tank, is explained in Chapter 11. The correct intensity of light for corals is roughly four watts per gallon. A 135-gallon reef tank may have two 175-watt metal halide (incandescent) lamps plus two 40-watt ordinary fluorescent and two 60-watt high output fluorescent lamps for a total of 550 watts. Metal halide lamps emit lots of heat and, if enclosed in a hood, should be cooled with a built-in fan. The fans, light timers, and submersible water pumps for circulation and operating the skimmer may add another 100 watts. We've already reached 650 watts, but that could easily go to 1,000 watts with bigger air-cooled pumps, stronger halide lamps, and optional ozone generator (Chapter 9). Finally, your tank may run so hot from metal halide lamps and submersible water pumps that a chiller unit (Chapter 10) is required to hold temperatures at healthy levels (72–78°F). Chillers use 500 or more watts.

The combination of salt water with this much electrical demand is good reason to provide a separate line to the reef tank with a ground fault interrupter (GFI) outlet. Have an electrical contractor run a 15- or 20-amp line to the indoor location of the reef tank. Install a GFI outlet first on the line, and then additional multiple outlets downcurrent, with all outlets about a foot above the top of the tank to protect from salt spray.

Chapter Three
Water Quality

The stability of coral reefs has resulted in the evolution of a group of marine invertebrates that decline outside narrow values. A water temperature below 65°F or above 90°F will stress or kill most corals. Stress at sublethal temperatures may encourage attack by bacteria, fungi, and fast-growing cyanobacteria (blue-green algae). Unlike fish, which have many physiological mechanisms for adjusting to various water conditions, invertebrates such as corals, flatworms, and some echinoderms such as sea stars are unable to adjust rapidly to salinities, temperatures, or pH values outside their normal experience. That is why the reef aquarium should be maintained within strict parameters. On the other hand, many aquarists have had great success with aquariums where pH values fall below 8.0, water heats to more than 82°F, alkalinity drops to a third its recommended range, and calcium is half again the concentration it should be. Occasional alterations are often tolerated, and frequent alterations from norms may even facilitate adaptation.

Seawater contains chemicals and trace elements necessary to support marine life; indeed, many marine organisms from algae to larval fish can absorb nutrients and trace chemicals directly from the surrounding water. In the old days, aquarists had to collect seawater for their aquariums by hauling water home from the ocean. Today we can buy synthetic salt mixes that, mixed with pure fresh water, provide all the necessary chemicals in the correct proportions to sustain and even breed marine animals.

Because the chemistry of ocean water doesn't vary much around the world, you might think that corals and other marine animals would have lost any tolerance for values away from typical seawater. In fact corals are tougher than you might imagine. Many of them can tolerate, at least for a time, changes in salinity, temperature, alkalinity, and other parameters quite removed from normal. However, some chemicals in even slight concentrations are lethal. An ordinary aquarium medication such as copper, used to treat fish diseases, is lethal to many invertebrates, while ammonia, lethal to most fish, is a nutrient for corals.

More important is what a variation from normal chemistry does to the entire ecosystem within the aquarium. Slight increases in nitrate or phosphate levels, not at all toxic to corals, can nevertheless promote blooms of some types of algae and microbes. Some algae compete for space with corals and can overgrow and kill them. Other algae and some microbes release toxins into the water as they grow. Water quality maintenance is important not only to promote the growth of corals, but also to avoid promoting the growth of noxious algae and microbes.

Municipal tap water, to which you will be adding the salt mix, is not pure water. Some municipal water contains troublesome chemicals such as chlorine or chloramine. Tap water also contains some nitrates, phosphates, and silicates, nutrients for noxious algae. The first time you set up an aquarium, you'll add all of the above to the tank. There may be a brown smear on the glass, sand, and rocks for a few weeks as diatoms bloom, feeding on the silicates; there may be a filamentous algal bloom, fed by phosphates and nitrates. These blooms are gone in a few weeks, dealt with by herbivorous snails and fish.

Noxious algae will bloom, using nitrates, phosphates, and/or silicates if these nutrients are not diluted by regular partial water changes or removed by the growth of desirable algae such as *Caulerpa*.

In many municipalities, surface water is treated to remove nutrients so thoroughly that it poses no threat of inducing reef tank algal blooms. On the other hand, groundwater wells may be quite rich in nitrates or silicates, and should not be used to make up evaporative losses. Call your municipal water supplier and ask for a copy of the most comprehensive laboratory analysis.

Makeup Water

After filling the aquarium, start the pumps and filters but leave the lights off for the next six weeks. Do not add any invertebrates. This period of very low light and new marine water will retard the growth of noxious algae while favoring establishment of coralline red algae. It will also provide time for the nitrogen cycle bacterial populations to develop.

During these weeks, the aquarist will be surprised at how fast water (but not salt) will evaporate from the highly agitated surface of the aquarium and from all the surfaces of the supporting equipment (sump, protein skimmer, trickling filter). This water must be replaced to stabilize salinity and the proper balance of chemicals. Ideally we would add pure salt-free and nutrient-free water. In some localities the tap water is of high quality, containing calcium, but not silicates, nitrates, or phosphates. In most cities, however, the concentrations of those chemicals in tap water is so high that they may promote noxious algae blooms. We need a substitute.

RO, DI, and Distilled Water

Evaporation can be made up with distilled, deionized (DI), or reverse osmosis (RO) water. Distilled water has no salts or nutrients, but does pick up atmospheric carbon dioxide during condensation. A still (apparatus for distilling) is a laboratory instrument too expensive for aquarists. You can buy distilled water at supermarkets for about a dollar a gallon. Tap water is usually unsuitable for makeup water, because its dissolved chemicals will alter the chemistry of the aquarium over time, its nutrients may promote growth of noxious algae, and municipal additives (chlorine, chloramine) may require the addition of even more chemicals, such as sodium thiosulfate, for neutralization.

Differences between DI and RO

Commercial DI and RO units for the aquarium hobby produce good water at a reasonable cost. Both require maintenance. RO membranes must be replaced when flow rates drop. Deionizer units must be recharged or have their cartridges replaced. RO water takes many hours to produce in multigallon quantities, whereas running tap water through a DI unit will produce all the water you need in a short time. RO units waste 75 percent or more of the water coming through the unit, while deionziers waste none. RO units are expensive to operate if your water/sewer service charges are based on water use. RO units must be run for long periods, and accidental flooding due to failure to turn off the unit is quite common. Both RO and DI product water ideally should be tested with

Recommended Water Quality Values for a Reef Tank

temperature	72–78°F
specific gravity	1.022–1.026
salinity	32–36 o/oo
pH	8.0–8.4
alkalinity	6–9 KH
carbon dioxide	2–5 ppm
calcium	400–450 mg/L
oxidation-reduction potential	+250–375 mV
dissolved oxygen	>5.5 ppm
Ammonia	<0.25 mg/L
Nitrite	<0.25 mg/L
Nitrate	<30 mg/L
phosphate	<0.03 mg/L
iron	0.1–0.2 mg/L
movement	>5 × tank volume (gph)

Symbols

°F	degrees Fahrenheit
gph	gallons per hour
KH	German degrees of calcium alkalinity
>	greater than
<	less than
mg/L	milligrams per liter
mV	millivolts
ppm	parts per million
o/oo	parts per thousand
o/o	percent or parts per hundred

a total dissolved solids meter to monitor effectiveness, but a hardness kit is a good substitute.

The combination of DI and RO units in series produces excellent quality water, provides backup in case one unit fails, and increases the lifetime of the resins and the membranes. It may be worth the cost in locales with very hard water or where house plumbing contains lead pipes or copper pipes with lead solder. Where lead in tap water is high because of plumbing,

let the tap run ten minutes before taking water for drinking or aquarium use. The effectiveness of an RO or DI unit can be increased by combining it with a mechanical prefilter and activated carbon adsorption filter. The best quality water combines all of the described techniques and equipment in the treatment train.

Deionized Water

Deionization removes some gases, and produces water purer than distilled water. A deionizer canister contains charged synthetic resin beads or granules that attract ions of opposite charge. Newer units use synthetic resins with differing attractiveness for calcium and magnesium and for the anions nitrate and phosphate (NO_3^-, PO_4^-). Units in series remove a broad spectrum of charged chemicals. Deionizers require replacement of the resins or recharge in a laboratory with strong acids or bases. As with distilled water, you can purchase DI water in supermarkets for about a dollar a gallon.

Reverse Osmosis

Reverse osmosis removes a high percentage (not all) of minerals, nitrates, and phosphates, but not silicates. Tap water is under pressure sufficient to squeeze the water through the RO semipermeable membrane while not allowing passage of minerals and salts. An RO unit requires several hours of breaking in, but afterward might produce 25 percent by volume of oxygen depleted, cation-poor and anion-poor water and 75 percent by volume wastewater containing 85–95 percent of the ions and other impurities of the tap water.

RO efficiency depends on the impurity of incoming water, water pressure, water temperature (room temperature is better than cold or hot water), and the type and age of the semipermeable membrane. Cellulose triacetate (CTA) membranes are readily degraded by bacteria and must be used in chlorinated water or they will break down. More expensive thin film composite (TFC) membranes are damaged by chlorine but work better on nitrates, yet in most areas nitrates are not a problem. Vendors will advise you on the type (CTA, TFC) and size unit (gallons/day) for your applications. All membranes have limited life expectancy, so product water should be tested every couple of months with an expensive total dissolved solids (TDS) meter or an inexpensive marine hardness test kit.

You can divert RO product water for storage and wastewater for disposal to remote locations in your fish room with tubing and connectors from a hardware or appliance store stocking parts for refrigerator icemakers.

A reverse osmosis unit consists of a membrane cartridge and one or more water filter cartridges. Tap water entering the unit is forced against the membrane. Relatively pure water passes through the membrane while wastewater, with concentrated minerals, is discarded.

Motion, Powerheads, and Wavemakers

Corals cannot survive in the ocean or in captivity without water motion to wash away waste products, expel eggs and sperm, deliver planktonic food organisms, exchange respiratory gases, and move the animal's stalk and tentacles for exposure to sunlight and other necessities. Outside power filters can provide near-surface current from their discharges and have the added value of containing packets of carbon for water purification. Submersible powerhead pumps are useful in moving water through all layers and corners of the aquarium, leaving no dead spaces above the sand to become oxygen depleted. Water flow across the bottom sweeps detritus (decomposing plant fragments) from corners. Water flow provides respiratory exchange for the sand surface, which is the lung for the minute animals living within the gravel and sand (meiofauna). If rocks cover the entire bottom, they should be elevated

on points to the extent practicable in order that the sand layer be readily washed by not fewer than two powerheads. Powerheads or water pumps for reef tank currents should turn over not fewer than five times the tank volume per hour. In very small reef tanks (ten gallons) where heat of powerheads is a concern, vigorous aeration with large, nonsplashing bubbles can provide sufficient current.

While powerheads in a freshwater stream tank are typically aligned unidirectionally with stream flow, the dominant currents on coral reefs are reversible surges. Here's how surges can be managed in reef tanks:

1. pointing the discharges of outside power filters or the discharge ports of powerheads toward each other or on intersecting paths
2. placing one or more opposing dischargers on timers so they alternate between blocking and not blocking their opposite number

3. use of wavemakers, buckets on spindles that fill and then dump their contents into the tank
4. use of large clamshell type bubble collectors
5. use of motor-mounted rotating spindles to which a powerhead or sump pump discharge is attached (e.g., AquaGate, Osci-Wave), providing up to a 90-degree arc of discharge at a slow pace to replicate natural surge.

Modern commercial wavemakers use 2–4 or more amps, but can handle several plug-in powerheads, and can even be programmed to provide a surge when a light sensor detects dimming in the evening. Rotating motorized spindles are simple and flexible for many applications, but cost about a hundred dollars. The spindles mount in a top corner of the tank and slowly turn an attached powerhead (or discharge from the sump) back and forth in an arc. One simple mechanical wavemaker is a bucket that tips over and empties after filling by a small powerhead. The spindle holding the bucket is mounted below the mid-level of the bucket's capacity. When

Powerheads are inexpensive submersible pumps used for creating current, running filters, and returning water from the sump to the aquarium.

the volume above the spindle is greater than the volume below, the bucket becomes unstable, tips, and spills its contents back into the aquarium in a sudden surge. Because water will leak from the hole carrying the spindle, the bucket must be mounted completely inside the aquarium at just above water level.

Nutrients

The water surrounding oceanic reefs is almost devoid of nutrients, while reefs associated with land masses must be free of excessive freshwater, silt, and nutrients. Areas of bright light, high heat, and low surge or low pounding, as in lagoons, often provide habitat for tolerant soft corals adaptable to aquariums. Shaded reef areas such as deep water, caves, and underhangs provide habitat for plankton-feeding corals that do not depend on symbiotic algae. These desirable corals can be maintained in a tank on a diet of live foods or bits of seafood fed with a tweezer or baster.

Reefs are efficient at recycling food and energy. While the symbiotic algae in corals are producing sugars, sugar alcohols, and alanine from carbon dioxide and sunlight, these algae are also recycling animal wastes by utilizing ammonia before it dissipates into the surrounding ocean. Calcareous and noncalcareous algae grazed from the reef by tangs, damsels, and parrotfish are returned to the reef as fecal matter, as are the feces of other fishes, invertebrates, and surrounding plankton. Nowhere is this so dramatic as in many tangs, which supplement their herbivorous diet by consuming the other fishes' droppings falling through the water.

Any aquarium quickly becomes a barrel of marine manure as foods are added and animals and plants excrete wastes. In a perfect world, the reef tank should be a closed system in which all nutrients are

Yelloweye tangs (Ctenochaetus strigosus) *feed on attached algae and recycle organic compounds by consuming the droppings of other fishes.*

recycled and there is never a buildup of waste. In reality, your reef tank is a closed system in which nutrients are hardly recycled at all and wastes rapidly build up. If you don't dispose of the old water and replace it with new, the increasing concentration of wastes will stress the inhabitants beyond tolerance. A good rule of thumb is to replace 1 percent of the synthetic seawater daily. A 125-gallon aquarium contains about 100 gallons of water, so removing a gallon of tank water a day and replacing it with newly mixed sea water accomplishes the 1 percent water change. For a tank half this size, change a gallon every other day.

Tap Water

Ideally we would set up our brand new reef tank with a hundred gallons of water treated through a DI or RO unit, but those quantities are beyond the capabilities of these units to provide. In practice, we usually mix our marine salts with tap water. We might also use tap water to dilute limewater or buffering additives, to top off the aquarium or sump in an emergency, or for myriad other purposes. Tap water typically contains additives provided by your municipal water purveyor.

Chlorine

Several tests can determine chlorine in water. In the diethylphenylenediamine (DPD) test, free chlorine causes the test chemical to turn red. This simple procedure can verify whether you used enough dechlorinator. Other tests rely on free chlorine to liberate iodine, which can then be stained and made visible. Avoid test kits containing orthotoluidine; tests based on that chemical are unreliable.

Ammonia

Don't worry about ammonia in tap water. The major source is from microbial decomposition. Early in the cycling of an aquarium, ammonia may build up to toxic levels. Only when ammonia cycling by microbes is under control (which takes weeks) will ammonia become an occasional problem associated with sudden massive decomposition due to overfeeding or the death of a large animal.

Tests for total ammonia do not distinguish between ammonia (NH_3) and ammonium ion (NH_4^+). As pH drops, the equilibrium shifts toward nontoxic ammonium ion. As pH rises, the equilibrium shifts to toxic ammonia. That is why there is no single "ammonia" level reading with a test kit that tells you what is toxic and what is safe.

The standard test for ammonia in freshwater relies on a chemical called Nessler's reagent that generates deepening shades of yellow with increasing ammonia concentration. In salt water, Nessler's reagent is precipitated by calcium and magnesium, preventing the yellowing reaction. This precipitation can be blocked by adding either of two other chemicals, EDTA or Rochelle salts, both of which keep Nessler's reagent in solution. Nessler-based ammonia test kits lacking EDTA or Rochelle salts are not reliable for salt water use.

An alternative test kit is based on formation of a blue pigment (indophenol) when ammonia in aquarium water reacts with the reagent chemicals phenol and hypochlorite.

Nitrite and Nitrate

The standard test for nitrite in water yields a reddish purple (azo) dye. The Hach Chemical Company has a highly sensitive version that can read nitrites down to 0.25 *micro*grams per liter (0.25 µgm/L). Nitrate (NO_3^-) in the water will not interfere with the results.

Phosphate

Organic phosphorus occurs in animal and plant tissues and in many agricultural compounds (organophosphates). In the dissolved inorganic (orthophosphate) state it is a plant nutrient that can cause blooms of nuisance algae. This dissolved inorganic state is also called soluble reactive phosphate (SRP) by ecologists.

Phosphate is an important zooxanthellae and macroalgae nutrient occurring in seawater at about 0.07 milligrams per liter (mg/L), and in synthetic salt mixes at even lower concentrations. Phosphate concentration in the reef tank should not exceed 0.02 mg/L, as excess phosphate can induce noxious algal blooms, whereas many algae will not grow at SRP concentrations below 0.02 mg/L. Phosphate gets into the reef tank with the animals and food, with some forms of activated carbon, and with some municipal tap water. Phosphate-free distilled or deionized water from supermarkets is far better for makeup water or for preparing limewater (calcium hydroxide solution). Commercial phosphate removers are pads impregnated with aluminum oxide, but they last only a short time and are expensive. Limewater added to the sump or aquarium reduces concentrations of phosphate by inducing its precipitation. Aquariums without gravel should be regularly vacuumed with a siphon to remove animal wastes, detritus, and precipitated phosphates.

The tests for phosphate rely on yellow or blue complexes. The yellow test reads down to 1 mg/L, which is too high for aquarium use. The blue antimony-ascorbic acid test reads down to 0.1 mg/L, ten times better. The blue tin method is best, with a sensitivity of 0.007 mg/L.

Phosphate removal pads must be replaced after 24 hours, and probably are ineffective in lowering phosphate levels. To

Milligrams per Liter (mg/L) versus Parts per Million (ppm)

Concentrations of trace elements and unwanted wastes (ammonia, nitrite, phosphate) are reported in ppm (parts per million). If a "part" in ppm refers to 1 gram, then ppm would refer to grams per million grams (= million parts). As long as the "parts" are identical units then using "ppm" is accurate.

The term "mg/L" is a measure of mixed kinds of parts, milligrams (weight) and liters (volume). It is incorrect to refer to 1 mg/L of salt in water as 1 ppm. Here's why. One liter (1 L) of natural sea-water has a mass of approximately 1.025 kilograms or 1.025 Kg/L (depending on temperature). Pure (e.g., deionized) water at 4°C has a density of 1.0000 or 1 Kg/L. If you measure nitrite in seawater

from a marine aquarium and the value on the test kit is "1.00" (either as nitrite ion or as nitrite-nitrogen), what the test actually reports is 1.00 mg/L. This means that each liter of water contains 1.00 mg of the substance.

This same value, 1.00 mg/L, if reported as "ppm," would actually be 0.9756 ppm. That is because 1.00 mg/L is equivalent to 1 mg per (1 liter × 1.025 kilograms per liter); or 1 mg per 1.025 Kg; or 1 mg per 1,025,000 mg; or 1 part per 1,025,000 parts; or 0.98 parts per million parts (ppm).

This difference is only 2.5 percent, but it is a real difference. Better quality test kits usually report results in mg/L, and not in ppm.

decrease SRP levels, feed less, siphon detritus and wastes, and remove algae, which store phosphates.

Salinity

The reef environment is remarkably constant. The composition of seawater everywhere in the world is about 35 parts per thousand of salts (35 ppt or 35 o/oo). Seawater is dilute in estuaries (to about 15 ppt), hypersaline in some lagoons (40 ppt), but the components and proportions of the elements are always the same. The Red Sea, an enclosed gulf that evaporates faster than it receives inflow from the Indian Ocean, is slightly more saline than the rest of the Indo-Pacific, but that's the only large exception. The majority of marine inverte-brates and fishes are quite comfortable at salinities of 30–40 ppt, and tolerant of tank evaporation by as much as 15 percent. Strict adherence to a salinity of 35 ppt or specific gravity 1.025 is unnecessary. Many

oceanic forms can penetrate far up estuar-ine rivers rich in calcium, and almost all marine fishes are tolerant of protracted freshwater dips to eliminate surface para-sites. These tolerances also occur in some invertebrates, but in general invertebrates

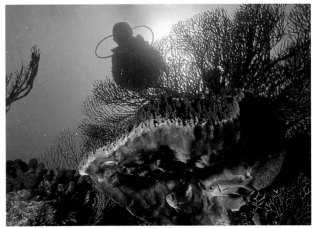

The salinity of the western Atlantic at St. Lucia is the same as that at coral reefs in other oceans around the world.

Temperature, Salinity, and Specific Gravity

ppt	sp.gr. at 60°F	sp.gr. at 70°F	sp.gr. at 80°F
20	1.015	1.013	1.012
25	1.018	1.017	1.016
30	1.022	1.021	1.019
35	1.026	1.025	1.023
40	1.030	1.028	1.02

cannot manage osmotic adjustments as well as fishes.

Aquarists measure salinity of marine aquarium water by determining the water's ability to displace a floating object. That floating object might be a glass hydrometer or a floating arrow in a plastic box. The latter is much easier to read and probably more accurate.

Salt Mixes

Seawater can be collected or purchased as a synthetic mix. Commercial marine mixes are 99.9 percent sodium chloride, potassium chloride, calcium chloride, magnesium chloride, magnesium sulfate, sodium bicarbonate, potassium bromide, strontium chloride, boric acid, sodium fluoride, plus minor elements (more than 1 microgram per liter or µ/L) and trace elements (less than 1 µ/L).

Calcium and strontium are rapidly taken up by corals and must be replaced by liquid supplements (calcium hydroxide and strontium chloride) or through the dissolution of aragonite sand. Iodine is a minor constituent of synthetic salt mixes, important for soft corals and fleshy macroalgae that may use iodine to detoxify excessive oxygen produced under intense light. Trace elements are provided by feeding brine shrimp nauplii or liquid supplements, or by regular partial water changes.

If you are using an ozone generator with your protein skimmer, select a salt mix with the lowest bromine concentration. The effects of ozone on bromine are discussed in Chapter 9.

Temperature

Water temperatures at coral reefs vary from the surface to the depths, seasonally, and with exposure to sunlight and oceanic or nearshore tidal currents. The greatest coral diversity, abundance, and stability are where temperatures are within 70–78°F, there is little seasonal variation in light levels (closer to the equator), and the populations are either outside the hurricane belt along the trade wind routes or deep enough to survive storms. Where temperatures seasonally drop below 60°F or rise above 85°F, few coral species occur. The marine reef aquarium should be maintained close to 75°F and never allowed to exceed 80°F.

Marine animals in the temperate zone tolerate summer temperatures not unlike those experienced by tropical species living in deep water and bathed in cold currents. A reef tank maintained in the mid 70°s F will support estuarine invertebrates acclimated to summer temperatures along the Pacific coast or the northeastern United States. Many brilliant red or blue anemones, sea stars, and nudibranchs will thrive in a reef tank, but often must be hand fed.

pH

In laboratories, pH—indicator of acidity (below 7) or alkalinity (above 7)—is typically measured with electronic meters calibrated against freshly prepared standard buffers. Electronic meters and replaceable probes are now available for aquarists.

In the field or the fish room, pH can also be measured by titration. Indicator dyes that change color allow us to determine pH. The test kit color change must be proportional to concentration to be valid; that is, it must follow Beer's Law. That's the basis of indicator dye tests.

The pH of tropical oceanic water is 8.0–8.4 everywhere. At this pH, carbonate deposition is optimal and corals and calcareous algae grow fastest. At lower pH, hard corals won't survive, soft corals slowly decline, and noncalcareous nuisance algae and cyanobacteria overgrow hard coral surfaces. In aquariums, the main contributors to lowering pH are bacterial nitrification and photosynthesis. The pH should be maintained at or above 8.1 by regular partial water changes, minimal supplementary feedings, avoidance of all liquified or suspension food supplements (despite commercial hyperbole), or (in an emergency) the addition of sodium bicarbonate (baking soda), sold as pH upward buffer.

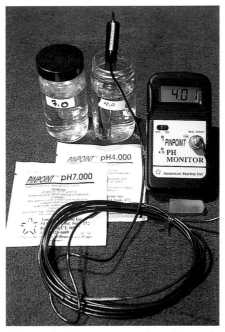

Electronic pH meters must be calibrated against freshly prepared buffer solutions.

Dissolved Oxygen

The most accurate way to measure oxygen concentration is with an electronic oxygen meter, which is expensive. Titration kits are trouble to use and inaccurate. The simplest way to assure a high oxygen concentration is with low temperature (not higher than 76°F) and strong currents. The appearance and health of the animals can be the most practical indicators of oxygen concentration.

Oxygen concentrations in the sea and in marine aquariums depend on temperature, salinity, and the oxidizable organic compounds in the water. Oxygen is saturated in tropical oceanic water at about 4–7 ppm at 75°F, but can be supersaturated in quiet, shallow, sunny waters rich in algae. Oxygen supersaturation is seldom stressful to

corals, but can be stressful to fish and gilled invertebrates.

Oxygen concentrations drop in stagnant waters with rotting organic materials, as in polluted bays. Occasional slight depressions from saturation are not important, but sudden massive depletions or chronically low levels are stressful. The sudden drop of 2–3 ppm when decay microbes grow on dead animals, dead algae, or leftover food is often accompanied by a rapid buildup of ammonia/ammonium, a drop in pH, and an increase in dissolved carbon dioxide, all of which contribute to stress.

Oxidation-Reduction Potential

Minireef aquarists are fond of oxidation reduction potential (ORP) meters. An ORP meter measures the change in electrical potential in millivolts—thousandths of a volt (mV)—across a probe. The actual ORP reading is less important than a sudden decrease of 50 or more mV, suggesting that water pumps have failed or that something in the tank has died and should be immediately located and removed.

The oxidation-reduction potential of ocean water around reefs has been measured with an ORP meter at +250 to +350 millivolts (mV). Although reported as the preferred level sought by minireef aquarists with ORP meters, your tank's ORP is less important than whether the fish and decapods are active and in good color, the corals are spread and their polyps open, and the animals look as healthy as if they were in the ocean. An ORP meter by itself is an expensive gadget of limited usefulness; hooked up to a carbon dioxide delivery system, other pH adjustment equipment, or an ozonizer, it can be a useful tool.

If the creatures look stressed, first check for unacceptably high or low temperatures; if temperature is not the problem, look for a dead animal decaying in the tank.

Note: The quickest, easiest, and safest way to correct noxious water conditions and reduce stress on the animals in any aquarium is with a large water change.

Ozone

Oxygen (O_2) energized with electricity or ultraviolet light forms ozone (O_3), a highly reactive oxidizer. The pungent odor accompanying a thunderstorm is ozone from lightning strikes, as is the odor from some office copiers. In aquariums, ozone oxidizes all organics, including rubber gaskets, O-rings, and ordinary airline tubing. It can also damage fish and invertebrate tissues. Its major use is destroying bacteria, single-celled algae, parasitic protozoa, and in clarifying yellow (organic-rich) water by oxidizing tannins, lignins, phenols, and other organic

Health Hazards of Ozone

Ozone is produced by UV in sunlight acting on smog, by high energy welding equipment, and from other synthetic sources. Ozone exposure is expressed in ml of ozone per 1,000 L of air or parts per million by volume (ppm_V). You can smell it at 0.05 ppm_V or less, and may suffer coughing and irritation from 1 ppm_V after 8 minutes or 4 ppm_V after 1 minute. The U.S. Occupational Health and Safety Administration (OSHA) limits industrial exposure to 0.3 ppm_V in 15 minutes, not to exceed 0.1 ppm_V in 8 hours. Ozone exposure has been estimated to be fatal in less than a minute at 10,000 ppm_V. But don't worry about using it in an aquarium. If you can't smell it, the concentration is below harmful levels.

compounds. The side benefits of removing color and odor are the primary reasons to use ozone in reef aquariums.

Ozonizers use a stainless steel ground electrode separated by a gap from a ceramic or glass dielectric material, the unit enclosed in a protective plastic case so you don't splash water on the unit or burn yourself. Filtered air from a high-output vibrator air pump enters the influent port of the ozonizer, passes across a dessicant to remove moisture, and then proceeds across the electrical gap. High voltage AC generates a charge across the gap that reacts with oxgyen in the air, or with pure oxygen if provided. The higher the energy, the more ozone is formed. A portion (about 1–10 percent in industrial units) of the oxygen is ionized, reacts immediately with molecular oxygen, and produces a small amount of O_3 (ozone), which will then react with anything organic.

Waste air and ozone leave the unit for skimmer or sump, and are then released by an air diffuser constructed of sintered glass or sandstone. (Wooden air diffusers are destroyed by ozonization.)

Situate the ozonizer well above water level to protect it from backflow water damage in a power outage. Every six months the unit should be disassembled, the generator tube and contacts cleaned of accumulated grit, and the dessicant replaced or regenerated. The efficiency of a unit drops rapidly with humidity in the air and with the accumulation of sediments, grit, or dust. These wastes also block heat dissipation, which can damage the unit.

How much ozone is enough? You can rely on an ORP controller to manage output by turning off the ozonizer when ORP is high, but that's complex and expensive. Just 10 mg/hr per 50 gallons of aquarium water will deliver a substantial prophylactic dose to the aquarium with little danger of overdosing. Be aware that UV sterilization also produces ozone.

Ozone reduces the output of a protein skimmer by breaking large, sticky molecules into units too small to capture on the water-air interface. Ozone also oxidizes effluent in the collection cup, producing a noxious odor that can be neutralized with activated carbon in the path of the waste air.

Ozonizers are more often used on fish tanks to control bacterial and protozoan diseases than on reef tanks where they also destroy plankton. Ozonizers are particularly useful for reef tanks with algal mat filtration because that system produces yellow water due to organics leaking from the macroalgae.

Burning in marine fish subjected to ozone is sometimes corrected by cutting back ozonization, but this may be the wrong approach. Excessive bromine in some salt mixes forms excessive, stable hypobromite (OBr^-), a powerful oxidant that can irritate gills and skin. Compare salt mixes and select one with a low bromine level that will allow a relatively safer use of ozone. Alternatively, simply reduce the generator output directly or through the program to your ORP controller.

Carbon

Carbon is the backbone of all life, the defining element of organic compounds. It is the element of coal and of diamonds, adsorptive, hard, and reactive. Charcoal is the carbon residue when organic substances (usually wood or coconut husks) are smoldered. Coal is the carbonaceous residue of ancient plants and animals subjected to geologic heat and pressure. Diamond is carbon subjected to greater heat and pressure from the earth's interior, associated not with fossils, but with volcanoes.

Activated carbon is carbon treated with high temperatures to burn and drive off substances blocking its pores. It is more effective than charcoal or coal for adsorption of organic substances, colors, toxins, and medications. The two general forms are powdered (finely ground) and granular (coarsely ground). The finer the grind, the more surface area, the higher the cost, and the greater effectiveness. The principal commercial terms are granular activated carbon (GAC) and powdered activated carbon (PAC).

Many water treatment plants use GAC to adsorb colors and odors in drinking water. It is also used in wastewater treatment plants for these same attributes, and also because the pores become colonized by anaerobic bacteria that feed on dissolved nitrates and release free nitrogen gas (denitrification).

PAC is finer and has greater adsorption capacity than GAC. Its absorption capacity is measured in how much of its own weight (milligrams of substance per gram of carbon) it can absorb of small molecules (iodine and methylene blue) and large molecules (molasses). A good grade of PAC will have an iodine number of 1,000 (1,000 milligrams of iodine per gram of carbon). That PAC then can adsorb its own weight of iodine.

Contact time (Tc) is a measurement used in treatment plants. It describes the period necessary for optimal reactivity to occur. For substances requiring a short Tc to be effective, such as PAC, a small volume in the filter may work quite well. For GAC with its much longer Tc, you can increase effectiveness by using a larger volume of carbon or a small volume for a longer period during which water passes through the activated carbon.

PAC is useful with diatomaceous earth filtration for emergencies (yellow coloration of the water, noxious odors, accidental excessive doses of chemicals). GAC can be used routinely to remove noxious gases and colors before they become nuisances. GAC can be placed in nylon net bags in the sump, in the overflow chamber, or mixed with a surface layer of aragonite gravel. GAC should be replaced at the first hint of yellowing of the aquarium water. Replace no more than a third of the total at a time. Old GAC becomes colonized by nitrogen cycle bacteria and is useful forever in this capacity; its capacity for substance adsorption is limited to a couple of months at most.

Activated carbon might remove some trace elements, but these substances are replaced by occasional feeding, use of additives, and normal water changes.

Note: Some activated carbons leach excessive phosphates and oxides to the water, and should not be used in a reef aquarium until soaked and leached in freshwater. You can test for phosphate leaching of any carbon with a simple aquarium phosphate test. Poor quality carbon, when new (unsoaked), will give a reading above 2 mg/L orthophosphate; the preferred level is below 0.1 mg/L.

Biological Oxygen Demand, Chemical Oxygen Demand, and Total Organic Carbon (BOD, COD, and TOC)

Carbon-containing substances are excreted, leached, and emitted from living and dying animals and plants as organic wastes, sexual products, hormones, pheromones, pigments, and other metabolic products. The water and the surfaces of the rock have bacteria, protozoans, fungi, algae, and broken cells of these microbes that also leach organic substances. Excessive waste substances cause yellowing of the water. The sum of this material from all sources is called total organic carbon (TOC). High quality water has low TOC; low quality or nutrient-enriched (or simply enriched) water has high TOC.

TOC is removed by foam fractionation (protein skimming)—see Chapter 8—and/or activated carbon adsorption. No simple test kits are available to aquarists, but yellow water is a good indicator of high TOC. Protein skimmers remove large molecule TOC, and very small molecules can be removed by activated carbon adsorption.

A standard water quality testing procedure is analysis of biological or chemical oxygen demand (BOD or COD). In different ways, these tests measure the organic constituents in the water and provide an estimate of dissolved organic substances. The lower the value, the higher the water quality. One company currently provides a test based on permanganate demand, a form of COD. This is an inexpensive if less accurate substitute for measuring ORP.

Carbon Dioxide

All the corals, algae, and macroinvertebrates, and many of the microorganisms in a reef tank require oxygen for aerobic respiration, and expel carbon dioxide (CO_2) as respiration's waste product. The dissolved carbon dioxide in the water is a nutrient for the algae and some of the microbes. The CO_2 is a growth promoter for the symbiotic algae in hermatypic corals and tridacnid clams and for the macroalgae attached to live rock. Most importantly, CO_2 also reacts with carbonates to form the bicarbonates that buffer sea water at about pH 8.3.

Ordinarily we don't measure dissolved carbon dioxide in the aquarium, but rather its effects on pH. Commercial carbon dioxide pH controllers monitor aquarium pH and, upon detecting an elevation in pH above 8.3, slowly inject compressed gas from a refillable cylinder into the aquarium water to bring the pH back to 8.3. These controllers are suitable for both freshwater and marine applications, as the desired pH can be programmed to the controller unit. However, controllers are expensive.

There are no simple test kits to measure carbon dioxide in seawater. Even if there were, the results would vary with temperature, pH, alkalinity, and time. Laboratory methods to compute carbon dioxide concentrations are not adaptable to home aquariums.

Calcium

Calcium is essential to the growth of hard corals. Hard corals and coralline algae rapidly deplete calcium, which must be replaced with additives if coral growth is to continue. Soft corals need far less calcium. Therefore an aquarium containing only soft corals (especially a tank with aragonite gravel) will maintain adequate calcium levels if merely provided periodic water changes.

Calcium dissolved in seawater is limited by chemical competition with magnesium for carbonate ions, and by rapid uptake by coralline red and green algae, hard corals, and other calcareous invertebrates. Without high concentrations of magnesium (1,350 mg/L in natural seawater), all the calcium would combine with carbonates and precipitate out of solution. The average calcium concentration in natural ocean water is 400 mg/L. Many synthetic marine salts, when dissolved in municipal tap water, meet this concentration because tap water usually contains calcium. When marine salts are dissolved in reverse osmosis (RO), distilled, or deionized (DI) water, calcium should be added.

Calcium's constant removal from solution by hard corals requires its replacement by a saturated solution of calcium hydroxide ($Ca(OH)_2$, limewater, "Kalkwasser"), calcium oxide (CaO), calcium chloride ($CaCl_2$), through the slow dissolution of an aragonite gravel base, or through regular water changes. (Calcium chloride requires an additional step of buffering with bicarbonate.) You can make "Kalkwasser" by adding 2 tablespoons of granular calcium hydroxide per gallon of RO, DI, or distilled water in a 5-gallon bucket and mixing with a submerged powerhead. (Delbeek recommends 1.5 grams of calcium hydroxide per liter, which is about 6 grams per gallon.) Should you decide to make the Kalkwasser in phosphate-contaminated municipal tap water, mix it for not less than half a day to induce phosphate precipitation, then discard both surface scum and sediments before use.

Kalkwasser (about 800 mg/L Ca^{++}) is best added directly to the aquarium or sump at night, when reef tank pH is normally slightly depressed to 7.8–8.0. The pH 12–13 calcium hydroxide solution can elevate tank pH, but at night this remains well within normal tolerances. Addition of the high pH solution during the day might push the reef tank above pH 8.3, which is not advised.

How much and how often calcium hydroxide should be added to replace calcium ions depends on your tank's coral and coralline algae community (soft corals do not need calcium additives), hours of bright light during which calcium ions are taken up, and the growth rates of the inhabitants. Measurements of calcium concentrations with a test kit are the only way to tell when and how often to add supplements. Aragonite gravel often eliminates the need for supplementary calcium in soft coral tanks, as the gravel (if deep) may dissolve fast enough to maintain a 400 mg/L calcium concentration. Moderately higher concentrations (450–500 mg/L) are not harmful.

Note: Calcium carbonate cannot achieve its benefit of maintaining alkalinity in the absence of carbon dioxide gas. Calcium reactors are automated units that mix calcium carbonate granules and injected carbon dioxide gas with aquarium water. This eliminates the need for periodic hand mixing and delivery of Kalkwasser. Levels of calcium must still be monitored. Problems with reactors are their tendency to induce filamentous algal blooms (too much carbon dioxide) and elevated phosphate levels. Kalkwasser does not induce those side effects.

Hardness and Alkalinity

Hardness is primarily the concentration of calcium (Ca^{++}) and magnesium (Mg^{++}), the two most important metal cations with more than a single positive charge, but in aquarium usage it sometimes also refers to alkalinity. Real alkalinity is the acid-neutralizing capacity of all the negatively charged ions, but mostly phosphate (PO_4^-), carbonate, bicarbonate, silicate, and borate.

Alkalinity, Hardness, and pH

Of all the concepts inherent in aquarium water chemistry, the two most confusing are hardness and alkalinity. One reason these two concepts are often confused is that German aquarists, who introduced the concept to the American hobby, use the term "general hardness" to refer to hardness and "carbonate hardness" to refer to alkalinity. In reality, the term "carbonate hardness" is an oxymoron. Anions such as phosphates, silicates, borates, hydroxide, carbonate, and bicarbonate work together to produce alkalinity.

In the ocean, the constant influx of clay (anionic aluminosilicates) into the water from coastal rivers provides the alkalinity that buffers oceanic pH. In aquariums, bicarbonate and carbonate provide the alkalinity to stabilize pH. Do not use clay to buffer your aquarium! Think of alkalinity as "acid-neutralizing capacity."

Hardness is the ability of water to form soluble suds when mixed with soap, and varies with the concentration of polyvalent metals. Polyvalent metals mixed with soap form insoluble salt, so suds are not formed. The major polyvalent metals that determine sea water hardness are calcium (Ca^{++}) and magnesium (Mg^{++}).

Hardness does not determine pH or alkalinity. However, in healthy seawater systems a high hardness is usually associated with a high alkalinity and with a high pH. Nonetheless, these parameters need to be monitored with test kits and adjusted when necessary. It is not unusual to have a high calcium concentration but an inadequate alkalinity that will prevent coralline algae and hard corals from taking up calcium for growth.

Aquarium "alkalinity" and "hardness" can also be expressed as mg $CaCO_3$/L or milliequivalents per liter (meq/L). Aquarium "hardness" is usually reported as mg/L of calcium carbonate, but in reality hardness should refer only to the calcium concentration. When we talk about milliequivalents, we are really referring to the amount of base or alkali (OH^-) it will take to neutralize the concentration of anything with a positive or acidic charge (H^+) or more than one charge if it is a metal rather than an acid (Mg^{++}).

One test for hardness is the EDTA method. A dye added to the test water complexes with calcium and magnesium and turns the water wine red, after which EDTA is added until the red solution turns blue. The number of drops of EDTA needed for the change to blue is proportional to total hardness. We measure alkalinity in a somewhat similar manner, using a drop-by-drop test with either of the common indicator dyes phenolphthalein or metacresol purple.

It is important to raise aquarium concentrations of calcium to that of seawater and alkalinity even higher for three reasons:
1. Calcium, depleted by stony corals and coralline algae, must be replaced
2. Alkalinity helps maintain a high pH
3. Calcium saturation will precipitate phosphates, protecting the aquarium against nuisance algae blooms. (Calcium carbonate is less soluble than calcium phosphate.)

Note: Should you use baking soda (sodium carbonate) to adjust alkalinity? Absolutely not. Commercial preparations for raising alkalinity are balanced mixtures of sodium carbonate and sodium borate. In the right ratios, they can adjust alkaline reserve without suddenly raising pH. Baking soda alone will rapidly raise the pH and stress the inhabitants.

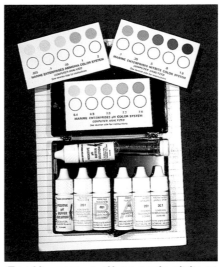

Test kits measure pH, ammonia, nitrite or nitrate, hardness, or other water quality parameters by titrating a water sample to a color change that must match the color provided by the manufacturer.

Strontium

Strontium's concentration in natural sea water is 8–9 mg/L, and varies from 0.2 to almost 14 mg/L in synthetic mixes. You can purchase commercial supplements of strontium chloride to be added to your aquarium weekly or make your own. It's easy. Mix a 10 percent (w/v) solution of strontium chloride ($SrCl_2$) or 100 grams per liter, and then add 1 ml (20 drops) of this solution to each 30 gallons of reef tank water volume (not total tank size) weekly. Strontium supplements improve the growth rate of hard corals. Aragonite gravel releases so much strontium that it may eliminate the need for supplements.

Strontium is difficult to detect because it is masked by calcium. At present, there are no reliable and practical kits for measuring strontium in a reef tank.

Measuring and Relating Alkalinity and Hardness

In a nutshell, hardness refers to the concentration of calcium and magnesium cations, and alkalinity refers to the concentration of carbonate and bicarbonate anions.

Americans measure total hardness in meq/L or in grains of $CaCO_3$ per gallon. In all but soft water, alkalinity and cation hardness are expressed as calcium carbonate equivalent. The relationships are as follows:

$$1 \text{ meq/L} = 50 \text{ mg/L } CaCO_3$$
$$= 2.8 \text{ KH, GH, or dH}$$
$$= 2.92 \text{ grains } CaCO_3/\text{gal}$$
$$1 \text{ mg/L } CaCO_3 = 0.02 \text{ meq/L}$$
$$= 0.056 \text{ KH, GH, or dH}$$
$$= 0.058 \text{ grains } CaCO_3/\text{gal}$$
$$1 \text{ grain } CaCO_3/\text{gal} = 0.34 \text{ meq/L}$$
$$= 0.96 \text{ KH, GH, or dH}$$
$$= 17.9 \text{ mg/L or ppm } CaCO_3$$

mg/L Ca	mg/L $CaCO_3$	meq/L $CaCO_3$	dH, GH or KH
40.00	100.00	**2.0**	5.6
100.00	250.00	5.0	14.0
200.00	500.00	10.0	28.0
300.00	750.00	15.0	42.0
400.00	1000.00	20.0	56.0
440.00	1100.00	22.0	61.6
460.00	1150.00	23.0	64.4
480.00	1200.00	24.0	67.2
500.00	1250.00	25.0	70.0

Note: dH, GH, or KH are alternative terms for the German hardness scale measuring alkalinity.

These relationships are for calcium or for calcium carbonate equivalent. Seawater has 400 mg/L of calcium and an alkalinity of just over 2.0 meq/L, one tenth the concentration predicted by the relationship in pure water.

In practice, we keep the calcium concentration and alkalinity of a reef tank higher than natural seawater to promote rapid growth of corals and coralline algae.

Iodine

Iodine as the iodide ion, I^-, is a micronutrient for macroalgae, symbiotic zooxanthellae, and many soft corals. It is used up rapidly and must be replaced for good growth. Commercial supplements typically consist of 1 percent potassium iodide, with instructions to add 1 ml per week per 20–25 gallons. Delbeek and Sprung recommend weekly dosing of 1 drop per 20 gallons with pharmaceutical over-the-counter tincture of iodine. Overdosing can cause blooms of noxious filamentous algae in the presence of high nitrate concentrations. Some synthetic salt mixes provide iodine; daily water exchanges of 1 percent may provide sufficient iodine and preclude the need for supplements. Poor red algae growth may improve with a combination of supplementary iodine and calcium, and a longer but not brighter photoperiod.

Copper

Trace amounts of copper, found inside living tissues, are micronutrients for algae. However, a few drops of free copper solutions are toxic to invertebrates, and medicinal concentrations will kill algae. The principal source of copper in aquariums is fish medications, which should be avoided. Copper leaching from old pipes is not dangerous if you let the water run before use. Lead from solder in old copper plumbing can leach into water and is a health hazard, but modern solders used on new pipes are lead free. A copper test good for marine tanks is the neocuproine method, which works at pH 3–9 to yield a yellow (not orange) product.

Iron

Iron is a nutrient for macroalgae and for the symbiotic algae in corals, but we don't know how much to use. In one outstanding reef aquarium, the iron concentration was found to be 0.15 mg/L, but there is no generally accepted level. We don't have any good tests for iron, but testing is probably not important anyway. When using iron supplements, watch the aquarium. If you get an algal bloom, cut the dose.

Trace Elements

Molybdenum (Mo), manganese (Mn), zinc (Zn), and cobalt (Co) are important trace elements for plants, including the motile algae used to feed rotifers or copepods, the symbiotic zooxanthellae of corals, attractive macroalgae, and nuisance filamentous algae. Trace elements in salt mixes are used up quickly, and should be replaced by liquid preparations or regular water changes. Combinations are safer than single element preparations because they're mixed in the biologically correct ratios (10 Fe: 4 Mn: 5 Zn: 2 Co: 4 Mo). Daily 1 percent water replacement with new synthetic seawater will reduce or obviate the need for trace element supplements. Supplements sometimes produce lush growths of desirable macroalgae and improve the growth of soft corals, but can also stimulate outbreaks of hair algae, particularly in water high in nitrates and phosphates. The noted German aquarist Peter Wilkins changes only 1 percent of water per month to replace trace elements, noting that tap water in his city will replace manganese and iron as well as liquid supplements, yet not induce algal blooms.

Wrapping Up: The maintenance of low concentrations of total organic carbon, phosphates and nitrates, high levels of calcium, and specific levels of strontium and iodine, are the most important chemical parameters of the reef aquarium under control of the aquarist. These chemical and physical parameters pale, however, compared with the importance of brilliant (intense) lighting (Chapter 11).

Chapter Four
Rock, Gravel, and Sand

The rocks, gravel, and sand of the reef aquarium have several functions. The more obvious are as decoration and as platforms for corals. The less obvious are filtration and chemical stabilization of the water.

Live Rock

The term *live rock* refers to coral rubble colonized by marine organisms and cleaned for reef tank use. Its most important characteristics are porosity, origin, cleanliness, and what grows upon it.

Live rock is one key to the reef aquarium (the other is intense lighting). Some corals are sensitive to the high levels of nitrate ordinarily found in marine aquariums with large carnivores. Live rock provides a vast surface area of deep pores where denitrifying bacteria take up the nitrate, thereby keeping its concentration below that which might stress corals.

Natural live rock consists of storm-broken pieces of weakened coral that have tumbled to the reef base as rubble. It originated as healthy coral of years past. But coral is home to more than the animals that made it, and the older it gets, the more it is invaded, drilled, dissolved, and weakened. Unseen by humans, boring clams, mussels, worms, protozoans, and sponges live within its structure, or they find protection for just their soft parts. Other plants and animals grow on the outer surface of both dead and live stony coral, finding habitat in strong cur-

rents and surges or above a sandy bottom. Instead of producing an adhesive such as the barnacle's glue or the blue mussel's byssus threads, many marine creatures dissolve the coral's skeleton, forming a deep hole in which to live or a shallow hole to give firm anchorage. Over time, the myriad holes created by invaders weaken the calcium carbonate reef structure. A storm arrives, enormous forces pound the most exposed parts of the reef, and the most weakened corals are broken from their supports to tumble down and about, killing the polyps, and becoming rubble.

In most parts of the world, it is the *Acropora* group of corals that grow fastest and suffer most during storms. Caribbean coral rubble consists mostly of elkhorn coral (*Acropora palmata*) and staghorn coral (*Acropora cervicornis*), for no reasons other than their abundance in the storm susceptivity zone. There are other corals making up the rubble rock, and a walk on the beach will hint at the great diversity of corals out from the shore.

As the rubble is rolled, ground, broken, and eroded, it is invaded by more boring organisms. Over time the rubble will be pebbles, then gravel, and finally coral sand. The base of the reef is covered in coral rubble in various stages of demolition, sorted by the surge into areas of rock, gravel, and sand. The rock and sand continues to support myriad algae and microorganisms between the grains and pebbles and within the pores, and provides habitat for bottom-dwelling invertebrates and small fish. It is a valuable habitat still, and that is why the State of Florida and the federal South Atlantic and Gulf of Mexico Fishery Management Councils placed it under legal protection, so that, since 1996, it has been illegal to collect submerged wild rubble in south Florida.

Live reef rock can also be cultivated from mined limestone, from concrete and seashell aggregate, or other materials. Several aquaculturists in Florida are placing mined Caribbean limestone (ancient dead reef rock) on shallow bottoms leased from Florida or the U.S. government. Florida limestone would work as well, but the lease laws require that the rock be from a remote site in order to prevent illegal trade in black market rock from U.S. waters.

Natural wild coral rubble continues to be legally available from outside United States territorial waters. Both wild and cultivated rock come from the Caribbean, Singapore, and the Philippines. Names such as Tonga rock, Fiji rock, and Marshall Island rock are often used as marketing ploys unrelated to actual origins.

The quality of live rock depends on its structure and how it was treated prior to sale. In nature, coral rubble is overgrown with algae and invertebrates simultaneously, with the complexity of the community varying by water depth and increasing over time. The best pieces for the reef aquarist contain an encrusting layer of red coralline algae and little else. Nature, however, is not that cooperative.

Larger rocks are valuable to marine aquarists for denitrifying microbial surface area, for coralline algae that encrust exposed portions not buried in sand, for the attractive invertebrates or plants that may live on them in quieter waters, and as decorative pieces for forming bridges and caves. The best pieces for microbial denitrification are large and flat, derived from

Live rock from around the world differs in porosity, weight, and colors of the encrusting communities. Gulf of Mexico rock (left) is rich in red sponges. Florida east coast rock (right) is lighter. Highly porous Fiji rock (center) is very light and its coralline algae are purple.

outer branches of elkhorn coral. More massive pieces derived from boulder corals or elkhorn coral bases are heavier and often support attractive live invertebrates and denser concentrations of coralline algae that develop on rubble not subject to tumbling.

Wild rock must be cleaned and cured. Commercial collectors remove clumps and layers of green, red, or brown algae, sponges, sea squirts, noxious worms, crabs, and other life. Most of it is too massive to adapt to shipping or life in a reef aquarium. After clearing away the excessive growth, the coral is stored away from bright lights for one to six weeks. During this period of light deprivation, most of the remaining animals and algae on the rock die off and decompose, but a few of the smallest invertebrates and algal holdfasts survive, as do the encrusting coralline algae and microbes. As surface area is made available by die-offs and decomposition of competitors, some of the coralline algae, which require little light, spread over the rock.

When the rock has only a slightly fishy odor or none at all, and all the mud and debris have been removed, the rock is ready for the reef aquarium. Adequately cured live rock will not develop a fuzzy, white or gray film. If film develops, the rock should be removed from the aquarium and placed in a barrel of seawater for further curing with strong aeration. Otherwise, the rock should remain in the newly set up reef tank for not less than two weeks for further curing with the lights off and all the water pumps operating to provide good current, aeration, and circulation.

As the remaining marine life on the rock continues to die off and the coralline algae and microbial population in the rocks increase, the fungal, bacterial, protozoan, and worms comprising the decomposer community digest the remaining organic material to carbon dioxide, water, and toxic ammonia (NH_3). Ammonia at the high pH of seawater (about 8.3) ionizes to ammonium ion (NH_4^+). This initiates the nitrogen cycle (Chapter 5), because ammonium is food for a group of bacteria known as *Nitrosomonas*. These bacteria consume and oxidize the ammonium, producing nitrite (NO_2^-) as a waste product. When the nitrite concentration rises, that triggers a bloom of another group of bacteria (*Nitrobacter*) that consume the nitrite, excreting nitrate (NO_3^-) as a waste product.

Both *Nitrosomonas* and *Nitrobacter* are called nitrifying bacteria, and they are on all the surfaces of the aquarium, wherever there is enough oxygen and food. Now the value of live rock comes into play, for without it the nitrate would accumulate to toxic levels.

Nitrate removal (denitrification) is an anaerobic process. The live rock's pores are deep enough to become anaerobic at the bottom. And here is where denitrifying bacteria, with an excellent source of nitrate

Larval Recruitment or Supply-Side Ecology

How do mollusc and coral larvae decide where to settle? How are larvae of sessile invertebrates recruited to specific habitats? Studies of artificial reef materials have compared cement, steel, and old tires, but scientists were looking for love in all the wrong places. In fact, corals and other larvae reconnoiter by sniffing out chemicals. Here's how. Some encrusting coralline algae leak an amino acid attractant plus a peptide containing a neurotransmitter (a chemical that triggers impulses between nerve cells). According to Daniel and Aileen Morse at the University of California at Santa Barbara, coralline red algae known in the food industry as *isoyake* produce lysine and a peptide containing the tiny molecule gamma-amino butyric acid (GABA). Lysine attracts nearby larvae to home in on the red algae. The GABA-peptide then induces attachment and metamorphosis of at least 13 species of abalone and probably other molluscs. Another neurotransmitter, dihydroxyphenylalanine (DOPA) induces settlement and metamorphosis of other molluscs, including clam and oyster larvae. That's not all. The plant cell walls of some isoyake algae contain a sulfated polysaccharide (glycosaminoglycan) that induces settlement and metamorphosis of two species of *Agaricia* larvae (lettuce coral and leaf coral). Species of coralline algae differ in their chemical messengers and presumably induce different species of invertebrate larvae to settle and metamorphose. If you want your reef tank's coral larvae to settle and grow, try growing coralline algae from both Atlantic and Indo-Pacific live rock.

in the water diffusing down through the rock, now undergo an explosive population bloom, converting the abundant nitrates to harmless nitrogen gas (N_2) and oxygen gas (O_2), which rapidly dissipate out of the pores and out of the aquarium.

If the protein skimmer is turned on when the rock is introduced to the tank, the skimmer will remove much of the dissolved organic material from the water before it can be broken down into ammonia by the decomposers. That slows the development of the nitrite peak and nitrifying bacteria bloom.

Bottom Media

Reef tanks can be maintained with or without a sand or gravel bottom. A bare bottom aquarium is easy to clean, whereas detritus is difficult to remove from a tank with gravel, sand, or shell hash. Tanks with gravel/sand bottoms also risk developing anaerobic pockets generating hydrogen sulfide gas, lowering pH, and releasing bacterial toxins into the water. The advantages of a gravel/sand bottom are increased reflective light, another medium in which to conduct both nitrification and denitrification, and as a supplementary habitat to support more diversity.

The media available for the bottom of marine aquariums are gravel, sand, shell hash, and crushed coral. These materials are mined from different locales and have varying concentrations of different minerals. Most sand is finely eroded quartz rock (silica base). Some sands are mixes of silica and limestone (calcium carbonate base). The black sands of some Hawaiian beaches are volcanic, rich in phosphates and unsuitable for reef aquariums. Shell hash is rich in calcium and magnesium carbonates, but may have phosphate-rich inclusions. Crushed coral may consist of ground surface materials of recent age

Coral rubble becomes live rock over a period of months if submerged in shallow water and given abundant sunlight and water changes. Live rock is cultured most commonly at artificial reef and aquaculture sites off both coasts of Florida.

(aragonite) or of mined fossilized limestone of different chemical composition.

The best material for reef tanks is the unique gravel and sand that accumulates around the base of the reef itself, the product of erosion. It may be collected where it accumulates on south Florida beaches near shore or from under the sea. This aragonite gravel and sand is available dry in uniform grades of 1.25–1.75 mm (fine), 1.75–3.00 mm (coarse), less than 1.25–1.75 mm (sugar), and sold as reef sand. It is also collected from submerged localities and shipped out immediately for use in reef tanks. This fresh material is sold as live sand and, because of its enhanced weight from water, is more expensive than dried product.

Aragonite

Aragonite is recently deposited crushed coral, a marine limestone or oolite secreted by modern corals and coralline algae. (Ancient reefs were laid down by other kinds of organisms.) Its composition is 97 percent calcium carbonate, less than (<)1.5 percent magnesium carbonate, with traces of aluminum oxide (<0.15 percent), sodium chloride (<0.25 percent), and strontium oxide (<0.125 percent). Strontium, an element similar in chemistry to calcium, is essential for the growth of coralline algae and coral skeletons. Magnesium, also taken up by corals and algae, is adequately replaced by gradual solubilization of aragonite gravel, so supplements are not required.

Aragonite sand should be placed in a reef tank to a depth proportional to grain size. Coarse gravel is filled to a depth of up to four inches, while "sugar"-sized aragonite is effective at less than an inch deep. Too deep a layer in a nutrient-rich aquarium risks creating deep anoxic conditions that promote growth of noxious black colonies of hydrogen sulfide-producing iron bacteria.

New aragonite gravel should be briefly washed (one or two rinses) to remove dried black fragments of plants. Continued washing will never result in clarity, as aragonite dissolves during washing. Washed aragonite will initially cloud the water, but the tank will clear in a few days.

Aragonite sand has several advantages over limestone or shell hash. Its composition and particle size promote a population explosion of microbes and minute invertebrates (infauna). These infauna protect the sand from blooms of noxious hydrogen sul-

What to Do About Hydrogen Sulfide

Anaerobic bacteria produce hydrogen sulfide (H_2S), a gas with the odor of rotten eggs. Stripped from the water by an ordinary protein skimmer, it is then passed into the surrounding air. A new process for removing H_2S in a skimmer oxidizes the H_2S with ferric ions, keeping the ferric and ferrous ions in solution with a chelating agent. The final product is elemental sulfur, which is removed by adsorptive plastic balls. The overall process is $H_2S + \frac{1}{2} O_2 \rightarrow S + H_2O$. Used for treating drinking water supplies, the process can probably be adapted to reef systems having deep sand layers. See Nagl (1996) References, page 184.

fide-producing anaerobic iron bacteria (gray-black pockets and gas in the gravel). As high pH (8.1–8.4), highly oxygenated water diffuses into the sand, the oxygen is depleted by the infauna. The mostly aerobic infauna feed on the detritus from the reef corals and fish, stirring it into the sand as the infauna consume oxygen diffusing downward from the overlying water. Their metabolism releases carbon dioxide, water, and simple acids. The acids produced by decomposition immediately react with the carbonate of the aragonite sand, dissolving it and releasing calcium ions that now diffuse outward and upward back into the overlying aquarium water. The reaction is fastest at lower pH and accelerates in the deeper sands. With time, the sand becomes filled with life and dissolves, dropping up to an inch in depth per year in some cases. This pH-mediated release of calcium ions into the water may replace the calcium ion uptake by coral growth. At the least, aragonite sand calcium release reduces the need to make up the calcium deficit by addition of limewater.

In the deeper parts of the sand, the oxygen concentration is low enough to allow development of a large population of denitrifying bacteria. These bacteria complement those in the deeper pores of the live rock, often doubling the capacity of the aquarium to remove nitrates.

If the sand goes from microaerophilic (very low level of oxygen) to anoxic (no oxygen at all), acids and hydrogen sulfide gas will be produced, threatening the corals and fish. The sand should be deep enough to encourage denitrifying bacteria, but shallow enough that some oxygen can diffuse to all areas. With aragonite sand, the proper depth is 1–3 inches. Shell hash, though coarse, should be no more than an inch deep because of its abundant stagnant pockets that promote anaerobic decomposition. Media other than aragonite will promote development of denitrifiers, but not aragonite's continuous calcium (and strontium) release into the water.

The Plenum System

Dr. Jean Jaubert at the Monaco Aquarium described an effective way to rid aquariums of nitrate with a carefully designed system of deep gravel beds separated by a screen, and containing a subterranean space (the plenum) filled only with water. The upper gravel layer was aerobic, rich in small invertebrates and microbes, promoting nitrification. The lower layer was screened from small invertebrates, and oxygen-deficient, promoting denitrification. Diffusion from the lower layer and stirring by the invertebrates of the upper layer moved the decomposable substances downward and free nitrogen gas upward. Jaubert operated this aquarium as a completely self-sufficient, virtually closed system.

A few reef aquarists in the United States have set up plenum systems, but it is easier to manage a reef aquarium with water changes, additives, and good husbandry than to create a working plenum aquarium that operates as a closed system. If you would like to try it, here's a simple method.

Lay an undergravel filter plate or plastic egg crate on the bottom of the aquarium to a depth of 0.75–1.0 inch, and cover with plastic window screening. Place a 1–2 inch layer of calcareous gravel on the screen and cover with another layer of screening. Then add a final top layer of 1–3 inches of calcareous gravel.

This results in two layers of sand above a layer of water. The top sand layer supports a diverse infauna of small invertebrates and microbes. Wrasses, gobies, and jawfish also stir this layer, so that it stays aerobic to microaerophilic.

The lower sand layer is screened from invasion by the fishes and infauna. It doesn't become stirred, and develops a microaerophilic community of denitrifying bacteria.

The lowest layer (called the plenum or space) is just stagnant water. It exchanges minute amounts of oxygen and carbon dioxide with the sand above, preventing complete anoxia of the water or sand. The water layer must be wide enough that temperature differences cause it to slowly circulate within its confined space. The water layer is close enough to the very top surface of the sand layers (not more than a few inches deep) that gasses can diffuse from bottom to top. There should be just enough light available to see the plenum, but not enough to promote algal growth that can crash and cause a bloom of anaerobic bacteria.

The system has been emulated by some aquarists, but no differences are reported between using a plenum and not using one beneath a sand layer. A simpler approach is 1–3 inches of aragonite gravel rather

Actinodiscus caeruleus, *a mushroom coral, does well in nutrient-rich aquaria containing fishes.*

than a thicker layer, and 1–2 pounds of live rock per gallon of water. The rock and the deeper layers of gravel provide sufficient nitrogen-cycle bacteria. Elimination of the plenum and very deep gravel eliminate the risk of a large confined space that can become anoxic.

Note: Sand collects detritus. Although it is unsightly, it is also a good food source. Rather than siphon or vacuum it out of the aquarium, blow it about with a powerhead every few days to feed the corals. Excessive detritus will be captured by the sump or skimmer.

Chapter Five

The Nitrogen and Carbon Cycles

Fish, corals, and other invertebrates feed on plants and animals, breaking down proteins into peptides, peptides into amino acids, and finally to wastes. The principal wastes of protein metabolism are eliminated as urine in mammals, uric acid in birds, urea in sharks and rays, and ammonia in bony fishes and most invertebrates.

Ammonia (NH_3) is toxic to many reef fishes at 0.2–0.5 mg/L, and can cause stress at less than 0.1 mg/L. The ionized form or ammonium ion (NH_4^+) is non-toxic. Both forms are in equilibrium in water, with their relative concentrations affected by total ammonia-ammonium, pH, and temperature.

Ammonia is an energy source for certain aerobic bacteria in soil and in marine environments. The bacteria (*Nitrosomonas, Nitrosococcus, Nitrosospira, Nitrosocystis*) oxidize ammonia to nitrite (NO_2). Nitrite is toxic in marine aquariums at concentrations of 5 mg/L. Unlike ammonia, nitrite cannot be converted to a nontoxic form by pH.

Still another group of aerobic bacteria use nitrite as an energy source. These genera (*Nitrobacter, Nitrocystis, Nitrospira, Nitrococcus*) oxidize nitrite (NO_2) to nitrate (NO_3).

Nitrate is relatively nontoxic to fish. High concentrations can be useful to macroalgae and even to some soft corals, but stressful to some fish and many invertebrates including shrimp, at levels exceeding 40 mg/L. Most important, nitrate triggers nuisance algal blooms. There is no particularly dangerous level of nitrate for all organisms, although its removal cannot but benefit the reef aquarium. Nitrate is removed by plants, tridacnid clams, and by denitrification in the live rock pores and in deeper, oxygen-poor layers within deep aragonite gravel. Nitrate is most efficiently removed by water changes. Chemical nitrate removers sold in the pet industry for marine use are resins; clinoptilolite (zeolite), a water-softening mineral, and an ammonia remover in fresh water, is ineffective in marine water.

The toxicity of nitrite to many aerobic animals is due to competition of NO_2 with O_2 for attachment sites on the hemoglobin molecule. Because nitrite binds irreversibly, affected animals develop methemoglobinemia and suffer oxygen starvation that can cause death or chronic debilitation.

Although nitrates have not been demonstrated to generally damage corals, prudent reef-keeping warrants keeping the level as low as possible in minireef aquariums.

Not all nitrates are taken up by plants. Certain bacterial species in the genera *Denitrobacillus, Micrococcus, Thiobacillus, Pseudomonas*, and *Sulfomonas* can live aerobically or anaerobically. Under anaerobic conditions, these bacteria reduce nitrate for energy. They often live deep in the soil or in oxygen-deprived sediments in lakes and oceans. In the minireef aquarium, some of these bacteria grow deep inside thick sponge filters, down under the gravel, and most importantly at the bottoms of

Ammonia and Ammonium Toxicity

At high pH (as in a marine aquarium at pH 8.3) and at increased temperatures, the ammonium-ammonia equilibrium shifts to the toxic ammonia form. Slight amounts of ammonia in a marine tank can kill the inhabitants. (Many freshwater swamp-dwelling fishes can live in virtual organic soups at pH 5.0 because almost all ammonia is ionized to ammonium.) For the marine aquarist, there is a danger in adjusting pH upward to normal seawater levels of 8.3, required for fish and invertebrate health. At high pH, nontoxic ammonium is converted to ammonia and the animals are stressed or killed from ammonia toxicity. Aquarium industry shippers do not put buffers into shipping water. As the pH in shipping water drops (from animal respiration and wastes), the shift from ammonia to ammonium ion helps protect the animals from the toxicity of their own wastes.

pores of live rock. At low pH (as deep within the gravel) reduction of nitrate (denitrification) breaks the NO_3 into nitrogen and oxygen gas (N_2 and O_2) that is eliminated as bubbles or dissolved into the surrounding water.

Without these microbes, nitrate concentrations would continue to rise beyond the capacity of algae to utilize them until they stressed the more sensitive invertebrates.

Tactics available to aquarists for reducing nitrate concentrations are water changes and anaerobic bacterial decomposition. Water changes dilute more than nitrates and are good husbandry in any aquarium. Anaerobic microbial decomposition is safe, easy, and efficient, promoted by moderately deep (1–4 inch) beds of gravel or by an abundance of live rock. Nitrate

decomposition can also be provided by a large block sponge filter in the sump of a trickling filter.

Two other methods are commercially available. The first, low-voltage electrical decomposition, is unsafe for marine aquariums. The second is the dedicated coil denitrator. The principal of a dedicated denitrator is that water with organics enters a small diameter coil such as 15–50 feet of airline tubing, and moves through very slowly, perhaps at the rate of three quarts an hour. As water passes slowly through the coiled narrow tube, aerobic bacteria on the tube walls near the entrance oxidize the organics. Eventually, somewhere along the tube, the oxygen is used up and only anaerobic bacteria are available for organic decomposition. At this point, the anaerobes begin reducing nitrate in the tube to nitrogen gas and oxygen. If oxygen levels fall completely but too high an organic load continues through the tubing, there is danger of hydrogen sulfide-generating bacteria blooming in the tube and producing noxious H_2S gas. If organics are low but nitrates are high, then the bacteria need supplementary food. The system depends on a long and slow passage through a coil with an extensive anaerobic component and low organics.

Drawbacks: Cutting to the chase, live rock does the job with a lot less care than coil denitrators. Coil denitrators require a food source (70 percent lactose, 30 percent sucrose dissolved in RO water to a final concentration of 15 percent or 15 grams per 100 ml of water). This sugar solution is delivered to the reaction vessel mounted above the sump at a rate of 5 percent of tank capacity four times a day (use a timer). Tank water enters the reaction tubing for denitrification at the rate of 3 ml/minute. It takes several weeks for the tubing in the reaction vessel to develop stable anaerobic bacterial flora with denitrifiers predominating and hydrogen sulfide producers only a minor component. Finally, before dripping into the sump, the effluent should pass through granular activated carbon to remove traces of hydrogen sulfide. The coil units are expensive, require constant monitoring of the effluent, and can undergo sudden microbial population shifts resulting in failure to denitrify, production of excess hydrogen sulfide, or the production of other noxious chemicals.

Cycling the Aquarium

Bacteria increase by cell division. One bacterium becomes two, two become four, four become eight, and so on. Mathematically, the growth of the population is logarithmic to the base 2. This doubling of the population can occur every 24–32 hours if the temperature is optimal, nutrients are freely available, wastes are rapidly eliminated, and nothing else interferes with reproduction. That's a theoretical rate that seldom continues very long, but the more conducive all conditions, the faster the population increases.

In a new aquarium, there are few ammonia-oxidizing and nitrite-oxidizing aerobic bacteria other than those introduced with rock, coral, contaminated hands, nets, and the like. There is little ammonia and virtually no nitrite. Gradually animal metabolism adds ammonia to the water. When the ammonia builds up to optimal levels, *Nitrosomonas* and related ammonia oxidizers grow at a logarithmic rate and suddenly are able to metabolize all the ammonia as fast as it is produced. In the meantime, *Nitrobacter* and other nitrite oxidizers await the conversion of ammonia to nitrite by the *Nitrosomonas* group. Eventually, the nitrite level will be high enough to allow *Nitrobacter* also to undergo logarithmic growth, and the nitrite levels in the aquarium will suddenly plummet.

Goniopora **have polyps and tentacles long enough to sting other corals and don't need sweeper tentacles to defend a territory. All need intense light, moderately low current, supplemental large zooplankton, and exceptionally good water quality. They are not recommended for beginners. Many of them waste away after a few months in captivity.**

This 4–6 week period for growing large populations of ammonia- and nitrite-oxidizers is the break-in time for an aquarium, during which, to promote the process, the tank should have only hardy animals (damselfish, hermit crabs) tolerant of ammonia and nitrite, and vigorous aeration. Alternatively, one could start the cycle chemically by adding ammonium chloride to the water.

The end product of this bacterial metabolism is nitrate. Over time, the concentration of nitrate can increase markedly. With ordinary marine aquariums, the only control of nitrate levels is through water changes and algal growth and harvest.

Until recently, we had no way to eliminate nitrates sufficiently to keep corals in captivity. With the advent of live rock and an understanding of its microbiology, all that has changed. In the minireef aquarium *with live rock and/or deep gravel*, nitrate levels will first peak and then plummet as anaerobic bacteria at the bottom of the rock pores and in the gravel attain logarithmic growth and maximum population size. At this point, chemical readings for ammonia, nitrite, and nitrate should all be near zero. The tank is now completely cycled.

Cycling of the minireef tank takes about 8–10 weeks. The cycle can be accelerated by adding lots of live rock or a large dose (a five-gallon bucket) of live sand (soaked sand/gravel/shell hash from an underwater source rather than dry sand from the beach) to increase the initial numbers of bacteria. Once cycled, large fluctuations in feeding and livestock populations should be avoided as they can promote overgrowth by other bacteria that displace the nitrifiers, allowing a buildup of nitrites to harmful concentrations (>0.1 mg/L)—faster than the bacteria can metabolize these nitrites to harmless nitrates.

Carbon

Carbon dioxide in the atmosphere freely dissolves in water. That's important, for dissolved CO_2 then can be incorporated into living tissues. In fact, carbon is literally the backbone of living tissues. Chemical structures containing carbon atoms are called organic compounds. The study of these compounds in living systems is called biochemistry.

Water is not quite H_2O. Its reactivity will be better understood if we write it as $H^{+-}OH \underset{\leftarrow}{=} \rightarrow HOH$. In other words, a certain percentage of the proton (H^+) and hydroxyl (^-OH) ions making up water is available to react with other molecules. One of those molecules is carbon dioxide (CO_2).

Carbon dioxide reacts with water to form carbonic acid ($H_2O + CO_2 \rightarrow H_2CO_3$). Carbonic acid in turn is in equilibrium with free protons (H^+) and carbonate (HCO_3^-) and bicarbonate ($CO_3^=$).

The pH of water is affected by the relative concentrations of carbon dioxide, acidic carbonate, and alkaline bicarbonate. Ocean water is stable at pH 8.1–8.4 because the bicarbonate and carbon dioxide equilibrium absorbs and disposes of acidic protons (H^+). In aquariums, pH can vary dramatically and should be monitored.

Calcium Carbonate Deposits

Carbonate reacts with calcium ions to form calcium carbonate ($CaCO_3$). It also reacts with strontium, magnesium, and other elements to form strontium carbonate, magnesium carbonate, and other compounds found in the deposits of clams, corals, fishes, algae, and other marine life. Most limestones and shells are mixes of deposits of carbonates of calcium, magnesium, and strontium. The most common mix in ancient limestones and modern shellfish is calcite. Dolomite is another type of calcium carbonate. The most common mix in corals and coralline algae is aragonite. These materials are capable of buffering water by breaking apart the calcium from the carbonate, feeding the carbonate/bicarbonate equilibrium. Most of these materials are stable and slow to dissolve. Aragonite (oolite), deposited by corals and calcareous algae, is the least stable and most recent limestone. The pH of deep gravel beds is low so that aragonite can dissolve, releasing calcium ions and carbonates/bicarbonates. The released carbonates once more are taken up by growing corals and calcareous algae, while the bicarbonates buffer the seawater by neutralizing acids (protons) from waste and decomposition.

Chapter Six
Powerheads and Water Pumps

All powerheads and water pumps are centrifugal pumps that must be at or below the level of the water; they cannot pull water upwards, but they can push it upwards to different heights depending on design (head pressure) rather than electric power consumption. You need to select the right one for the specific application, and that means how many gallons you need delivered to a certain height. Powerheads that have the same rated flows on the package may differ in head performance.

For those unfamiliar with the term, head pressure is pump output in pounds per square inch; for water pumps, it is an indicator of how high water can be pushed (for air pumps, it is an indicator of how deeply air can be pushed below water level or how far it can be pushed through narrow pipes). If you just want to stir water about, you don't need head pressure, and submersible powerheads are all you require. If you want to raise water several feet from a sump below the tank back to the tank, then you need a pump that offers several feet of head pressure. That can be either a large submersible powerhead or a typical external water pump. With that in mind, let's look at pumps for reef tanks.

Powerheads: Simple submersible powerheads are most often used in the aquarium hobby to drive water flow through under-gravel filters. These powerheads use little electricity and are inexpensive. Because powerheads are submerged,

water flows into the vane cavity to prime the pump, so they generally don't cavitate. Reef tank keepers use submersible powerheads to create currents in tanks, to return

A nylon impeller spins rapidly within the electromagnetic field of its powerhead drawing water into and pumping it out of the unit. Some powerheads must be mounted near the surface to take advantage of an optional venturi air supply (note airline). The water intake is screened to keep mobile livestock out of the attractive nuisance of a dark tube.

Large external water pumps move huge volumes of water to considerable heights. Their flow is controlled by placing a gate valve or ball valve in the outflow. Were it placed at the inflow, back pressure would damage the pump.

water from sumps, or to drive some (not many) venturi protein skimmers. Very few powerheads can push water a height of six feet.

Powerheads of different sizes drive 20–200 gallons per hour at zero head. Most are inadequate for running the larger venturi skimmers or the returns to very high tanks. Powerheads typically run water through a half-inch port. They shed waste heat to the tank (or sump) water, and will burn out if run dry. The metal spindles (on which the vanes are mounted) can corrode; the better, newer powerheads have corrosion-free ceramic spindles. Because there is no filter between their intakes and the tank water with all its debris, the spindles also become wrapped in algal or polyester fibers, causing the unit to slow and finally fail.

Water pumps: Big air-cooled water pumps are not submersible. Mounted outside the aquarium, they move larger volumes of water, often at considerable head pressure, some pushing 1,000 or more gallons per hour even at five feet of head. These pumps are protected from damaging fibers by filter pads, and can be further protected by inserting a settling basin barrier to collect debris between the tank or sump and the pump's intake port. Some have air slits and fans to disperse heat, while others radiate heat through the metal skin. Some small pumps produce little heat that can be carried away by the water passing through. Most pull 85–250 watts, the larger ones in the 1/10th horsepower range. Water pumps must be primed by flooding before being switched on or they cavitate and fail to work. Most have thermally protected motors that shut off if they overheat.

Caution: Most external water pumps require flow restrictors to produce just the flow you need, rather than all the pump is able to put out. Otherwise, the pump may flood the aquarium, pull the sump dry, or overflow the skimmer to which it is rigged. The most common flow restrictors are ball or gate valves that can be finely tuned to control output. The valve must always be mounted on the discharge side of the pump. If mounted on the intake side, it will cause the pump to work very hard and burn out. For the same reason, the intake side should be kept absolutely clean to prevent flow restriction into the pump.

Chapter Seven
Filters

There are all kinds of filters for all kinds of applications. Some types are very popular today, but all types have value and roles in marine aquarium husbandry. Rather than focus on what's hot and what's not, this chapter will describe how filters work, what types are available, and the most appropriate applications.

Filtration of reef aquariums requires mechanical, chemical, and biological removal of wastes. Early in the history of the reef hobby, most tanks were equipped with undergravel filters to break down nitrogenous wastes. That gave way to trickling filters with their much higher level of organic decomposition. Subsequently some aquarists rediscovered a series of old articles by Eng reporting the use of no filters at all, just sunlight and collected wild rock. Eng noted that in his "natural system tanks" there was no measurable level of nitrate. Pioneering reef aquarists took the Eng reports, correctly interpreted the results as due to the deep pores providing denitrification, and began adding wild (live) rock to tanks already equipped with trickling filters and protein skimmers. Subsequently the Germans published reports that removal of the trickling filter in a tank equipped with live rock actually lowered nitrogenous waste levels from very little (with trickling filters) to practically zero without them. Aquarists rushed to disconnect their trickling filters.

This combination of brilliant lighting, live rock, and a protein skimmer (but no trickling filter) is called the Berlin system, and is the most widely used reef tank technique today.

The Berlin system relies solely on protein skimming (foam fractionation) to remove organics and on porous rock and/or aragonite gravel to provide nitrification (mineralization) and denitrification. It would seem that other types of filtration are superfluous, but that is not the case. Activated carbon is important in removing noxious chemicals emitted by some soft corals and other invertebrates and in removing yellow tints produced by the metabolism of green macroalgae. The activated carbon must be positioned for ease of replacement, cleaning, or regeneration, and there is no better place than in a separate mechanical filter such as a box filter, an outside power filter, or a canister filter. These filters provide additional benefits.

Hang-on Power Filters

Hang-on outside power filters provide a simple means of placing and replacing activated carbon. The simple ones are best. Avoid hang-on power filters professing trickling filter capability; the claim is just hyperbole to create a market niche or to justify an uncompetitive price. Air-driven units, and especially those driven by open-vented electric motors, should be avoided. Get a unit with sealed magnetic drive, replaceable parts, adequate finger space for removing the impeller for cleaning, UL-listing, and replaceable, inexpensive filter cartridges combining floss and activated carbon. Measure the width of your aquarium rim to be certain that the reverse U-shaped lip with which the filter hangs onto your aquarium is sufficiently wide; most of these units are not built for very large aquariums that, of necessity, have very thick frames.

Canister Filters

Canister filters are very efficient for forced water at high rates through compact layers of granular activated carbon and alternating layers of foam, coral, or shell

A prefilter allows you to place a trickling filter on an undrilled aquarium. The prefilter skims water from inside the tank, delivers it to a sponge-filter box outside the tank via a siphon tube, and then allows it to fall to the trickling filter below mounted in a sump. Bubbles of air in tank water will collect in the tube and break the siphon if the flow rate is insufficient to rush the bubbles through to the outer box.

hash pebbles that provide a biological bed for nitrogen-cycle bacteria. Canisters are most important in tanks without an aragonite gravel/sand substratum. Use about one pound of GAC in the canister filter for each 25 gallons of aquarium water, and change a third of the GAC when the water begins to yellow. More than any other aquarium equipment on the market, canister filters vary in quality of fabricating materials, so rely on dealer recommendations and guarantees and never forget to use the O-ring. Avoid units with multiple pored discharge wands, as the pores tend to clog and the suction cups on the wands tend to slip. Avoid top-heavy units (motor mounted above rather than at the base), those with thin toggle line switches (they get wet and fail), and units with flimsy internal media baskets. Look for the capacity for diatomaceous earth filtration, various possible configurations, and interchangeable parts among models. Seek ease of starting and disconnecting, and visible discharges; should a filter clog and restrict flow, the motor can burn out (a vexing problem with submerged powerheads).

Internal canister filters may be difficult to service, may clog and not reveal the interrupted flow, and may be overdesigned, offering unneeded and unwanted extras, such as heater ports and bioballs for nitrification.

Trickling Filters

Trickling filters are not popular in reef tanks today because they mineralize nitrogenous compounds to nitrate, rather than remove those compounds entirely from the system, as do protein skimmers. However, low levels of nitrate have not been found harmful to corals. The trickling filter is beneficial in tanks with a large bioload of (especially carnivorous) fish that excrete and eject quantities of wastes.

Ammonia Stripping, Fact or Fantasy?

There are various sizes and configurations of void spaces in so-called bioballs, and some advertisements claim that their products have the optimal void space to drive off ammonia. That may be true in industrial applications, but it isn't in the home aquarium. In industrial plants and massive public aquariums, ammonia stripping is possible. There, great volumes of compressed air are driven at high speed from the bottom of the filter bed up through the trickling medium to provide a very rapid counter-current rich in oxygen; with eight feet or more of vertical space and a powerful air flow, and at an adjusted pH of around 10 (which is then adjusted downward after treatment), void space (the ratio of air to water film) increases the efficiency of ammonia stripping. For home aquarium applications, ammonia stripping is a myth. That's because trickling filter height is too short, you don't have a massive volume of compressed air to rush over an eight-foot column of packed bioballs, and there is no safe way to raise the pH to 10 and assure that it comes down to the pH 8 range before returning to the aquarium. Without the right pH and enough height for a long run of rushing air over the thin layer, the void space becomes irrelevant.

Note: For the limits that are possible in home aquariums, any inert medium, including scrap plastic, hair curlers, and loose filter floss, will work as well as plastic spheres, so long as the medium *remains loosely packed* and air can reach all parts of the thin layer of biological organisms. Be alert, however, to the danger of gradual packing down from a heavy organic load, which will reduce aerobic decomposition in favor of inefficient microaerophilic (low oxygen) oxidation, and even less efficient anaerobic (no oxygen) decomposition.

Trickling filters are excellent backup systems should your protein skimmer's air injector or limewood diffusers clog. Their production of nitrates is a minor concern; their enhanced evaporation is far more relevant, but this is a nuisance rather than a water-quality issue.

With trickling filters, water bearing heavy organic loads, but without silt or debris, falls or trickles as a thin film over an inert medium such as rock or plastic "bioballs." Water running on any inert substance anywhere will develop a growing film of bacteria and other organisms that utilize the organic substances in the water as an energy and food source, and leave the water cleaner than when it entered the system. The difference between trickling filtration and submerse filtration is that, when a thin film of water in air is used, the colonizing organisms are much more efficient. That's because the surrounding air (which is adjacent to the wet bacteria) is 21 percent oxygen, while water might contain only 8 percent oxygen. The higher the oxygen concentration, the more efficient the aerobic bacteria. In a trickling filter, the organisms degrade virtually all the organics coming into the system, rather than only a portion limited by the oxygen in deeper water.

When the organisms (bacteria, fungi, protozoa, rotifers, algae, nematodes, and others) initially coat the inert surfaces, they form a very thin film, and oxygen is available to all the "bugs." As the population of microbes takes nutrients out of the water and converts them into new biological biomass, the thickness of the living layer

You can retrofit an undrilled tank with a hang-on trickling filter. The small box prefilter (right) skims the surface inside the aquarium. A siphon transfers this water to the bulk of the unit hanging on the outside. Particles are removed by filter floss, then trickled down in the air over a layer of inert material such as these bioballs where aerobic nitrifying bacteria convert ammonia and nitrite to nitrate. A totally submerged and oxygen deficient layer at the bottom promotes denitrifying bacteria that consume some of the nitrate before the water is returned to the aquarium.

increases, becomes visible, and eventually unsightly. Now the biological community is thick enough (and this varies with the system and flow rate) to cause the inside "bugs" to starve for oxygen, and they die off, lose their grip on the surface, and the entire colony sloughs away from the plastic, falling to the bottom of the sump as "mulm." Immersed under water, the surviving biological mulm organisms also die from lack of oxygen. This mulm or gunk must be removed as it becomes a source of anaerobic decomposition with its attendant production of organic acids (a great deal) and hydrogen sulfide gas (very little while the pumps are running, but possibly a great deal during a power outage). That's why a trickling filter requires cleaning. Never just set it and forget it.

I strongly believe that a trickling filter is a useful appendage to a basic Berlin system built on intense light and lots of live rock. Some low levels of nitrate are not a prob-

lem; high levels that might ensue should a skimmer fail are a very real danger.

Building a simple trickling filter: Take a five-gallon plastic bucket filled with bioballs and build a discharge port at the bottom. Locate a marina, and purchase a through-hull fitting that consists of a port and locking nut. At a hardware store, purchase a plastic cutting head for a power drill and matching starter drill bit. Be certain that your through-hull fitting and plastic cutting head are the same size. Bring along a powerhead from home, and at least six feet of plastic tubing that will fit over the powerhead discharge. Get a smaller length of wider tubing that will fit over the discharge port of the through-hull fitting. Your discharge port and tubing should always be much wider than the intake tubing. Drill a hole an inch above the bottom of the plastic bucket (to allow room for the locking nut) and insert the fitting, then tighten the locking nut until it deforms the bucket. A glob of silicone sealant will protect against leaking. A powerhead on the undergravel filter stem or lying among rocks takes up tank water, and through the long plastic tube on its discharge port delivers the water into a small hole cut into the top of the bucket. Driving a long stainless steel nail through that end of the hose within the bucket will keep the hose from pulling out. The pumped-up water trickles down the bioballs and exits the bucket at the lower port, falling by gravity back into the aquarium.

Trickling filters range from simple hang-on retrofit units to monsters that could drive the space shuttle's wastewater treatment needs. In some units, one can add carbon and media canisters to the trickling filter water path to remove other dissolved substances from the water; or one can provide fittings for dripping in trace additives, in effect using the trickling filter sump and bioball box for adding a variety of chemical treatments and physical media out of sight, and away from direct contact with the tank's inhabitants.

Trickling filters are less critical in reef tanks with very small biological inputs (foods), especially those with big protein skimmers and abundant live rock. A rock-laden system with one or two protein skimmers on one tank can replace the need for trickling filtration and achieve even greater reductions in nitrate and phosphate levels. Double skimmers are the latest variation on the Berlin system. It is fine for reef tanks with very small organic loadings, but is risky where meats are fed to fishes or invertebrates, in that case, supplemental trickling filtration is preferred. What is the explanation? Trickling filtration is an aerobic process that mineralizes ammonia to nitrite and then to nitrate, so nitrate is always found at the end of the process. Live rock provides both aerobic (on the surface) and anaerobic (in the deep pores) conversion of ammonia with both processes occurring in close proximity. As a result, nitrate produced on the surface of the live rock is transferred deep into the rock for denitrification by anaerobic bacteria, and nitrate levels in the water become undetectable.

The effectiveness of the Berlin system has been tested by many aquarists. When you remove the media from a trickling filter after several months of active use, the nitrate and phosphate levels should drop from a normally achieved 5 mg/L and 0.5 mg/L, respectively, to zero. You will achieve the same result by simply removing the trickling filter from the reef system.

Fluidized Bed Filtration

The fluidized bed reactor is a recent application from the wastewater treatment industry to the aquarium hobby. Surface area is colonized by microbes to provide nitrogenous waste mineralization in richly

Most trickling filters are made to be mounted inside a sump. This one trickles water down over double layered spiral (DLS) and a totally submerged sponge to promote denitrification.

oxygenated water. Wastewater is slowly forced into the lower end of a column containing water rushing upward fast enough to keep sand in suspension, the turbulence driven by a powerhead. Excess water, now mineralized, exits the top through an overflow located above the highest level reached by the elevated sand-water column. Both entrance and exit can be through the top of the unit, so long as entering wastewater is delivered to the bottom of the column by an inside tube.

Advantages to fluidized bed filtration:
1. High degree of mineralization
2. Continuous removal of sediment and particles in the overflow
3. Small space required
4. Elimination of need to change sand, because tumbling and friction prevent formation of thick biological mats on sand, as they form on bioballs in trickling filters
5. Evaporation, enhanced in trickling filtration, is reduced.

Fluidized bed filtration is rapidly finding new converts in both the wastewater and aquarium industries. Costs of equipment

A fluidized bed reactor's sandstorm should rise to about halfway within the reaction chamber, as in this hang-on model.

are low and continue to fall. You can easily build a system at home from clear polyvinyl chloride (PVC), filling with ordinary silica sand, and powering with a powerhead. The powerhead should be mounted above or outside the filter to keep it from clogging with sand when electrical power goes off. A tube from the powerhead extends to the bottom of the tall, narrow, clear PVC cylinder. A hole drilled in the upper side (or a notch at the top) allows water to overflow back into the sump. The cylinder is filled a few inches at a time with ordinary play sand to provide surfaces for aerobic nitrifying bacteria and the powerhead energized. The sandstorm within the cylinder should reach just above the halfway mark, well short of the overflow. Add sand until the correct level is attained. Always use silica sand, because aragonite sand dissolves, defeating the purpose of the sand's providing a self-cleaning aerobic bacterial bed.

Note: The powerhead intake port should be covered with a sponge filter to keep particles of detritus out of the fluidized bed.

Algal Mat Filtration

Growing plants on animal wastes is nothing new. Farmers spread cattle manure on potato fields. Third world farmers use algae fertilized by human waste (night soil) washed off crop fields to grow tilapia. Municipal wastewater treatment plants grow duckweed on wastewater settling ponds to take up nitrates, phosphates, metals, and other materials that are then converted into cattle or poultry feed, or used as a soil amendment for crops. Pondkeepers keep their koi and goldfish ponds cleansed with edible duckweed.

Algal mat filtration is one alternative for eliminating wastes. It is no more natural than foam fractionation (equivalent to wind-blown foaming), but the production of masses of vegetation appeals to some aquarists; it is measurable, like the green gunk in the skimmer collection cup.

Methods of algal mat filtration are in-tank algal growth, plant growth in a refugium, and use of an algal turf compartment.

In-tank algal growth: These algae can sometimes be controlled by herbivores. In most cases, algal growth is insufficient for removing nitrates, organics, phosphates, metals, and toxins. Too many herbivores are required (more than two snails per gallon and more than one tang per 25 gallons, for example). In-tank excessive algal growth occurs during nuisance (hair) algal blooms, and blooms can kill valuable corals. Nonetheless, algal blooms remove excess nutrients and noxious metals. Blooms can also produce noxious chemicals such as algal toxins.

The refugium: This accessory tank accomplishes waste removal by algae (or vascular plants) in a separate aquarium connected by piping to the minireef tank. Water is pumped between the two aquariums, and algae are allowed to grow luxuriantly, free of grazers, in the refugium. The refugium requires intense round-the-clock light to keep the algae and/or vascular plants net oxygen emitters; should the lights go off, the vegetation will take up oxygen from both aquariums. Preferred refugium algae are fast growers that take up waste nutrients as fast as they are produced. The fastest growers are those considered nuisance algae in minireef aquariums. In fact, the refugium can become a constant source of nuisance algae that infest the minireef aquarium if the refugium flow is not filtered.

Fast-growing, attractive *Caulerpa* species are also excellent refugium waste absorbers. The advantage of the refugium is its ability to grow organisms that would not survive in the minireef tank, such as the small crustacean amphipods that can later be used as minireef food. The refugium can also be used to grow colorful shrimp or baby marine fish. Because the purpose of the refugium is removal of excess wastes, the algae must be periodically harvested and discarded. A refugium without supplementary foam fractionation or carbon filtration can lead to yellowing of the minireef aquarium water.

The algal turf compartment: The usual accessory for algal mat filtration is a plastic box placed above or beside the minireef, fitted with large amounts of surface area (plastic window screening or 1–3 mm plastic grids), and provided flowing tank water and intense, close, 24-hour light. Over time, the grid surfaces become coated with microbes and then with a mixed community of nuisance algae. As this algal turf grows, it absorbs increasingly more wastes, converting them to plant biomass. Unattended, the mass can grow so large that fragments break off and wash into the minireef tank, or water flow becomes blocked. The mass

The intake port of the powerhead driving a fluidized bed reactor must be covered with sponge material to protect the sand bed from detritus particles.

should be kept cropped to provide a balance between mass and growth rate. If the mass is cropped too short, its volume is insufficient to do the work required. An algal mat should grow fast enough to be harvested and washed once or twice a month. If the mat is cropped and washed less often, it is either not doing its job or is overgrown with noxious cyanobacteria. If you crop and wash the mat more often, you may be washing away important algal base growth. An entire book has been devoted to the promotion of this system (W.H. Adey and K. Loveland, Dynamic Aquaria, Academic Press, San Diego). The system is used by some aquarists and several public aquaria. The plastic light boxes and grids are available commercially, but the technique has not become widespread in the hobby because of its complexity, need for a separate lighted system, and the leakage by plants of organic substances that tint aquarium water yellow.

Chapter Eight
Protein Skimmers

Protein skimmers (foam fractionaters) have been in the marine hobby almost fifty years. The importance of fine aeration from wooden air diffusers to increase oxygen saturation was an early finding, along with the observation that ugly slime and gunk accumulate at the waterline. An early idea was to adhere a four-inch wide strip of glass catercornered and just up from the bottom of the tank, extending a couple of inches above the water level. A wooden air diffuser was affixed to stiff tubing inside the chamber. Water entered from the bottom, rose with the fine bubbles delivered from a powerful air pump, rolled around randomly inside the chamber, eventually exiting from the same bottom slit. The fine bubbles at the top confined gunk and deposited it within the chamber, so that the waterline of the tank was no longer dirty and ugly. The accumulated gunk was wiped from the top of the chamber by hand.

The significance of that large volume of gunk was recognized at once, and so the protein skimmer was born.

What do skimmers do, and how do they do it? You've seen skimming in nature in the form of foam on an ocean beach during a windy day. The foam is least noticeable in the nutrient-poor tropical oceans, and most pronounced in the Intracoastal Waterway where salinity is brackish but the dissolved organic load is higher than in the ocean.

Skimming or foam fractionation consists of two events occurring simultaneously and continuously. The initiating action is denaturation (modification of molecular structure) of proteins and peptides that are produced by the tank inhabitants or added to the tank as food. Wastes are also produced by algae and cyanobacteria. These proteins and peptides are fragile compounds. When you heat the white of an egg (albumin is virtually pure protein), the hydrogen bonding that gives that protein its unique chemical structure is broken, and the protein collapses upon itself; what you observe is denaturation (collapse) of the albumin pro-

Skimmer Care

Wooden air diffusers for countercurrent skimmers should be replaced when bubble size increases or total air release drops noticeably, about monthly or every two months. The air intake on a venturi skimmer should be cleaned by inserting flexible airline tubing into the pore, then inserting the other end into a quart of very hot water, letting the hot water be sucked up to wash out dust and grease. All skimmers should be disassembled and cleaned when the walls are heavily coated.

Some experts believe that skimmers work best when used intermittently (the surge cleans the air passages), and at night, so that putting the skimmer on a timer to operate only after dark will increase skimmer longevity and efficiency.

tein. You can also get denaturation by adding vinegar or lime juice (hydrogen ions) to egg white (changing the pH). In short, heat, acid, alkali, and many other chemical and physical insults to the very weak hydrogen bonds of proteins can cause denaturation, visible as an opaque precipitation out of a clear solution. One of those precipitating insults is violent exposure to oxygen in air or some other highly reactive gas (such as ozone).

Fine air bubbles, and lots of them in violent motion, are effective denaturers of sensitive protein. That's the first stage of foam fractionation, and it generates myriad particles of—and this is important—sticky, sticky, sticky precipitated protein. In the second stage, other materials adhere to the denatured protein, things like drifting algae, bacteria, protozoa, fungi, small molecules (including nutrients), and even heavy metals and pigments. All this takes time, so the longer that bubble remains in the water, the more it can collect.

The earliest skimmer was a catercorner plate inside the aquarium, open at the bottom, and enclosing an air diffuser. The water in the chamber rolled around in all directions and eventually was replaced through random movement as it leaked out of the reaction chamber. Gunk was concentrated at the top of the chamber.

Cocurrent Skimmers

The first real protein skimmer offered to the hobby was the cocurrent skimmer, also installed inside the aquarium. Air and water delivered at the base allowed the water to escape through pores in the reaction chamber just below the water level, while air bubbles continued to rise inside the elevated tube, pushing the foam upward into a collection zone. The problem with the cocurrent skimmer is that water and air move in the same direction, contact time between the water and air is short, and the water is only partially cleaned before leaving the contact chamber.

Countercurrent Skimmers

A significant step up is today's countercurrent skimmer. Air is delivered at the base, but the water is fed into the top of the skimmer and driven out the bottom. The bubbles are slowed as they fight the downward current, and contact time between water and air is greatly increased, resulting in greater efficiency. The reverse water flow can be driven by a second air diffuser inserted in the other side of a U-shaped unit; its only function is to move the water—downward out of the contact chamber, through the connecting base, and upward

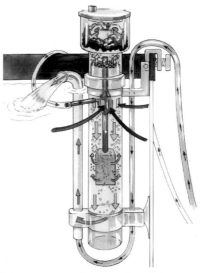

A hang-on countercurrent protein skimmer takes little space and requires no water level adjustment. If the air supply is from a pump passing water to a limewood air diffuser, that diffuser must be replaced when the bubble output is reduced or the bubbles seem larger. Both indicate the diffuser is becoming clogged and ineffective, and putting backpressure on the air pump.

How to Buy a Skimmer

Which is better, the lime wood air diffuser countercurrent skimmer or the venturi? Neither is better. Both can do a good job based on the quality and quantity of the dark green gunk. Individual models of either type differ in ease of takedown for cleaning and in the frequency of cleaning required. Generally, the larger the unit, the less often it needs disassembly for cleaning. The flip side is that large units with considerable bioload can themselves pollute the tank if they should shut down, then suddenly come back on line, breaking off and releasing large volumes of oxygen-deprived gunk to the aquarium.

Among countercurrent skimmers, those with replaceable wooden diffusers are best. Avoid units in which the diffuser and hard plastic tubing are a single unit available only from the manufacturer, those with tight space that require you to use small replaceable diffusers (try to replace the wooden diffuser in the store before you buy), and any units "guaranteed" to never need cleaning!

Does height make a difference? The optimal air-water interface has been reputed to be 30 inches in a single pass. From this, many have assumed that shorter skimmers are less efficient, while taller skimmers would provide no additional benefits. There is no substance to this claim. Many industrial and public aquarium skimmers, designed for maximum efficiency by engineers, are more than three times this height.

out the release chamber of the U—faster than the precipitating bubbles from the other air release move water upward. This can be accomplished using equal air releases, but making the contact chamber wider than the water discharge chamber; the narrower the chamber, the faster the water will move through it. Alternatively, you can control water direction using a powerhead or water pump. Moving the water with a pump now allows the skimmer to be placed outside the tank, with longer chambers with more air-water contact time.

Countercurrent skimmers rely either on compressed air supplied by an air pump and released into the contact chamber through air diffusers, or upon a fine hole inside a cone within the water path to draw air by venturi suction from the atmosphere into the water stream.

Important: These are the basic skimmer types. Contact time (Tc) between bubble and water is fundamental, but so is bubble size. The finer the bubbles, and the more you can crowd for the longest time into the contact chamber, the greater the removal efficiency of the skimmer. (It's analogous to using very fine carbon rather than large granules.)

There are intrinsic and extrinsic limits on bubble size. Intrinsically, certain woods (especially lime wood) can produce the finest bubbles from a compressed air source. Extrinsically, bubble size is also a function of the salinity and pH of the water; at high salinity and pH, you get fine bubbles. That's why you can get some foam fractionation in fresh water, but only if the water is hard (lots of dissolved solids), alkaline (as in African reef tanks), and heavily laden with organics (otherwise you won't see any results of the mechanical work).

Wooden air diffusers are effective, but clog with use and degrade when used in ozone delivery systems. They need replacing every month or two.

Venturi Skimmers

All venturis rely on powerheads or water pumps to circulate water in rapid circular motion inside the reaction chamber, pulling air into the water stream (the venturi effect) by friction. Some require a separate pump to deliver water to the skimmer from the aquarium.

Venturi skimmers last indefinitely, need only occasional cleaning but not diffuser replacement, produce a great volume of bubbles, can be made of ozone-resistant materials, and rely on long-lived water pumps or inexpensive powerheads rather than short-lived diaphragm air pumps. Large venturi skimmers require large pumps, but today's smaller models can be operated with powerheads.

A particularly vexing problem when hooking up some skimmers, both venturi and lime wood, is determining the correct elevation in relation to water level in the tank or the sump. Often a minor adjustment in skimmer elevation will obviate the need for a larger, more expensive pump. Manufacturers usually recommend the correct level in relation to sump or tank. A nice innovation is the hang-on skimmer. When draped over the tank frame, only minor adjustments in tank water level or powerhead output will result in optimal skimmer efficiency.

Skimmer size: There is no standard volumetric relationship in the industry of, for example, × cubic inches of skimmer reaction chamber per gallon of tank. It is organic loading of the tank that matters. The best advice is to get the largest unit you can afford for any tank over 50 gallons; hang-on skimmers of high quality are adequate for smaller tanks.

Depending on pump output, air output, organic load, and skimmer elevation, the bubbles might rise too fast, carrying too much water and not enough gunk. In that case, your skimmer might waste a lot of tank water for the work it does. You would prefer it to be otherwise.

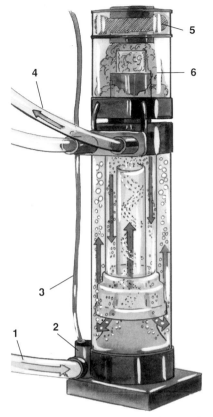

1. **water inlet from sump**
2. **venturi fitting**
3. **venturi air injector**
4. **water returns to sump**
5. **carbon chamber**
6. **debris removal chamber**

Larger floor or sump mounted venturi countercurrent protein skimmers are usually driven by an external air-cooled water pump. The venturi port draws in atmospheric air to fill the low pressure space where the pump-driven water suddenly flows into a larger chamber. The airline entering the venturi port should be placed into a glass of hot water once a week to clean the venturi and keep it from clogging.

One solution is putting a screen support into the bubble chamber, slowing ascent and letting the bubbles age. This increase in bubble age helps more heavily laden bubbles to get to the top of the column, and promotes a denser discharge, rich in gunk and poor in water.

The venturi nipple on top of the lower nozzle (intake) inserts air into the water stream of this countercurrent protein skimmer.

Fine tuning a skimmer usually requires flow control from the powerhead or water pump (if applicable), often accomplished through a PVC ball or gate valve.

"Good gunk" should be blackish green at first; if you're getting straw-colored water, and lots of it, your bubbles are inefficient, probably because the skimmer is at the wrong elevation or you're pumping water too quickly through the system, not allowing enough Tc. Too much air flow can also decrease skimmer efficiency. If you cannot get a dark gunk, then the unit is of poor design for the job or you've succeeded in removing all the gunk as fast as it is forming. Some skimmers never provide a dark gunk, only a thin green waste or none at all. It will still do the job needed. Simply set it to provide its thin watery waste and replace the waste with new water as necessary. Think of it as providing skimming and water changes simultaneously.

Note: Every reef tank should have as large a skimmer as possible. Does this mean skimmers are the holy grail and trickling filters should be retired? Many marine experts advise eliminating trickling filters in order to lower the nitrate level to zero. I disagree. There is no evidence that moderate levels of nitrate (e.g., 5–10 mg/L) harm corals. At the very least, the trickling filter is a redundant life support system providing supplemental mechanical and chemical filtration and additional aeration and degassing for a complex marine community whose existence is never far from precarious.

Chapter Nine
UV Sterilizers and Ozonizers

Ultraviolet Sterilizers

Ultraviolet light is invisible energy in the range of 1,900 to 4,000 angstroms (Å), which is the same as 190 to 400 nanometers (nm). Energies higher than 2,000 Å fall into the realm of X rays and then gamma rays (both produced by stars). These various types of radiation are capable of oxidizing atoms and molecules into unstable, reactive ions.

Ultraviolet light, the weakest of the ionizing radiations, can damage DNA. Some microbes can repair minor DNA damage shortly after it occurs, but excessive and prolonged UV exposure causes irreparable damage by breaking the chromosomes.

The ultraviolet range of wave lengths is often divided into categories of increasing energy, known as UV-A, UV-B, and (most energetic) UV-C. High energy UV-C can destroy the nucleic acids of microbes with minimal contact time and wattage. UV bulbs designed for water sterilization emit at 2,537 Å. Because UV rays are absorbed by glass, water, and dissolved salts, maximum germicidal effects require that the 2,537 Å bulb be enclosed in quartz through which the radiation can freely pass. To be most effective, sterilizers must operate above 100°F and must keep the water to be sterilized (to kill the entrained microbes) within millimeters of the emitting source for a prolonged contact time. Just as in photography, the effect depends on intensity, distance from the light source, and exposure time.

A sterilizer unit consists of a PVC tube to contain the water, electric ballast, quartz sleeve for the UV bulb, and O-rings to prevent leakage. The units are designed to slow the water outflow so the period spent around the emitting bulb is sufficient (dwell time) to kill the most resistant microbes and algae (50,000–100,000 microwatts per

Blue light from this canister-mounted UV sterilizer unit indicates that it is turned on. Water is retained for a long contact time to assure the germicidal UV-C is effective. (The other unit contains a diatomaceous earth filter requiring that water pressure be monitored to protect the pump).

second per square centimeter of UV bulb surface). Martin Moe has recommended a maximum flow rate of 30 gallons per hour per watt. Less gallonage per hour per watt increases effectiveness of the unit. Because effectiveness falls off with age and slime, bulbs should be replaced every six months and cleaned regularly, at least monthly. Cool aquarium water also reduces effectiveness, so a larger than necessary unit is recommended for maximum effectiveness.

Ozonizers

Ozone is another effective killer of microorganisms, better than UV ionizing irradiation because it remains in the water for some time and can be carried considerable distances where it continues to sterilize. Ozone is produced by electrostatic generators and by UV lights. An aerator supplies air to the ozonizer, and also sufficient pressure to force the ozonized air into a sump or directly into the aquarium. A container of dessicant between the air supply and the ozonizer will increase the

ozonizer's efficiency. Dessicant can be recharged by heating in the oven.

The use of ozone has drawbacks. Although toxicity to fish and fry is overrated, ozone is destructive to rubber and some plastics, including ordinary airline tubing. Skimmers receiving ozone-treated water must be constructed with Kynar, Neoprene, or other ozone-resistant plastics. Ozone escaping the sump, aquarium, or skimmer can irritate human mucous membranes and can harm pet birds. Excess ozone continues to oxidize the gunk in the collection cup on its way out of the skimmer, forming a particularly noxious odor.

Several skimmer manufacturers have dealt with the last two problems by providing a deodorizing and ozone-absorbing granulated activated carbon (GAC) container atop the collection cup through which discharged air, ozone, and odors must pass before entering the room. The GAC should be replaced whenever any sweet or foul odor is detected near the skimmer cup.

Aquarists using ozonizers for sterilization should avoid salt mixes containing excessive bromide, which reacts with ozone to

UV Sterilizer Unit Manufacturer Recommendations

	Angstrom	Rainbow Lifegard[1]	Aquanetics
4W	120 gph 75 gal	—	—
8W	180 gph 150 gal	320 gph	240 gph 120 gal
15W	450 gph 300 gal	—	480 gph 240 gal
25W	—	1000 gph	750 gph 520 gal
30W	750 gph 500 gal	—	1000 gph 800 gal
40W	—	1500 gph	—
80W	—	3000 gph	—
120W	—	4500 gph	—
160W	—	6000 gph	—
240W	—	9000 gph	—

gph = gallons per hour
Ratings are based on wattage, flow rate, and dwell time.
[1]Rainbow declined to recommend specific gallonages. Large-wattage units contain multiple small-wattage tubes.

form hypobromite ion (OBr⁻) that then oxidizes to bromate ion (BrO_3^-) at seawater pH (but not at pH 6.5). Bromate ion is a powerful oxidizer not unlike commercial bleach; it is stable in seawater for several hours and can accumulate to toxic levels. Bromate ion's toxicity is about the same as ozone's. The ion can be converted back to harmless bromide by some brands of granular activated carbon (GAC). Ozonization can also form potentially carcinogenic brominated hydrocarbons, so generate only the ozone necessary to decolorize, disinfect, or otherwise clean the water, and include GAC in the system, perhaps within an in-line container within the water return from the sump. In freshwater applications, lower pH and higher ammonia shift the equilibrium to somewhat less harmful hypobromitc ion.

Ozonizers come in many sizes and price ranges. Because ozone must be used at very low doses in marine systems, the smallest commercial unit will be more than enough for even a large reef tank. About 10 mg/hr/50 gallons of aquarium water is usually a safe and effective dose. See also the section on ozone in chapter 3.

At six feet, Dr. George Benz, Curator of Fishes, is no taller than the ozone generator serving the Tennessee Aquarium.

Chapter Ten
Temperature Control

Overheating

Corals do best at about 70–76°F, and can tolerate temperatures in the 60s for hours or days. Overheating is more common and dangerous than the occasional chill. The major sources of unwanted heat are metal halide lights, powerheads, intake clogging, and insufficient space between the aquarium and surrounding walls.

Metal halide lights within hoods or very close to the water should be cooled by fans; pendant bulbs should have not less than eight inches of open space between water and the rim of the lamp. Powerheads and larger water pumps can overheat water in several ways. First, there can be too many small pumps doing the work of a few large ones; consider sizing the pumps upward and cutting back on their number. Second, a restricted flow can cause the pump to overheat because of back pressure. Clean the intake strainers without removing them because an unscreened intake will capture and kill fish and invertebrates exploring dark recesses. Do not place foam covers over intake strainers because the minute pores clog over time; this produces back pressure on the pump, resulting in overheating, warping, and failure. When first setting up the aquarium, use the largest diameter piping compatible with your skimmer and sump pumps; narrow pipes restrict free flow of water, putting back pressure on the pump and resulting in unwanted and avoidable heat. Try to match piping diameters with intake and discharge port diameters, although it is often safe to step up to a wider pipe. If all else fails, consider (1) moving the aquarium 4–6 inches from all walls or barriers to allow total tank heat to dissipate or (2) maintaining a large room fan blowing continuously over the aquarium.

Heating

In very cold locations, reef tanks need a high-quality submersible heater set at 72–74°F. Many animals are killed in an overheated tank when an old-style thermostat consisting of two metal strips welds shut because of corrosion or age. If an older-type heater is used, it should be sized at 2 watts per gallon, so even if the metal thermostat strips weld together, the constant heat output will be insufficient to overheat the tank before you can detect a problem. Old-style heaters should be replaced yearly, before they fail.

Newer heaters offer silicon chip solid-state technology with no moving parts and no metal strips to weld shut. In situ or remote thermostats correlate well between dialed and actual generated temperature. There should be two solid-state sensors, one to sense water temperature using the glass wall as a probe, and the other to detect differences in different regions of the glass, signaling that the water level has dropped or the heater has been removed from the aquarium, either circumstance triggering the unit to shut off.

Cooling

Reef tanks in hot climates might be adequately protected by placing the aquarium beneath an air-conditioning vent or in the flow of a fan. Where heat buildup is caused by sunlight, lack of air circulation, or metal halide illumination, supplementary cooling may be necessary. Aquariums that use some degree of trickle filtration, either as a separate filter or by placing bioballs in the overflow well, benefit from evaporative cooling that can make a big difference.

Chilling

Tanks with multiple metal halide lamps often get so hot that a chiller becomes necessary. Chillers are small, fan-cooled, industrial refrigeration units with a grid of titanium coils, a compressor, and a motor. Unlike your home refrigerator, which takes heat from the internal air and releases it to the outside air, the aquarium chiller is a sealed box with inlet and outlet ports for water delivered by a water pump (not included). Heat is removed from the water and released to the air.

The two types of chiller are stand-alone and drop-in. A stand-alone chiller requires a pump to drive water to the chiller and push it back to the tank. Submersible powerhead pumps are cheap, but add heat to the water; compensate by going to the next larger size chiller unit. External water pumps are more expensive than submersible powerheads, so where you want to spend the money is a trade-off. Because the pump is necessary to operate the chiller, the pump should never be turned off while the chiller is operating. A stand-alone chiller can be placed away from the tank, but water lines between chiller and tank should be well insulated. All chillers must be well vented for efficiency, and must not be placed in confined spaces like closets.

The more popular alternative is the pumpless or drop-in chiller with drop-in titanium coil heat absorber. The coil is just like a plug-in hot water heater for making a cup of tea or coffee, except that the coil absorbs rather than delivers heat. The water around the coil must be in constant motion; the unit is made to drop into the current of a sump whose pump must not be turned off.

Chiller output is preset to each aquarist's specifications by the manufacturer or dealer. The options are 65°–80°F, 50°–65°F, and below 50°F. Ask that the compressor be filled with R22 or MP39 refrigerant rather than R12 freon. The coldest chillers used for North Pacific marine animals (below 50°F) cost about $125–$200 more than those used for most minireef tanks, which cost $400–$1,000 for a 1/6 to 1/2 hp unit.

The size of chiller needed for your reef tank is based on both water volume and the degrees of chilling. Thus you'll need a larger chiller for a 30-gallon tank of Icelandic lobsters than for a 100-gallon tank in which you're attempting to reduce heat by 10 degrees for corals.

The capital cost depends on horsepower. Operational costs increase with size. Most chillers run on normal household (115-volt) current, larger units (1 hp and up) on 220-volt current. You can estimate that capital cost in dollars of a chiller will about equal its wattage. Some typical relationships are:

hp	watts	cost
1/6	400	$ 450
1/5	500	550
1/4	670	650
1/3	850	750
1/2	1,140	1,150
1	1,820	1,750

These prices do not include the electronic thermostatic controller (another $100–$200, depending on whether it operates only a chiller, or a chiller and heater) or the power bill from your local utility.

Brands and models on the market include the Aqua Logic Cyclone, Aqua Logic Delta Star, New Ocean, West Coast Aquatics Micro-mini, and the Aquanetics Drop-in and Slim-line chillers. All come in 1/6 to 1/3 hp, the most popular sizes, and some come even larger. Consult the following major suppliers for recommendations and costs for your situation:

Aquanetics
5252 Lovelock Street
San Diego, CA 92110
619-291-8444

California Reef Specialists
740 Tioga Avenue
Sand City, CA 93955
800-268-2449

Champion Lighting and Supply
570 Bethlehem Pike
Fort Washington, PA 19034
800-673-7822

Universal Marine Industries
1815 Williams Street
San Leandro, CA 94577
510-352-9856

For do-it-yourselfers, Sea Life Videos (1678 North Woodland, Provo, UT 84604, tel. 801-375-9646) offers a $92 postpaid videotape on building a chiller at home. And if you're of scientific bent and need an extensive apparatus, see Wangaard et al., "Apparatus for precise regulation and chilling of water temperatures in laboratory studies," Progressive Fish-Culturist, vol. 53, 1991, pp. 251–255 (available from Carl Burger, USF&WS, Box 1328, Petersburg, AK 99833).

Monitoring

No heater or chiller is safe without a thermometer to monitor water temperature. Adhesive strips of temperature-sensitive liquid crystal are difficult to read, register room temperature more than tank temperature, and fail with age. Standard aquarium alcohol thermometers are inexpensive but unreliable. Purchase an expanded scale alcohol or mercury thermometer from a photography store or scientific supply house, mount it where you can easily read the temperature, and scrub off scale and algae regularly. Discard any thermometer with a space within the registering liquid.

Chapter Eleven
Light and Lighting

The basis of the reef aquarium is the growth of corals. Corals survive by feeding their wastes to enclosed symbiotic algae, the algae in turn providing the corals with nutrients. The symbiotic relationship is mutually obligatory; if the algae die, the corals cannot survive, and the algae cannot exist outside the coral host. To keep the algae and corals alive, we need to provide both with carbon dioxide, and provide the algae with the proper light for photosynthesis. The marine reef keeper must evaluate and select lights for a reef aquarium that will support this symbiosis. Reef aquarium equipment has specific characteristics of wattage, wavelength, intensity, and color quality, which are described in lux, nanometers, CRI, and other technical terms. To understand the needs of the corals and their algae and the capabilities of equipment to meet those needs, the aquarist needs to know these terms.

Wavelength

The wavelength of light is the distance between peaks or troughs, as measured in meters, nanometers, or angstroms (Å). A nanometer is a billionth of a meter (10^{-9} meter), and an angstrom a ten-billionth of a meter (10^{-10} meter). Various wavelengths of light promote photosynthesis in green plants, red algae, brown algae, different

· Relative Distribution of Solar Energy (red curve) and Distribution of Visible Light (blue curve)

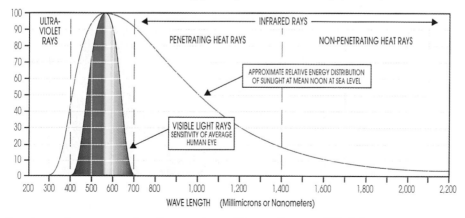

Spectrum of energy wavelengths, courtesy of Energy Savers of Virginia.

Photography and aquarium light meters measure lux, which is all radiation to which the light meter is sensitive. Botanists and coral scientists measure PAR or photosynthetically active radiation, that portion of the visible spectrum (4,000 to 7,000 Å) used for photosynthesis. PAR must be measured with a quantum meter in energy units called microEinsteins falling on a square meter of surface per second ($\mu E/m^2/sec$). In a discussion with me, Dana Riddle (*The Captive Reef*), suggests using a far less costly ordinary light meter and dividing by the following equations. PAR = sunlight lux/50, ordinary (6,500 K) metal halide lux/75, 10,000 K metal halide lux/30, actinic fluorescent lamp lux/18, or combination metal halide+fluorescent lux/150.

kinds of bacteria, and even in cyanobacteria (blue-green microbes).

Kelvin Degrees

Our eyes perceive wavelengths between violet (4,000 Å) and red (7,000 Å) as colors. When these colors are combined, we can describe the quality of the light in Kelvin degrees of color temperature (K). There is a degree of Kelvin color temperature that resembles the light of the sun at noon, another that resembles morning, one that resembles daylight at noon at 40 feet beneath the ocean, and so on.

Color Rendering Index

The Color Rendering Index (CRI) is a measure of an artificial light's similarity to the Kelvin value of the sun at noon at mean sea level at the equator. A color rendering index (CRI) of 100 would be equivalent to noon sunlight at mid-tide on the equator. High-quality stroboscopic lights for cameras approach a CRI of 100 because they are designed to mimic noon equatorial sunshine. Expensive aquarium lamps list a CRI next to the information on wattage. The higher the CRI, the closer the spectrum (mix of wavelengths) is to equatorial sunlight at noon. A standard incandescent lamp typically has a CRI of about 82, irrespective of watts.

Ultraviolet Light

The wavelengths of all kinds of light, visible and invisible, have energy. Sunlight energy can be harmful, but so can X rays, the radiation from radium and plutonium, and the radiation from your microwave oven. For marine reef aquarists, the energy of ultraviolet light is particularly important.

There are three areas within the ultraviolet (UV) portion of the spectrum, UV-A (least energetic), UV-B, and UV-C. The first two are the common causes of sunburn; in a reef tank UV-A and UV-B simulate exposure to sunlight in very shallow water and in the intertidal zone. UV-C, the most energetic form, is an industrial product useful for sterilization (Chapter 9), but too energetic and harmful to be used directly on clams, corals, other invertebrates, fish, or macroalgae.

VHO (very-high-output) and low-intensity (175 W) metal halide lamps emitting in the UV-A and UV-B ranges may be beneficial to tridacnid clams and some colorful branching stony corals if these animals are placed about eight inches from the light source. At closer distances, especially with brighter lights, the bulbs may burn the corals.

It had been thought that colorful pigments of the acroporid stony corals were UV-protective. However, recent studies suggest that UV-protective substances are colorless, and the enhanced colors of hard corals under brilliant lighting are a response to intensity rather than wavelength.

In the absence of intense light, colorful pigments may be lost and the coral fade to tan or white. Of equal importance, corals from deep water, where UV-A and UV-B waves are insignificant, may be sunburned when placed too shallow or too close to a metal halide lamp. Note that many colorful corals occur in deep water, placing further doubt on a UV-protective role of colorful pigments.

Intensity, Lumens, and Lux

Intensity is not the same as energy, as some of us older folks are only too aware. In light, intensity is the volume of radiation emitted all at once. Compare, for example, the output of a 25-watt lamp with a 500-watt lamp. Although the wavelengths (colors) of the two lamps are the same, they differ in radiation intensity. So what is intensity? Intensity is the instantaneous volume of light emitted or lumens emitted at the source. But that isn't very useful, because the effectiveness of light depends on how far away it is from the object upon which it shines. A 500-watt light 500 feet away will not do much for a reef aquarium, so intensity or lumens at the source is only half the story. The light that gets to the aquarium is what counts, and that light is measured in illuminance, or lumens per square meter of surface (lux). Lux matters most, because lux is the light actually received.

A summary so far: We see a small part of all the wavelengths (light quality) put out by the sun. Light quantity is measured in lumens or output at the source, and measured at the target in lux or lumens received per square meter. Which brings us to the photosynthetic algae inside the corals inside the reef aquarium.

Metal halide lamps mounted in pendants above the aquarium should have guards to protect the hot bulb from being shattered by splashed water.

Photosynthesis

The light waves responsible for photosynthesis on your lawn are not the same as the light waves occurring on deeper coral reefs. The red and yellow waves used by grass are rapidly absorbed by the first 40 feet of seawater. The visible light that penetrates more deeply is blue light in the 4,000 Å or 400 nm range. Algae living symbiotically inside corals at these depths use this blue light for photosynthesis. It has also been suggested (although a mechanism has not been described) that traces of red light are able to make it this far down, and deepwater algae are able to capture that minimal energy and survive.

Metal Halide Incandescence

Ordinary tungsten lamps of high wattage offer excellent intensity in the yellow and red range but are not useful in reef aquariums because they miss the blue spectrum of marine symbiotic algae.

High-intensity incandescent lights are usually oversized lamps on oversized mirrored reflectors, and they're filled with gas under partial vacuum (which can implode) or under 50 pounds per square inch of pressure (and can explode). Mercury vapor and sodium vapor lamps are of no interest to reef keepers, because they are deficient in the blue end of the spectrum. Halogen quartz metal halides are not expensive, but their spectra are also the wrong colors for photosynthesis by symbiotic coral algae.

Tungsten quartz metal halides put out a broad spectrum of light, and many of them include a good proportion of blues, making them suitable for growing symbiotic marine

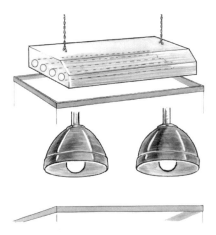

Heat is the enemy of reef tanks. Canopy or pendant lighting must provide either air space or fans for ventilation. The tank should also be far enough from the wall so that air can circulate all around and help cool the tank.

coral algae. Metal halide lamps offered in aquarium shops are smaller, brighter, and better color-balanced than earlier versions or those you'll find in a do-it-yourself hardware store. Heat and pressure in all metal halide lamps are reasons to exercise care; they are prone to explosive breakage if splashed while hot. Newer lamps have several layers of outer glass to block UV emissions. The UV emissions of some older lamps can damage your eyes and the bodies of corals.

Most metal halides mimic sunlight at sea level with an average output of 5,500–6,500 Kelvin degrees color temperature, but are manufactured in color temperatures of 4,300–20,000 K. They require remote ballasts specific to the wattage and type of lamp; one size does not fit all. Standard lamps with 150, 175, 250, and 400W, at a color temperature of about 6,500 K, all have enough blue radiant energy to support symbiotic algae in corals inside deep aquariums. For reef aquariums up to 20 inches deep, one or two 175-watt lamps eight inches above the water will suffice; 250- and 400-watt lamps may be needed for deeper aquariums. The lamps can be mounted in wall fixtures next to the aquarium, in pendant fixtures over the aquarium, in canopies, or in combination hoods that hold one or two metal halide lamps and one to six fluorescent lamps. Hoods containing metal halide lamps should always be fan-vented to dissipate the considerable heat, and the lamp must be far enough from water to avoid short circuits or splashes of chilling water that can shatter the lamp's glass. Newer models include compact units for tight spaces, and combination hoods that include metal halide and compact fluorescent lamps.

A new metal halide lamp contains a small, clear chamber at about the middle of the bulb. An old failing bulb flickers and overheats the ballast. Those familiar only with fluorescent lamps would assume that the ballast has gone bad, but it is probably the bulb that has worn out. Look for cloudiness in the center of the interior bulb and a large black spray of carbon deposited somewhere near the base of the bulb to confirm that the bulb has failed.

Fluorescence

Fluorescent lights are filled with mercury vapor that is energized by electricity and then radiates ultraviolet light. This UV light burns the lamp walls, which are coated with a dry chemical mix that fluoresces under ultraviolet radiation. Specialized coatings developed for the printing industry strongly emit in the 420 nm/4,200 Å blue range. These have been adapted to aquariums for coral-inhabiting algae. Today you can get a pure 420 nm lamp (the O3 type of actinic) with its dark blue light. While these lamps support symbiotic algae, they do not provide sufficient illumination for seeing the fish and colors of the other animals. On the other hand, actinic lamps cause many corals to fluoresce, a beautiful sight in a reef aquarium.

Some manufacturers sacrifice a small amount of energy in the 420 nm range to provide second and third minor peaks in the red and green range, obtained by including some rare earth phosphors in the fluorescent tube coating. The loss of 420 nm blue output can be made up with a second lamp or by increasing the lumens reaching the aquarium with a reflector. The combined blue, red and green is a bright lavender lamp that enhances colors, makes corals fluoresce, and keeps the symbiotic algae happy. The so-called 50-50 lamps consist of approximately 50 percent 6,500 K daylight and 50 percent 7,100 K actinic light, and are often available with mirrored reflectors.

A reef aquarium can be illuminated by

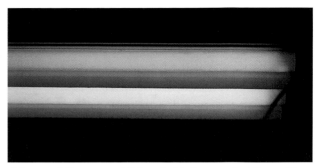

A four-unit fluorescent fixture holds two cool white and two actinic lamps.

four to six of these lamps or any combination of actinic O3 and color enhancers and even cool white. The best reef units are combination actinic fluorescent and mirrored metal halide fixtures that direct all light output downward into the aquarium.

Which Metal Halide Is Best?

Each of your metal halide lamps should be at least 175 watts. Two lamps are better than one for a four-foot or longer aquarium. The lamps should be positioned at least eight inches from the water surface to avoid heating, and the system should be fan-cooled if possible. Avoid halides less than 5,000 K, selecting the best-priced unit in the 5,000 K to 6,000 K range. For SPS corals, 10,000 and 20,000 K metal halides are better, providing greater intensity that brings out coral pigment formation at the tips. Although CRI is not critical, look for CRI values above 85 to provide a natural look to the aquarium. Metal halide lights do all they are meant to do within 4–6 hours, longer periods adding mostly heat; to provide additional hours of light, use supplemental standard, VHO (very-high-output), or HO (high-output) fluorescent fixtures.

Fluorescent fixtures tend to collect salt and to short circuit at the tips and inside the ballast. You can buy waterproof and salt proof sealed end caps and remote ballasts today, or you can try to save money by building your own, but I don't advise it. Commercial items are well built and inexpensive, and you won't save anything significant. The preferred approach is to position your end-capped lamps next to each other with plastic clips, and close to the water surface. The lamp must be close because intensity reaching the tank (lux) drops off as the square of the distance.

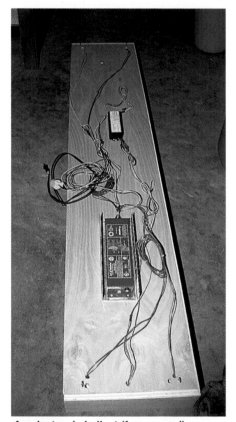

An electronic ballast (foreground) for VHO fluorescent lamps dwarfs an ordinary ballast (background).

High-Output and Very High-Output Fluorescent Lamps

A recent innovation is the high-intensity fluorescent lamp. These High-Output (HO) and Very-High-Output (VHO) lamps commonly come in 65W and 110W, 48-inch lengths, actinic and full-spectrum wavelengths, and require a remote electronic ballast. They're an alternative to metal halides for deep reef aquariums, but the cost of the electronic ballast is not much different from the cost of a metal halide fixture. Electronic ballasts are nonflickering, instant-starting, with little heat output. Located away from the aquarium, they are protected from salt water spray and salt creep. Note that the electronic ballast for a VHO unit cannot be used for HO lamps, and vice versa; the ballast must be matched to the lamp output type.

Compact Fluorescents

The new kids on the block are the compact fluorescents. Hardware stores carry them in a variety of shapes and sizes manufactured by Phillips, Panasonic, Osram Sylvania, General Electric, and others. The compact fluorescent discards the traditional both-end pin approach in favor of pins or a socket at just one end. The fluorescent tube is twisted back upon itself, and may resemble a bent-double small fluorescent, a light saber from Star Wars, or even an incandescent lamp.

The ballast may be built inside (an integral unit) or remote, and can be either magnetic (flickering and buzzing when you start up) or electronic (starting silently and instantly). The light output of an 18W compact fluorescent puts out about the same lumens as 75W of incandescent light. The CRI is not constant across the board and varies from 60 to more than 85.

Small compact fluorescents sold specifically for the aquarium market include a daylight lamp (5,000 K), an actinic model (7,100 K), and a 50–50 combination 5,000/7,100 K lamp. The ballast is remote rather than integral, and the pins require a special fixture. These units are available in fan-cooled combination hoods holding one or two compact actinic and daylight fluorescent lamps plus a metal halide lamp.

Compact fluorescents are not manufactured in high-wattage models, and consequently have limited intensity and application. Their low intensity limits their usefulness to tanks shallower than 14–16 inches or those in the 10- to 15-gallon size range holding soft corals requiring little intensity, such as demonstration aquariums for classrooms.

Combination Fixtures

A good rule: For the minimum acceptable lighting use ordinary fluorescent lamps for a small tank one foot deep containing soft corals, HO or VHO lamps for soft coral tanks 18 inches deep, and metal halides for tanks containing hard corals irrespective of depth.

A 20-gallon aquarium can maintain soft corals with four ordinary fluorescent lamps (two actinic and two full-spectrum daylight). A 29–55 gallon reef aquarium containing only soft corals is much deeper, and requires at the very least two VHO and two ordinary fluorescent lamps. Any tank with hard corals should, in addition to VHO and perhaps regular fluorescents, have one or two metal halide lamps.

You can get ready-made fixtures for one or two 175-250 watt metal halide lamps and one or two actinic-type (4,000 Å) blue fluorescent lamps in the 7,100 K range. To retrofit an existing fluorescent hood, install the actinic lighting or a full-spectrum lamp

and install a separate pendant fixture for the metal halide. For deep aquariums (150 gallons and up), increase the metal halide wattage (400-watt lamps and up) and look for a VHO actinic fluorescent fixture.

Timers

Each lamp type should be on its own 24-hour timer. Ordinary fluorescents should be on for 10–14 hours daily. Because flourescents emit the weakest light, they should be the first to come on in the morning and the last to turn off in the evening. VHO lamps should be used 6–8 hours a day. Metal halide lamps mimic sunlight, use a great deal of power, and should be plugged into a heavy duty (air-conditioning type) timer for 2–4 hours.

A few experts have induced Pacific corals to spawn in reef tanks by using long-term timers to slowly decrease daily light exposure and using the on-cycle of chillers to mimic the approach of winter, then reversing the cycle to mimic spring.

Replacement

All fluorescent and metal halide lamps undergo a weakening in intensity and a color shift over time. Fluorescent lamps should be replaced at six-month intervals or according to the manufacturer's directions. Replace one per week during the replacement period to avoid sudden shifts in color or intensity that might stress the animals. Metal halide lamps should be replaced when they begin to flicker.

Caution: Not only pretty colors are at stake, but the survival of the corals. Trying to squeeze another few months out of a $25 lamp may risk thousands of dollars in live coral and is a mistake rarely made more than once.

Chapter Twelve
Algae and Plants

The most important reef flora are the symbiotic dinoflagellate algae of reef-building corals, the red coralline algae that cement dead coral skeletons together, and the calcareous green algae that produce limestone beach sands. The nutrients required by corals, removal of their wastes, and dispersal of their offspring depend on both localized and area-wide water movement. Nutrient sources are sparse in the reef environment, and water movement facilitates nutrient recycling, essential to keep the reef engine running. Remote flowering plants (mangroves, marsh grasses, sea grasses) and macroalgae (kelps) on distant shores must be fragmented, pulverized, and in some cases dissolved to provide additional food (detritus and dissolved nutrients) to a habitat that can afford neither waste nor an interruption in its limited outside supply. Coral reefs take everything, reuse everything, and leave nothing but sand and rubble.

Detritus

Few species of higher plants have adapted to the marine environment, and then only at its edges. Upon these estuarine and nearshore marsh grasses, sea grasses, and mangrove forests depends the primary productivity of the coastal ocean. As mangroves and grasses are cropped by grazers or undergo seasonal leaf drop, they contribute plant remains to smaller consumers below. This debris is churned and rechurned through the intestinal tracts of species after species of herbivorous, filter- and silt-feeding fish, shrimp, other crustaceans, worms, fungi, protozoa, and bacteria. The plant particles, at all stages, are called detritus, which is the fuel that maintains coastal fish and shellfish production. Out at sea, phytoplankton plays the same role.

Algae

Algae are important in primary productivity, shoreline stabilization, and reef formation. The most important algae of the reef are the coral symbionts and the green and red algae that contribute to reef structure and beach sand.

Green Algae

Green algae (Chlorophyta) occur as single cells, sheets, filaments, or complex associations. Many are microscopic, often freely drifting in the water and sometimes growing on or in other plants or animals. Others are large enough to be noticed by people, and we call these macroalgae. Green algae may be single cells, colonial, or acellular. They may multiply asexually by fragmenting, budding, or dividing.

Green algae are important food for many fishes and invertebrates on the reef. Some filamentous species grow into large mats or turfs, protected as private food sources by damsels until overwhelmed by schools of locustlike tangs. Many green macroalgae concentrate calcium carbonate, which stiffens them, enabling upward growth and protection against predation by herbivores. These algae may contribute to reef structure by cementing adjacent coral skeletons, or may become part of beach sand after they die or are eaten by herbivores.

Attractive Calcareous Green Algae

Segmented Algae

Halimeda. The particulate limestone remains of *Halimeda* and the other calcareous algae grazed and passed through the gut by parrotfish are the most important component of tropical beach sand. *Halimeda* plants are upright, supported by a fibrous holdfast that provides purchase on rocks, in coral crevices, or in sand. They are stiffly calcified except at the joints, allowing flexibility in currents. Some occur in bright shallows, others at great depths and caves in dim light. Their rapid growth and beauty are attractive to reef keepers. *Halimeda lacrimosa* has tear-shaped or bead-shaped segments; *H. monile* has segments resembling small, irregular cylinders; *H. incrassata* segments are thickly bilobed or trilobed. Species with flattened, platelike segments and a central rib include *H. copiosa, H. tuna, H. discoidea, H. opuntia*, and *H. goreaui*, distinguishable by segment size and shape, branching, and depth. In nutrient-rich minireef aquariums, *Halimeda* might require thinning.

Feathers and Grapes

Caulerpa. Over a hundred species of feather and grape algae grow in rock and rubble zones in the clear coastal ocean, on woody debris in brackish, blackwater, marsh drainages, and in Atlantic and Indo-

A neon goby (Elacatinus oceanops) *rests on a large growth of calcareous* Halimeda. *In the background are the grapelike growths of* Caulerpa racemosa.

Pacific tropical and temperate waters. *Caulerpa* spread almost entirely by asexual growth and fragmentation. They grow rapidly under the brilliant lighting of nutrient-rich reef tanks, requiring thinning. *Caulerpa* are not prominent on coral reefs, but are common on mangrove roots, sand, rocks, or rubble. These acellular algae (with nuclei dispersed in cytoplasm not divided by cell walls) have an upright growth from a horizontal rhizome or runner held to rock, sand, or mud by penetrating rootlike rhizoids. The upright may have a midrib from which lateral branchlets extend like the barbs on a feather. *Caulerpa* variety is extensive. Many species have forms that

Caulerpa *upright growths spread from a horizontal rhizome, anchored by rootlike rhizoids.*

spheres are enlarged, reduced in number, and flattened on top; *C. nummularia* is similar, but its flattened tops look like unribbed umbrella algae; *C. prolifera* uprights look like smooth-edged sea grass, while *C. serrulata* resembles rough-edged *Sargassum* weed; *C. cupressoides* looks like young spears of asparagus; *C. lanuginosa* looks the same, but has fine hairs along the rhizome providing additional purchase in the sand. In three very popular aquarium species, the uprights are fronds; *C. sertularioides* is either flat-bladed with very fine branchlets or has three-dimensional uprights with thickened branchlets and a very thick rhizome, and *C. mexicana* has straight-edged, tightly packed flat branchlets while *C. taxifolia* has loosely packed, tapering flat branchlets.

Caulerpa sometimes grows too rapidly in a reef tank, becomes a nuisance, and must be thinned by hand. Tangs and pygmy angelfish usually keep it cropped to a manageable level.

occur only under certain light and nutrient regimes. *Caulerpa racemosa* uprights resemble clusters of tiny grapes, but there is one variety (var. *peltata*) in which the

Cups and Brushes

Acetabularia. The finely ribbed umbrella, thin stalk, and cryptic holdfast of the mermaid's wineglass is a single, giant cell with a cup or dish up to 0.75 inch across. The stalk is attached to rock, shell, mangrove roots, coral fragments, or other hard objects on sandy, shallow flats. Calcium carbonate supports upright growth and protects against algae-grazing damselfish. *Acetabularia* reproduces asexually by division at the base of the stalk. Sexual reproduction occurs when cysts released from rays of the cups produce flagellated gametes. Two species commercially available from Florida are the pale white *A. crenulata* with tiny teeth around the margins of the disk, and *A. calyculus* which is greener with smooth edges. *Polyphysa polyphysoides* is similar, intensely white

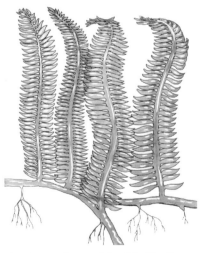

Caulerpa *species are identified by the form of the upright fronds, but all species grow over the surface by extending a runner or rhizome that attaches to the bottom by rootlike rhizoids.*

with lime deposits, and much smaller than mermaid's wineglass species.

Penicillus. The mermaid's shaving brush is a large, bristly, upright macroalga of shallow sand flats hardened by calcium carbonate tissue deposits. Its holdfast is a complex web of rhizoidal filaments anchoring it in deep sand. Three Florida species in commerce are *P. capitatus*, 2–4 inches tall with a long, slender stalk; *P. pyriformis* at almost 4 inches high, but with a stubby stalk and flat top; and *P. dumetosus*, the largest at 6 inches tall, with a stubby base and rounded top. Brilliant light is required.

Rhipocephalus. Similar to mermaid's shaving brush, the false shaving brush or ripweed is a calcified macroalga with plates instead of bristles. The single Florida species, *R. phoenix*, grows to 6 inches tall and ranges from shallow grass and mangrove flats to 120 feet deep on reefs, rock, or sand.

In reef tanks, cups and brushes require a deep sand base, intense light (they do best in shallow tanks at water depths of one foot or less), iodine and calcium supplements, and protection from tangs, pygmy angels, and snails. Their high nutrient requirements make them generally incompatible with hard corals.

Fans and Fingers

Udotea. Ranging from shallow grass flats to depths of 50 or more feet, the hard fan algae have smooth, calcareous green plates on or around a single stalk anchored by a holdfast in sand or muddy silt. The plates often have concentric lines of calcium carbonate deposits. The four Florida species are *U. cyathiformis* with a cup-shaped plate; *U. wilsonii* with a cluster of plates arranged radially around the central stalk; *U. flabellum* with dark green, leathery plates growing as a cluster; and *U. occidentalis* with light-green, stiff plates forming

The mermaid's wineglass, Acetabularia, grows abundantly in brightly illuminated shallows of the Florida keys, and requires intense light in a reef aquarium.

a cluster. *Udotea* species are grazed by parrotfish and are important contributors to beach sand.

Avrainvillea. The soft fans are blackish-green acellular macroalgae covered with very fine filaments providing a suedelike texture. The massive holdfast is a ball of filaments rooted in silty sand. The finger-shaped *A. rawsonii* occurs in grass flats. All the others have fan-shaped blades and range from mangrove and grass flats to deeper waters. The 8-inch high *A. longicaulis* has a more even outline than the irregular *A. nigricans*; the somewhat shorter *A. elliottii* has straight lower edges on the fan; and the dinner-plate shaped *A. asarifolia* has its foot-high fan completely surrounding the minute stalk.

Anadyomene. The veined fan algae are quite beautiful but infrequent survivors on live rock. Under the microscope, *A. stellata* has regularly arranged cells among the veins, while *A. saldanhae* has irregularly spaced cells. Both require good current.

Neomeris. Short, stubby green fingers of algae have calcified rings forming

Each green bubble of Valonia *is a single cell. Although pretty in small numbers,* Valonia *can spread and become a nuisance.*

concentric white lines throughout their length. Grows slowly as an upright turf, attractive in small amounts.

Codium. These thick, rubbery, dark-green algae may have simple or complex branching, grow low to the rock or be long and flowing in the wild. What appear to be thick fingers are really bundles of fine acellular strands bound together. They are usually picked off or die during preparation of live rock. Surviving fragments do not get sufficient light or nutrients in aquariums to become pests.

Bubbles

Valonia and *Ventricaria*. Smooth bubble algae are among the largest known single-celled plants, some attaining over an inch in diameter. Each bubble is a single cell with small particles of nuclear material scattered through the cytoplasm. *Valonia macrophysa* has large bubbles; *Valonia aegagropila* forms bubbles about three times as long as wide; and *Valonia utricularis* has sausage-shaped bubbles. *Ventricaria ventricosa* occurs as individual giant

rounded green bubbles up to an inch or more in diameter. All species can grow fast in aquariums, even in dark spaces, and should be thinned. They reproduce sexually and asexually. There is also a bubble stage of *Derbesia* (called the Halicystis) resembling *Ventricaria ventricosa*, but differs in drifting when detached (*Valonia* sinks).

Dictyospheria. Rough bubble algae, *Dictyosphaeria cavernosa* and *D. ocellata* (=*Valonia ocellata, V. verluyii*) form mats of tiny bubbles that encrust rock. They can be a nuisance in captivity because of fast asexual growth compounded by sexual reproduction. Rough bubble algae form fast-growing layers of 1 mm cells that cover rock, prevent attachment by corals, and may even overgrow corals. They are not controlled by reducing nutrients in the water, as they get their nutrients from the activity of worms, crustaceans, and other small fauna living beneath them. The only control is removal by hand.

Nuisance Green Algae

Many macroalgae and microalgae are noncalcareous. When present in small amounts, they are controlled in minireefs by grazing herbivorous snails, sea urchins, tangs, and pygmy angelfish. Further accelerating algal growth in minireefs is the supplementary iodine provided for soft corals. Iron and nitrates cause the algae to grow faster than they are consumed by too few grazers. Nuisance green algae overgrow the desirable coralline red algae on live rock, which then prevents these surfaces from being used by corals. Nuisance algae usually require removal by hand or prolonged immersion of the infested rocks in darkness or erythromycin solution. Other controls are activated carbon filtration, reduced iodine supplements, keeping the phosphate levels below 0.02 mg/L, water changes, and overskimming. The technique of connecting the minireef to a second aquarium (refugium) or to a lighted grid box where algal growth is promoted for chemical (algal mat) filtration can lead to repeated infestations of nuisance algae.

Ulva. Sea lettuce forms gelatinous sheets and blades attached to hard bottoms. *Ulva* grows so fast that it is harvested for food in the Pacific. *Ulvaria* is thinner and paler. Sea lettuce thrives under intense light in nutrient-enriched water, and can be killed by a few days without metal halide or other incandescent light.

Enteromorpha. Tubular green filaments occur on rock or shell collected near shore. Related to *Ulva*, *Enteromorpha* is quickly consumed by herbivorous fish, but the best control is scraping new rock and shell before placement in a reef tank. This nuisance alga seldom spreads in reef tanks because of the high light and nutrient requirements.

Bryopsis. The sea ferns grow as clumps of tuftlike, soft, feathery algae. A type of turf alga, it arrives on live rock and may be cultivated by damselfish.

Derbesia. A nuisance hair alga forming dense yellowish green mats of delicate branched filaments. It may develop a marblelike bubble stage (sea bottle) resembling *Valonia* that subsequently gives rise to the common filamentous form.

Chaetomorpha. Fine, light-green, unbranched filaments form small algal turfs (managed by damselfish) or vast masses of "mossy" nuisance algae. The variably sized cells have multiple nuclei, indicating incomplete wall formation following nuclear division. *Chaetomorpha linum* is the worst nuisance alga overgrowing Jamaican reefs and grass beds. It is a pollution indicator that responds to phosphorus by overgrowing everything in its vicinity, its 15-foot long strands wrapping around corals, grasses,

sponges, and other algae, cutting off their light and circulation.

Cladophora and *Cladophoropsis*. Dark-green, branched thin or thickened filaments form tangles or tufts with a greasy texture resembling Cyanobacteria. These coiled hair algae may be attached, floating, round clumps on or under the sand, or rolling clumps in current. Remove by hand.

Brown Algae

Brown algae (Phaeophyta) are abundant in cold waters (*Macrocystis* or giant kelps of rocky Pacific shores, and rockweed or *Fucus* of the northeastern Atlantic seaboard). Few hard bottom species of brown algae occur in the tropics, but drifting sargassum can cover acres of surface. A few calcareous species are attractive but difficult to keep. Browns require strong current and supplemental iodine, grow slowly, and are often smothered by epiphytic green hair algae and cyanobacteria. Brown pigment (fucoxanthin) completely masks the green chlorophylls.

Attractive Brown Algae

Stypopodium. Individual fan-shaped blades of this noncalcareous, tan to greenish alga with white banding are attached to hard surfaces. Noxious chemicals in the fronds discourage herbivorous fish.

Padina. Semicircular fan-shaped blades of this calcareous brown alga grow densely packed on hard bottoms. White bands or lines are colorless hairs and deposits of calcium carbonate that discourage herbivory.

Unsuitable Brown Algae

Lobophora. Leafy orange, brown, or green fronds resemble curved snack chips or tightly packed lettuce leaves. It is fast-growing and firmly attached by holdfasts. *Lobophora variegata* can be a nuisance alga on nearshore reefs exposed to excess nutrients. Its noxious-tasting chemicals protect it from herbivory by tangs, but it is eaten by *Diadema antillarum* sea urchins and ripped away by strong storms.

Dictyota. A large genus of highly branched, attached, rubbery algae with flattened fronds occasionally with attractive surface beading, and edges either smooth or toothed. *Dictyota cervicornis* and *D. jamaicensis* are fast-growing, nutrient pollution indicators rapidly overgrowing deeper coral reefs on densely populated islands. The delicately thin *D. bartayresii* is a translucent, iridescent blue. Species in the similar genus *Dictyopteris* are distinguished by fronds with midribs. Often attached to wild rock, no member of this group is suitable for minireefs.

Colpomenia. Brown bubble algae grow as gas-filled, rubbery spheres, irregular sinuses, or eruptions on hard surfaces, especially in nutrient-rich aquariums. Portions may break away and float. They would be pests were they fast growers.

Sargassum. Two drifting species (*S. natans, S. fluitans*) dominate the floating weed pooling in a vast oceanic circulation east of the Bahamas known as the Sargasso Sea. Storms and the Gulf Stream carry breakaway masses of weed northward along the Atlantic coast, where it is blown onto shore (Florida to North Carolina) or is caught by downwellings and sinks into the depths, providing food to the deep ocean. The floating weed contains over 200 species of fish and invertebrates, including endemics found nowhere else, such as the sargassum frogfish (*Histrio histrio*), the sargassum nudibranch (*Scyllaea pelagica*), and several kinds of sargassum shrimp. The marine community of the sargassum weed has its closest relatives on hard-bottom habitats, prompting ecologists to call it a floating benthic habitat. Fish of the sargassum weed com-

munity are the major foods for marlin, dolphin, and some marine birds; the floating weed is also a critical habitat for baby sea turtles.

The majority of *Sargassum* species grow attached (*S. hystrix, S. platycarpum, S. polyceratium, S. filipendula, S. bermudense, S. pteropleuron*), but broken segments may float into the masses of drifting weed. The species can be identified by the shape of the frond and whether it has smooth or toothed edges and a midrib, the presence, color, and location of floating bladders (berries) and whether berries have spiny tips. *Sargassum hystrix* responds to nutrient pollution by overgrowing deep coral reefs, along with *Dictyota* and *Lobophora*.

Turbinaria. One foot tall, with exquisite trumpet-shaped or mushroom-shaped branches, this is a shallow water alga requiring strong surge and brilliant light. *Turbinaria* is used for both human food and crop fertilizer, and will not survive in minireef tanks. (Note that *Turbinaria* is a generic name for both an alga and a coral.)

Red Algae

With more than 4,000 species, the red algae (Rhodophyta) are the most successful marine algae, living everywhere from the intertidal zone to more than 800 feet deep. Many have evolved to live far below the depth to which red light penetrates. The pigments of red algae are chlorophyll *a,* phycoerythrin, and phycocyanin. Phycoerythrin and phycocyanin absorb high-energy blue light and emit waste energy at longer red wavelengths. This light-conversion ability allows red algae to provide their chlorophylls with the needed red light at depths beyond the reach of the red wavelengths of sunlight.

Some red algae contain unusual chemicals that discourage herbivores and may have application to medicine.

Red algae range from rubbery fronds with thick holdfasts to delicate membranes to dense masses of finely branched filaments. They include calcareous encrusting species critical for the successful minireef aquarium. The encrusting calcareous coralline algae cement hard corals to the reef base, holding the reef together, and their growth builds up the reef crest, which in some places can be algal rather than coral animal in origin.

Encrusting Coralline Red Algae

Goniolithon, Amphiroa, Jania, Corallina, Neogoniolithon, Lithothamnion, Mesophyllum, Titanoderma, Peyssonelia, Porolithon, Spongites, Sporolithon, Hydrolithon. These are pink to dark red calcareous algae growing as a single crust or as overlapping layers. Species occur from the intertidal zone to great depths, and may be confused with sponges, bryozoans, or red protozoans, which form similar patches.

Porolithon pachydermum in the Atlantic and *P. onkodes* in the Pacific are the most important reef-building red algae, producing much of the hard calcium carbonate (calcite) that cements the reef structure together and absorbs the shock of waves, protecting the reef structure from destruction.

Live rock, both collected from the wild and cultured, should have abundant encrusting coralline algae surviving after weeks of darkness. The pink or red patches spread if provided supplementary calcium (>450 mg/L) even in dim light. In the established minireef tank, encrusting coralline algae cover the glass, filters, and other hard parts, providing a solid pink base for attachment of anemones and corals. Without a liquid calcium supplement or aragonite gravel, coralline algae grow poorly and may be overgrown by undesirable green hair algae and cyanobacteria.

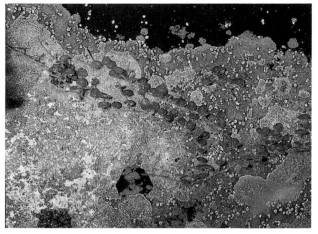

Encrusting plates of coralline red algae cover live rock, providing a substratum for corals if not first occupied by spreading green algae like this Caulerpa.

Nonencrusting Red Algae

Erect red algae are usually discarded during live rock preparation. Surviving fragments may grow in individual aquariums. Most are bushy types of little interest, while others are quite pretty.

Gracilaria. Cultivated throughout Asia for industrial extracts (cosmetics, antiinflammatory drugs, microbial media, food and food additives), and ubiquitous in reef tanks, but not usually a nuisance.

Botryocladia. Small, dull-red bubble algae or sea grapes, usually two or more bubbles on a short stalk in rock crevices. The bladders contain a sticky mucilaginous fluid.

Porphyra, Halymenia, and *Flahaultia*. Spreading sheetlike fronds suggesting a translucent, yellow to dark red version of sea lettuce (*Ulva*). In aquariums, each frond may collect within its fold a single large gas bubble.

Anotrichum, Antithamnionella, Bostrychia, Callithamnion, Ceramium, Griffithsia, and *Wrangelia*. Microscopic to fine filaments form tufts of turf algae, common

A recently discovered disease of coralline red algae caused by a bacterium has been named coralline lethal orange disease (CLOD). Resembling black-band disease of corals in its rate of spreading, and its demarcation by a distinct line and total necrosis leaving only bare coral skeleton behind, CLOD has been spreading on both Atlantic and Pacific reefs. It probably arose recently in the eastern Pacific. Early stages are marked by orange dots, then circles of destruction, then fingers of infection throughout the algae surface. In later stages, the mucilaginous bacterial colonies, consisting of gliding rods, protrude as eruptive globules called propagules that are carried by waves to other coral heads and reefs. In laboratory tests, all species of encrusting red algae were susceptible. This emerging disease calls for vigilance.

on rocks in the wild and often developing in algal mat scrubber communities. *Ceramium* is an indicator of nutrient pollution, masses of this fine, red, "mossy" alga overgrowing corals in shallow waters near sewage discharges.

Golden-brown Algae

The diatoms are members of the golden-brown algae (Chrysophyta) characterized by a marvelously complex external skeleton or protective capsule (the frustule) made of interlocking silica (glass) valves. With forms as numerous as snowflakes, entire books are devoted to diagrams of diatoms. They're the most important component of phytoplankton, without which there would be no zooplankton. Diatoms occur as single cells or filaments, some-times as clumps, attached or drifting. In aquariums, they form a light brown film over the glass, gravel, and rocks when silica in makeup water is unusually rich and there are too many nitrates (silica alone will not cause a bloom). Attached diatoms are usually controlled by grazing herbivorous *Astraea* snails, *Ctenochaetus* bristle-tooth tangs, and *Centropyge* pygmy angelfish. Drifting diatoms are removed by protein skimming.

Dinoflagellates

Dinoflagellates (Pyrrhophyta) are diverse and important single-celled algae. They consist of two cellulose plates divided by a transverse groove between the plates and a longitudinal groove across them. One groove has a short flagellum and the other a longer one for motility. Virtually all are members of the phytoplankton community, but some form unique and important symbiotic relationships.

Symbiotic Zooxanthellae

Many invertebrates contain in their tissues symbiotic dinoflagellates called zooxanthellae. *Symbiodinium microadriaticum* is the most common species inside cells of corals. Zooxanthellae photosynthesize using light as an energy source and the wastes of the coral (phosphate, ammonia, nitrate) as plant nutrients, and leak their own excess production of sugar alcohol and other animal nutrients to the host. The zooxanthellae in tridacnid clams occur between cells; these are cultured by the clam as whole food, and are periodically swept inside and digested.

Red Tide

A number of dinoflagellates (*Gonyaulax, Gyrodinium, Alexandrium*, and others) produce noxious waste products of metabolism. Under nutrient-rich conditions certain species bloom, and their wastes can reach concentrations toxic to fish, crabs, and other creatures. At times the free toxins in seawater can cause eye and lung irritation to people. When highly concentrated in shellfish consumed by people, these toxins are capable of killing a person. Red tides are natural periodic phenomena that may be increasing in frequency because of coastal enrichment with nutrients (eutrophication). Red tides have not been documented in aquariums, but only an algae expert (phycologist) would be capable of the diagnosis.

Blue-green "Algae"

The most primitive self-reproducing microbes (bacteria) have their nuclear material dispersed through the cytoplasm (prokaryotes), while the algae have distinct envelopes packaging genetic material into nuclei (eukaryotes). Blue-greens (cyanobacteria), although resembling algae to the naked eye, have the former arrangement. Additionally, the cell walls of cyanobacteria are structurally different from those of algae, they can produce strange chemicals no alga can make, and they can live where no alga can survive. Today's blue-greens are remnants of early life forms that played the most important role of any life on earth, photosynthesis; their waste product became our oxygen atmosphere.

Blue-greens usually look like greenish black discolorations or glistening dark films on rock. In moderation, they play important roles in biological systems, providing stability, nitrogen fixation, oxygen, and uptake of organic nutrients. Because they are distasteful, few are grazed by higher life forms. Under low light they outgrow algae and form thick, slimy, sheets, especially when the phosphate to nitrate ratio is higher than normal. Their benefits are offset by secretion of cyanotoxins that stress

or kill other aquatic life. Blue-green blooms have a distinctly acrid odor.

Blue-greens are divided into three orders. The Chroococcales are most primitive, occurring as single cells or colonies. The Stigonematales form filaments with true branches, that is, they divide in two planes. *Microcystis* is in this group.

The most important order in marine aquariums, the Nostocales, divide in one plane to form unbranched filaments. *Oscillatoria* often grows as a mat or turf on hard surfaces. *Schizothrix* forms gelatinous sheets and *Lyngbya* slimy turfs, both common in nutrient-enriched habitats, and important in artificial algal turf scrubbers. *Phormidium* is parasitic, causing black-band disease of corals.

For most higher plants and algae, nitrogen is the limiting nutrient; when it is used up, the plants stop growing. Blue-greens are not nitrogen-limited because they typically fix atmospheric nitrogen gas (or in aquariums, dissolved nitrogen gas) into all the nitrate they need. They are, however, limited by the availability of phosphorus. You can control their growth by restricting phosphorus availability with phosphate removal pads or the use of deionized or reverse osmosis water rather than tap water to make up evaporation. Other control methods are copper sulphate or the antibiotics erythromycin (about 20 mg/L), Chloromycetin (about 10 mg/L), or neomycin (about 4 mg/L), but effective concentrations vary with specific strains. Only phosphate starvation is safe in a reef tank. All other methods are likely to adversely impact the useful and essential microorganisms.

Nuisance Algae Control

Fast-growing algae (red, green, brown, golden-brown) and cyanobacteria are controlled in the wild by constant cropping and a paucity of nutrients. Nutrients in the minireef aquarium must be mobilized into living matter and then harvested. The minireef tank with too much algae can also be deprived of nutrients to stop excess growth. In practice, aquarists use many methods, but on occasion the algae overwhelm our controls.

Limiting Nutrients

The principal nutrients that must be limited are nitrogen as nitrate, phosphate as the inorganic form or orthophosphate, and silica as silicic acid, a nutrient for diatoms. Nitrates and phosphates can be introduced with tap water or well water, and well water might also contain silicates. Coastal communities and western communities in the Great Basin often use aquifers high in orthophosphates.

Nutrients in normal relative concentrations may cause an increase in nuisance green hair algae. Nutrients in abnormal relative concentrations, such as too high a ratio of orthophosphate to nitrate, can stimulate noxious cyanobacteria blooms. These microbes are distasteful to algal grazers and often secrete toxic chemicals. Avoidance of orthophosphate is especially critical to good husbandry; keep it below 0.02 mg/L.

Reverse osmosis reduces nitrates and phosphates, but will not block passage of silicates. Distilled or deionized water will eliminate or reduce all three nutrients. A wise investment is a deionizer or reverse osmosis unit to minimize nutrients in makeup water used to replace evaporation.

Protein Skimming

Algae, bacteria, and blue-green "algae" (cyanobacteria) form thin layers or biofilms on all surfaces. These films eventually change into visible mats through biological succession. The last successional stage is determined by the nutrient mix. Among the most important nutrients for cyanobacteria are the dissolved organics secreted by the microbial biofilm and algal mats. Foam fractionation (protein skimming) reduces dissolved organics in water, removing the very substances that promote cyanobacterial growth, shifting the advantage to red and green algae. This dramatic shift in dominant algae occurs within two weeks after an established marine aquarium has been provided with protein skimming.

Housekeeping

The bare bottoms of minireef tanks without a substratum of aragonite sand/gravel must be siphoned to remove animal wastes and the fungi, cyanobacteria, and other microbes living within the waste layer. Nuisance algae on rocks and glass should be scraped, clipped, and power-washed with tap water; alternatively, the rocks should be removed to a separate darkened barrel of seawater with erythromycin (Maracyn). This will kill the algae on the rock. The rock is then rinsed and placed in clean seawater under quarantine until it is suitable for return to the minireef aquarium.

Herbivores

Herbivorous snails, fish, sea urchins, and other animals graze excess noncalcareous algae. Keep about two small herbivorous snails (*Turbo, Astraea*) per gallon of tank capacity, fewer if you can get large snails. Some hermit crabs (*Clibanarius*) and sally lightfoot mangrove crabs (*Grapsus*) are algae eaters that, unlike the snails, even consume cyanobacteria. Not all tangs and angelfish are herbivores; yellow, yelloweye, and sailfin tangs, Moorish idols, and many pygmy angelfish are voracious grazers, but powder blue tangs and lyre-tailed angels are planktivores, attractive but useless for algae control.

Chapter Thirteen
Corals

Introduction

The Phylum Cnidaria or Coelenterates are the jellyfishes, soft corals, stony corals, fire corals, sea fans, anemones, and other hydroids important to reef aquarists and familiar to divers and snorkelers. The related Phylum Ctenophora contains the comb jellies. A few have been kept in aquariums, but some of them feed on soft corals and are not recommended for reef tanks. Stony corals usually contribute to reef structure through their skeletons, but some are free-living on sand and make no direct contribution to growth of the reef. Soft corals, with rare exceptions, do not contribute to reef structure. Several emit terpenoids, natural fat soluble polymers similar to lemon oil, which are toxic only to other corals (allelopathic). These may be concentrated by grazing nudibranchs immune to the toxin, and may be of medical importance. Other nudibranchs concentrate stinging cells of corals for their own defense; those are discussed in the chapter on molluscs.

Corals should be positioned according to light and current regimes found by other aquarists to provide the best survival and growth under aquarium conditions, irrespective of their depth distribution in nature. Ahermatypic corals such as *Tubastrea* do well in shade with currents to bring them plankton, while some delicate hermatypic forms like the mushroom anemones need light but cannot withstand the tearing action of currents from a direct powerhead dis-charge. Hard free-living corals should be placed on the sand. Hard reef-building corals should be sandwiched at the calcareous base between pieces of live rock, tied with rubber bands or plastic twist ties, or cemented to rock with nontoxic adhesives such as Thorite (Harris Chemicals, 7800 NW 38 Street, Miami, FL 33166, tel. 1-800-327-1570) or Aqua Stik (Two Little Fishies, Inc., 4016 El Prado Blvd., Coconut Grove, FL 33133). Soft corals may be attached to live rock by rubber bands, plastic ties, or toothpicks through the base and into the rock. If already attached to a shell or rock, soft corals may then be emplaced as for hard reef-builders.

What all cnidarians have in common are the unique structure called a cnidocyte and two embryonic layers, the ectoderm and endoderm. The ectoderm becomes the adult outer layer containing the cnidocytes and can grow tentacles; in some (the reef-builders) it also secretes a crystalline form of calcium carbonate called aragonite. The embryonic endoderm becomes the layer that lines the gastrovascular cavity or gut, where the polyp feeds, excretes, and respires.

Cnidaria occur in two forms, often accompanying different life stages. These are called the (sedentary) polyp form and the (drifting) medusa form. Some cnidarians have both stages in the life cycle, while others have abbreviated life cycles in which one or the other stage is reduced or absent.

The polyp is flat on the attachment end. The gastrovascular (gut and respiratory) cavity at the other end is surrounded by tentacles. Hard coral polyps secrete an aragonite cup, the corallite, from the outer layer's lower sides and base. Many free-living corals consist of but a single large polyp. Colonial polyps are those that bud at the edges to produce more polyps, each then producing its own corallite. Growth is accompanied by the accumulation of many daughter corallites budding laterally and vertically. With time, the colony becomes massive and rocklike, and is called a corallum. A single polyp, free-living stony coral may have a corallite the size of a man's hand, and it is then both corallite and corallum. More often, typical corallums are massive brain corals, extensive branching staghorns, or large crusts.

1. stony coral skeleton (corallum)
2. gastrovascular cavity
3. polyp tissue
4. individual polyps in a shared corallum

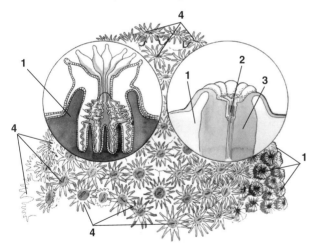

Each stony coral polyp is an individual animal that secretes its own calcium carbonate cup or corallum, often on top of an existing old cup. It divides at the base, and may remain attached or may completely separate from its sibling polyps. Food is supplied by symbiotic algae in the tissues of hermatypic corals, and by capture using sticky or stinging tentacles in ahermatypic corals, although many corals do both. The gastrovascular cavity, opening at the top, plays a role in respiration, digestion, excretion, and sexual reproduction.

Mixing Hard and Soft Corals

You can keep hard and soft corals in a long tank, provided that they are widely separated, that the soft corals are distant and downcurrent from the hard coral, and that the aquarium has carbon filtration. Soft corals emit noxious chemicals capable of poisoning hard corals; these chemicals are removed by carbon. Soft corals may sting and digest competitors, and should be far from immovable, vulnerable hard corals that have no defense. Soft corals secrete mucus that breaks off and can smother and kill a hard coral, so keep the hard corals closest to the powerhead discharge, and the soft corals downstream and more distant. Fire corals (hydrocorals) are not true hard corals, but have a calcareous skeleton that makes them appear hard. Their powerful stingers and rapid growth are reasons to keep them away from all other species. The safest reef tank is one that contains only hard corals or only soft corals, and fire corals apart from either.

The medusa drifts with the gastrovascular opening and tentacles pointing downward. It's a plump animal, with a thick, jelly-like substance between the two body layers. That's why the common name for most well-known medusa forms is jellyfish. The medusa develops sex organs for production of eggs and sperm. The zygote develops into an embryo that differentiates into a ciliated larva called a planula. The planula drifts, swims, and settles down to become a single polyp. The polyp grows into one large animal, or divides repeatedly into hundreds or thousands attached to each other. Reef-building polyps that secrete an aragonite corallite eventually

Sweeper Tentacles

Many anemones, soft corals, black corals, and stony corals have long, searching epidermal tentacles called *acrorhagi* that are used like military defensive patrols. *Acrorhagi* can sweep out great distances beyond the feeding tentacles, their nematocysts stinging other anemones or corals that have come too close.

Other cnidarians have specialized, elongated gastrodermal filaments called *acontia* that can extend far outside the gastrovascular cavity to sweep the surrounding area. These nutritive filaments digest other anemones or corals. Gastrodermal filaments are effective against enemies immune to the coral's stinging cells. In anemones, they've also been called fighting tentacles.

Epidermal stinging tentacles and gastrodermal nutritive filaments are mostly active at night; look for them with a flashlight after dark.

separate from the base and produce a new layer on top, leaving a cavity between. The corallum thus becomes ever more layered and massive.

The epidermis contains the cnidocytes. The most common cnidocyte is the nematocyst, a pressurized capsule with a coiled, barbed filament that shoots out when the cell is stimulated. Some nematocysts are warheads within warheads, the barb at the tip piercing the prey, and the barbs along the filament injecting a paralyzing neurotoxin. Nematocysts sting zooplankton, phytoplankton, and ichthyoplankton for food that is then brought to the gastrovascular cavity by the tentacles. Another type of cnidocyte, the spirocyst, has a sticky filament used to capture hard-shelled crustaceans that cannot be penetrated by stinging filaments. Many sea anemones feel sticky to the touch (spirocyst), but being brushed by the tentacles of a Portuguese Man O' War will cause searing agony (nematocyst).

Classification

The Phylum Cnidaria is divided into the jellyfish and their allies (subphylum Medusozoa), and the soft and stony corals (subphylum Anthozoa). I closely follow David and Jennifer George's *Marine Life, an Illustrated Encyclopedia of Invertebrates in the Sea* (1979, John Wiley & Sons, New York, 288 p.). Following are notes on species from this and other books, consumer periodicals (FAMA, AFM, TFH, others), scientific literature, reef group meetings (MACNA, Western Marine Conference), news-group postings on the Internet, and interviews with scientists, importers, dealers, and minireef aquarists.

I provide the classification scheme first, and then discuss the members of the Cnidaria most important to minireef aquarists and skin divers. The myriad species in most families of Cnidaria are not currently available to marine aquarists because of geographic or depth inaccessibility, difficulty in keeping these species alive, rarity or protected status, or simple lack of interest. The hobby will continue to expand, and many corals unavailable today will become available through captive-breeding programs. Some new corals may arrive in the hobby identified only to the family level. This list will help to find relationships that may provide starting points for considering their care.

Hydrocorals

Hydrocorals are members of the Medusozoa, which also contains the jellyfish and box jellyfish. The Milleporidae or fire corals,

Corals and Medicine

Some terpenoids and other unusual chemicals with potential medical value are found in corals. Some of the chemicals originate in marine algae and/or later concentrate in coral-grazing nudibranchs making them bad-tasting or toxic to predators.

Coral	Chemical
Sinularia	Sesquiterpene Furanoic Acid[1]
Lemnalia africana	Napalilactone[2], 16 Sesquiterpinoids[2]
Telesto riisei	Punaglandins[2]
Euplexaura erecta	Guaiazulene, linderazulene[3]
"blue gorgonian"	dimethylamino-Guaiazulenylmethane[4]
Paramuricea chameleon	Linderazulene[3]
Placogorgia sp	Virginolide[4]
Anthelia edmondsoni	Waixenicin (diterpenoids)[5]
Gerardia sp	Tetrazacyclopentazules (zoanthoxanthin)[6]
Plexaura homomalla	Prostaglandin[7]
Lobophyton depressum	Prostaglandin[7]

[1] Inactivates bee venom
[2] Antileukemia
[3] Blue and purple pigments
[4] Yellow pigment
[5] Possibly antileukemia
[6] Blue pigment
[7] Hormonal activities

unlike most Medusozoa, secrete a hard corallum. Fire corals are also unique in developing tiny medusalike reproductive organs in cups on the corallum. These release eggs and sperm that result in drifting planula larvae.

Fire corals have two kinds of pores on the otherwise smooth surface, central gastropores (holes for the feeding polyps) surrounded by smaller dactylopores (holes for the nonfeeding but strongly stinging defensive polyps). Both the hairlike tentacles of the polyps and the smooth surface of the corallum are armed with stinging cells. Contact causes a burning sting, and snorkelers thrown by surge onto the smooth plates learn not to get so close again.

Fire corals are grazed by filefish and damaged by storms, but are seldom overgrown by algae and are less vulnerable to pollution than scleractinians. They are hermatypic, the zooxanthellae-bearing polyps hidden beneath a stony yellow-brown crust. The Caribbean *Millepora alcicornis, M. complanata*, and *M. squarrosa* are differentiated by growth form. Pacific *Millepora* include the upright, leaflike *M. platyphylla* and *M. dichotoma*, staghornlike *M. tenella*, and the lumpy crusted *M. exaesa*. The number of fire coral species worldwide is unknown.

Fire corals in a reef tank grow rapidly but should not be housed close to other corals, which fire corals will sting and badly damage. They've reproduced sexually in

Symbiotic Zooxanthellae

Many Cnidaria contain zooxanthellae in their tissues. Corals with zooxanthellae are called hermatypic; those without are called ahermatypic. Polyps usually do not digest the zooxanthellae for two reasons. First, the algae are within the polyp's cells, rather than on the outside where they could be washed with secreted digestive enzymes. Second, most coral polyps, like most animals, lack the enzyme cellulase, required for dissolving plant cell walls. In some algae, the cell walls are porous or leaky, allowing digestive enzymes to get through. Corals that digest certain types of phytoplankton may use this method to feed.

Zooxanthellae leak half their production of the sugar alcohol glycerol, the sugar glucose and the amino acid alanine to the host polyp. In return, the polyps provide a place to live, protection from predation by zooplankton, and plant nutrients (phosphates, ammonia, other substances) acquired from the capture of prey by their tentacles and excreted as metabolic wastes.

During extreme cold or heat, symbiotic algae may be expelled (coral "bleaching"). If these algae remain expelled very long, the corals may die; if temporary, the corals will recover. So important are symbiotic algae to reef-building hermatypic corals, that they are passed on inside the fertilized egg during sexual reproduction.

Symbiotic zooxanthellae are limited by light to depths of no more than 200 feet and surface temperatures that year round do not fall below 68°F. Corals that live deeper or colder do not have symbiotic algae (they're ahermatypic), and rely on zooplankton and phytoplankton for nutrition and on their own excretory functions for disposal of waste ammonia.

Upright fronds of golden-brown fire coral, Millepora alcicornis, *cover the nearshore bottom at Bonaire, while orange* Tubastrea *corals grow in their shadow. Bar jack* (Caranx ruber) *hunts reef silversides in the shallows.*

captivity, turning the aquarium milky white and odoriferous as a swamp.

Stylasteridae

The stylaster corals are similar to fire corals, but are ahermatypic and often live in caves and shade as fan-shaped or bush-like colonies. The name derives from the star-shaped gastropores, which, as in *Millepora*, are surrounded by dactylopores. *Stylaster* occurs in the Atlantic and Pacific, *Distichopora* suitable for reef aquariums occurs only in the Pacific.

Anthozoa—Soft Corals

The Subphylum Anthozoa contains the anemones and corals, 6,500 species of cnidarians without a medusa stage. Reproduction is by budding or division, and occasional sexual reproduction leads to a planktonic larva that settles and grows into a miniature polyp. Many in plankton-poor waters rely on nutrients from symbiotic algae for their dietary needs, while those in dark caves and plankton-rich waters use cnidocytes to feed on zooplankton.

Classification within the Phylum Cnidaria

Subphylum Medusozoa
  Class Hydrozoa
    Order Athecata (= Hydrocorallinae, = Anthomedusae)
      Suborder Capitata
        Families Moerisiidae, Sphaerocorynidae, Tricylusidae, Candelabridae, Acaulidae, Euphysidae, Corymorphidae, Paracorynidae, Tubulariidae, Margelopsidae, Halocordylidae, Dicylocorynidae, Corynidae, Velellidae, Cladonemidae, Eleutheriidae, Halocorynidae, Hydrocorynidae, Solanderiidae, Cladocorynidae, Zancleidae, Teissieridae, Milleporidae
      Suborder Filifera
        Families Eudendriidae, Calycopsidae, Protiaridae, Pandeidae, Niobiidae, Cytaeidae, Bougainvilliidae, Russelliidae Rathkeidae, Rhysiidae, Stylasteridae, Hydractiniidae, Ptilocodiidae, Clavidae, Polyorchidae
    Order Thecata
        Families Campanulariidae, Campanulidae, Lafoeidae, Bonneviellidae, Haleciidae, Syntheciidae, Sertulariidae, Plumulariidae, Mitrocomidae, Laodiceidae, Melicertidae, Dipleurosomatidae, Eutimidae, Aequoridae, Phialellidae, Calycellidae, Lovenellidae, Eirenidae, Timoididae, Phialucidae
    Order Limnomedusae
      Family Olindiidae
    Order Siphonophora
      Suborder Physophorida
        Families Physaliidae (=Chondrophoridae), Rhizophysidae, Apolemiidae, Agalmidae, Pyrostephidae, Physophoridae, Athorybiidae, Rhodaliidae, Forskaliidae
      Suborder Calycophora
        Families Prayidae, Hippopodiidae, Diphyidae, Clausophyidae, Sphaeronectidae, Abylidae
    Order Trachymedusae
        Families Geryonidae, Ptycogastridae, Petasidae, Halicreatidae, Rhopalonematidae
    Order Narcomedusae
        Families Cuninidae, Aeginidae, Solmarisidae
    Order Actinulida
        Families Halammohydridae, Otohydridae
    Order Pteromedusae
      Family Tetraplatidae
  Class Scyphozoa
    Order Stauromedusae
        Families Eleutherocarpidae, Cleistocarpidae
    Order Coronatae
        Families Nausithoidae, Atollidae, Atorellidae, Linuchidae, Paraphyllinidae, Periphyllidae, Semaeostomeae, Pelagiidae, Cyaneidae, Ulmaridae
    Order Rhizostomae
        Families Rhizostomatidae, Stomolophidae, Cassiopeidae, Cepheidae, Mastigiidae, Versurigidae, Thysanostomidae, Lynchnorhizidae, Catostylidae, Lobonematidae
  Class Cubozoa
    Order Cubomedusae
        Families Carybdeidae, Chirodropidae

Classification within the Phylum Cnidaria (continued)

Subphylum Anthozoa
  Class Ceriantipatharia
  Class Antipatharia
    Order Antipatharia
      Families Antippathidae, Leiopathidae, Dendrobrachiidae
    Order Ceriantharia
      Families Cerianthidae, Botrucnidiferidae, Arachnactidae
  Class Alcyonaria (= Octocorallia)
    Order Stolonifira
      Families Cornulariidae, Clavulariidae, Tubiporidae
    Order Testacea
      Families Telestidae, Pseudocladochonidae
    Order Alcyonacea
      Families Alcyoniidae, Astrospiculariidae, Nephtheidae, Siphonogorgiidae, Viguieriotidae, Xeniidae
    Order Coenothecalia
      Family Helioporidae
    Order Gorgonacea
      Families Briereidae, Subergorgiidae, Coralliidae, Melithaeidae, Paramuriceidae, Anthothelidae, Paragorgiidae, Parisididae, Keroeididae, Acanthogorgiidae, Plexauridae, Gorgoniidae
    Order Pennatulacea
      Families Veretillidae, Echinoptilidae, Renillidae, Kophobelemnidae, Anthoptilidae, Funiculinidae, Protoptilidae, Stachyptilidae, Scleroptilidae, Chunellidae, Umbellulidae, Virgulariidae, Pennatulidae, Pteroeididae
  Class Zoantharia (= Hexacorallia)
    Order Actinaria
      Families Gonactiniidae, Boloceroididae, Edwardsiidae, Halcampidae, Ilyanthidae, Andresiidae, Actiniidae, Alciidae, Phyllactidae, Bunodidae, Stoichactidae, Minyadidae, Aurelianidae, Phymanthidae, Actinodendridae, Thalassianthidae, Discosomidae, Actinostolidae, Isophelliidae, Paractidae, Metriidae, Diadumenidae, Aiptasiidae, Sagartiidae, Hormathiidae, Stichodactylidae
    Order Corallimorpharia
      Families Corallimorphiidae, Actinodiscidae
    Order Zoanthiniaria (= Zoanthidea)
      Families Epizoanthidae, Zoanthidae
    Order Scleractinia
      Suborder Astrocoeniina
        Families Thamnasteriidae, Astrocoeniidae, Pocilloporidae, Acroporidae
      Suborder Fungiina
        Families Agariciidae, Siderastreidae, Fungiidae, Poritidae
      Suborder Faviina
        Families Faviidae, Rhizangiidae, Oculinidae, Meandrinidae, Merulinidae, Pectiniidae, Mussidae
      Suborder Caryophylliina
        Families Caryophylliidae, Flebellidae
      Suborder Dendrophylliina
        Family Dendrophylliidae

Several meats are good foods for corals. Guppies, other small fishes, or cut segments of clam, oyster, scallop, shrimp, and mussel are all suitable meats for carnivorous corals that can be fed to corals with a stiff rod. Other meats, such as live or frozen brine shrimp, are best squirted at the carnivorous corals with a baster.

Carnivorous cnidarians should be fed no more than once a week or once a month. If the coral appears inflated with water, it is still digesting its last meal. Cut one end of a 3-foot segment of rigid airline tubing to provide a sharp point. Impale the meat on the point and, keeping your hands out of the water, brush the cnidarian with the meat until it adheres to the tentacles. Always emplace cnidarians requiring supplemental meat in a location readily reached with the rigid tubing, and not within a cave or beneath a ledge.

Cerianthus, *the tube anemone, has a strong sting and cannot be kept with small fishes.*

Ceriantharia

Tube anemones are popular and inexpensive, but should never be kept with fishes or under intense light. The stinging tube anemones (Order Ceriantharia: Family Cerianthidae: Genera *Cerianthus, Isarachnanthus, Pachycerianthus*) have both outer and inner rings of tentacles. There is no foot nor calcareous skeleton. When frightened, the anemone withdraws into a mucus tube up to a meter long. Walls of the tube are strengthened by particles of shell and sand. Tube anemones sting other corals and even small fishes, which they eat.

Antipatharia

The black corals are basically anemones that secrete a calcarous skeleton. Legal protection on many islands is given to precious deepwater black corals of the genera *Antipathes, Cirrhipathes*, and *Stichopathes*. Black corals are mostly branching, bushlike, or whiplike colonies with a dark, horny support resembling the skeleton of sea fans; collection for jewelry has depleted their numbers. Those remaining are jealously guarded by dive operators. Black corals are, of course, not kept in reef tanks.

Alcyonaria

The Alcyonaria or octocorals are a thousand species of colonial soft corals with each polyp divided into eight segments, from tentacles to the partitions down its gullet. The major groups of aquarium interest are the branchlike gorgonians, and sea pens, and the typical or fleshy soft corals. Also included are the popular star polyps.

If a skeleton occurs, it is internal and either calcarous or horny. Spicules are the only certain way to identify many species; they are ornate in gorgonians, smooth in sea pens.

As a general rule, soft corals can be maintained under a mixture of full-spectrum daylight and actinic VHO (very high output) lamps, not less than 5 watts per gallon, for 12 hours a day. Soft corals also require strong currents (but not directly on the coral body) to sweep away frequent extrusions of slime and waste tissue, which sometimes contain organic chemicals called terpenes. Terpenes are toxic to other animals, including stony corals, but terpene concentration is usually too low to be a hazard in reef tanks with carbon filtration and a protein skimmer. Some types eat zooplankton, others do not. To determine feeding preferences, squirt live or thawed adult brine shrimp or newly hatched brine shrimp nauplii directly onto the tentacles with a food baster. Soft corals will either wrap tentacles around the food and deliver it to the mouth, or they will ignore the food. Gorgonians also capture and feed on meiofauna (tiny sand-dwelling invertebrates) and detritus stirred into the water column by physical disruption (hand stirring, powerhead blasting).

Mushroom anemones are piscivorous, and appreciate an occasional dead guppy.

Clavulariidae and Cornulariidae

The Cornulariiae and Clavulariidae (star and daisy polyps) are good corals for beginners, some even fluorescing under UV light. Both have a weak internal skeleton of calcareous spicules. *Clavularia* resembles multiple white palm trees with green centers. *Pachyclavularia* has green polyps with white centers that live inside tiny purple tubes, similar to organ pipe skeletal material. *Cornularia, Clavularia*, and *Pachyclavularia* should have actinic and metal halide light for their zooxanthellae. Provide moderately good current, but do not place these corals directly in the effluent of a powerhead. They do not take and may not need

The colonial polyps of Clavularia *are green or brown with a bright central spot.*

supplemental feeding of zooplankton (brine shrimp, bloodworms). New polyps arise from runners that spread out over rocks and even onto glass. You can propagate them by placing a rock adjacent to the colony. After the runners spread onto the new rock, slice the connecting runner with a single-edged razor blade, then remove rock and new colony to a separate location.

Tubiporidae

More difficult to keep is the closely related organ pipe (Tubiporidae: *Tubipora*). The dark-red calcareous skeleton is common in shell shops. A slow grower, it usually fares poorly in captivity because the pieces for sale are fragments rather than whole colonies, and the torn interconnected polyps seldom heal. Unbroken colonies of the brown polyps need high-intensity (high wattage) metal halide light, moderate current, and supplementary feedings with zooplankton (brine shrimp, mysids, bloodworms, small euphausid shrimp).

The red skeleton of **Tubipora** *sold in shell shops as pipe organ isn't as beautiful as the living polyps.*

Helioporidae

At first glance, blue coral might be mistaken for fire coral. However, *Heliopora coerulea* uses iron salts to construct a unique blue calcareous skeleton that is hidden by the overlying dull brown polyps. This shallow and quiet water coral is hermatypic with symbiotic zooxanthellae, and the only octocoral contributing to calcareous reef structure. It is seldom seen in the hobby.

Alcyonaceans

Most soft corals in the hobby are the leather corals or Alcyonaceans, fleshy animals with tiny polyps on top (the capitulum) that withdraw into the body mass (basal stalk), leaving behind a shiny surface on top. The polyps may be nocturnal, diurnal, or oblivious of light. Most have symbiotic zooxanthellae, but grow better with supplementary feedings of brine shrimp and regular additions of iodine to the aquarium water. Alcyonaceans discourage competition for space by stinging with sweeper tentacles, discharging mucus, or by emitting noxious allelopathic toxins of a chemical class known as terpenes. These toxins are distasteful to some predatory fishes, poisonous to others. Some Alcyonaceans are mobile and may migrate over *Acropora* and *Pocillopora*, leaving a trail of dead stony corals in their wake. Several multiply in captivity by dividing from the base of the main and branch stalks, none more prolific than the pulse corals (*Xenia*). Many take up sperm and brood embryos in their bodies, the minute offspring then migrating a few inches from the parent to start a new colony.

Alcyoniidae

The Family Alcyoniidae contains the hardy leather corals (*Alcyonium, Lobophyton, Parerythropodium, Sarcophyton, Sinularia*) and *Cladiella* or colt coral. *Sarcophyton* feeds on products of its zooxanthellae by day, capturing plankton at night. It has two kinds of polyps, large ones for prey capture, and smaller polyps (siphonozoids) that aid water circulation over the surface. Its powerful toxins will kill hard corals in nature, and are capable of even killing other soft corals (allelopathy). Killing competitors allows it to spread and colonize a large area. It multiplies by buds, and is readily propagated by cuttings.

The similar *Lobophyton* has fingerlike processes in the margins instead of mushroomlike folds, and ridges radiating from the center. It also has different kinds of polyps for feeding and circulation. *Sinularia* is distinguished from these other genera in having but a single type of polyp. *Cladiella* species are hard to identify, and you must examine their spicules with a microscope. Most of us hope the exporter or breeder has done that.

Sarcophyton elegans *is among the easiest soft corals to keep and propagate from cuttings.*

Many unidentified species of Sarcophyton *are being imported. The one pictured above has a trade name of "Tonga."*

The polyps of Sarcophyton glaucum *resemble miniature anemones.*

Sarcophyton lobulatum *has a massive body form.*

Making Cuttings from Soft Corals

You can make cuttings of mushroom anemones and leather, colt, pulse, and other soft corals established a long time in the same tank. You'll need a sharp razor blade or fine-point scissors, and either toothpicks, thin rubber bands, or Super Glue (cyanoacrylate adhesive). First, find a rock to receive the cut piece. If using a toothpick to nail the fragment in place, locate a hole to receive that toothpick and mark it. Although you can cut a soft coral completely through, it is best to take a one-inch or two-inch branch or lobe. Slice or cut in a single quick motion (do not saw). Insert the toothpick through the wall and out the base, and stick it onto the hole in the rock. Or, slip the rubber band around the base of the fragment and then around the rock. It's less work to lean a small piece of rock on top of the fragment to keep it in its new place, but the piece should be light to keep from squashing the fragment, which then would disintegrate. The raw tissue of the fragment should heal and attach within three weeks, after which you can remove the leaning rock, cut the rubber band, or ignore the toothpick, which will disintegrate. The wounded donor, after a sharp reaction, will rapidly recover. Some reef aficionados add vitamin C to the cut surfaces and tank water in the belief it aids wound healing. Commercial coral farmers put the cuttings in pots with gravel or shell hash as an attachment base.

A new method in commercial use is as follows. The soft coral, while attached to its rock, is cut into multiple (often six) longitudinal segments, but not completely through, and then returned to the aquarium. After some three weeks of healing, the divided soft coral is removed to a working bowl of seawater, and the segments are severed from the rock through their bases. The bases are briefly blotted on paper towels, and a drop of Super Glue is applied to the wound. After ten seconds, the sticky base is attached to a dry rock surface and held in place for 10–20 seconds. You can also attach the coral to a submerged rock, holding the glued end in place for 30 seconds, but more than one attempt may be needed.

All need a moderate current (not in direct flow from a powerhead) under a mix of actinic and full-spectrum fluorescent light, VHO or metal halide when more than two feet from the light source. Adding live baby brine shrimp or rotifers to the aquarium with a baster just before the lights go off is beneficial to many invertebrates, from corals to feather duster worms. Always first strain the brine shrimp in a net and resuspend them in tank water, discarding their old culture water rather than allowing it to pollute the aquarium. For directed feeding of just a single coral at a time, use a 3-foot segment of rigid airline tubing to suck up the cleaned and resuspended brine shrimp and blow them out onto the coral's tentacles.

Nephtheidae and Siphonogorgiidae

The Nephtheidae (*Dendronephthya, Nephthea, Lemnalia, Litophyton*) and Siphonogorgiidae (*Catagorgia, Scleronephthya*) are the tree corals. Some are hermatypic (with symbiotic zooxanthellae in their tissues) and others ahermatypic (without symbiotic algae).

Many are not particularly difficult, with one important exception. The spectacular

You can make cuttings of Litophyton *tree corals if the coral has grown well for several months.*

Xenia, *the pulse corals, may multiply profusely, then divide at the base to release polyps that are carried by currents to new locations.*

Dendronephthya is spiny to the touch. It requires light for its symbiotic algae, and doesn't last long in captivity in the absence of supplementary feeding with cultured phytoplankton. On the other hand, the similar (and smooth-skinned) *Scleronephthya* is not difficult to keep and even propagate from cuttings, but it does need strong currents and supplementary feedings of zooplankton; it does not have symbiotic algae.

Xeniidae

Very popular are the spectacular Xeniidae (*Xenia, Anthelia, Efflatounaria*) or pulse, pom-pom, or waving hand corals. *Xenia* grows from a massive central stalk, individual polyps fragmenting and taking root elsewhere to start new colonies. The similar *Anthelia* forms a spreading mat. Both may pulsate and rapidly multiply under metal halide light supplemented with actinic and full-spectrum daylight fluorescent. They tolerate very strong cur-

rents, but not directly on the colonies. Ravenously taking supplementary zooplankton, they also do well with bright light alone.

Anthelia *or pom-pom corals grow by multiplying at the base of the existing colony, and do not fragment to start new colonies as often as pulse corals.*

Plexaurella *is a sea whip common throughout the Caribbean.*

Gorgonacea and Pennatulaceans

The Gorgonacea are the mostly shallow-water sea fans, sea plumes, and sea whips, and the more widely distributed Pennatulacea or sea pens. Within the gorgonian group, Holaxonia skeletons are made of horny gorgonin and resemble miniature dark trees attached to rocks by a short holdfast, while the Scleraxonia are supported by calcareous spicules. A few gorgonaceans are encrusting. In sea pens, the stalk is the lower end of a large central polyp embedded into the sediments and strengthed by calcarous spicules; there is no horny material. Smaller polyps grow along the sides of the main polyp. Some

sea pens can retract into the sediments when disturbed. Sea pens are so successful that they even grow in the cold black abyss of the deep ocean.

Sperm are shed into the sea, collected by a female, and the egg incubated within the female. The hatched planula larva swims about for a time, and finally settles and divides to form a colony that will be either male or female.

All require strong current and surge, strong light for shallow water forms, blue light for deepwater forms, calcium additives, iodine, trace elements, and supplementary feedings of zooplankton such as brine shrimp, bloodworms, and daphniae squirted directly at the polyps through rigid airline tubing or with a baster. In good condition, gorgonians and their relatives grow rapidly. Sensitive to high ammonia, the polyps retract if anything in the tank has died. Because the polyps are connected, damage anywhere may kill the entire coral. In poor water or light, they decline fast and may not recover. High nitrate, phosphate, and iodine can lead to algal overgrowth.

Zoantharia

The Class Zoantharia (= Hexacorallia) polyps are divided into six radial segments, from tentacles to gut. The 5,300 species include solitary and colonial forms, with an external calcarous skeleton or none at all.

Actinaria

The sea anemones (Order Actinaria) are solitary, fleshy polyps without a skeleton, with few to numerous tentacles and a mobile foot for gliding over hard surfaces. Most reproduction is by asexual binary fission or multiple budding. *Nematostella vectensis*, an estuarine anemone with peculiar nematosomes in its gut (coelenteron), is one of only five anemones that divide

Getting Rid of *Aiptasia*

Aiptasia is a pest soft coral that stings desirable corals. It multiplies faster than desirable corals, occupying any available surface, and interfering with the spread of desirable corals.

Tricks for removing the aggressive nuisance, ubiquitous *Aiptasia* range from picking at them with tweezers, to injecting them using a hypodermic syringe filled with concentrated calcium chloride, brine solution, or vinegar. Peppermint shrimps (*Lysmata wurdemanni*) prey on *Aiptasia*. John Tullock has been tank-raising a species of nudibranch that preys specifically on *Aiptasia*; this nudibranch should soon be commercially available. If you have an elegance coral, you can copy a trick from the tool-bearing crabs that use *Telmatactis*. Lift your elegance coral by its base and press the tentacles quickly against those nasty *Aiptasia* anemones. One sting from an elegance coral should kill them.

Pseudopterogorgia *sea whips form large forests in shallows of the Caribbean Sea. They are harvested by bringing up the small piece of rock to which the holdfast is attached.*

transversely; all other anemones divide longitudinally. Many anemones adhere to rocks or shells. Many in the Family Actiniidae (*Actinia, Anemonia, Anthopleura, Bunodactis, Bunodosoma, Condylactis, Entacmaea, Macrodactyla, Physobranchia, Tealia*) require gravel or sand in which to bury. Others do well on rock. *Stomphia* (Actinostolidae) can chemically sense predators and detach from the bottom to swim away. People living in cold-water regions of the Pacific northwest or Atlantic northeast are familiar with tide pool Metriidae. *Metridium* species are prominent, often colorful, large anemones of rocky bottoms, suitable for coldwater aquariums.

The colorful tropical intertidal flower anemones (Phymanthidae: *Phymanthus, Ragactis*) are zooxanthellae-containing anemones with accessory pigments to protect against ultraviolet and infrared solar radiation exposure at low tide. Unlike many intertidal animals that withdraw under adverse conditions, these anemones stretch out as though sunbathing.

Many actinarians have symbiotic *Periclimenes* and other shrimps. *Bartholomea* (Aiptasiidae) is a white-ringed, brown anemone often symbiotic with *Alpheus* snapping or pistol shrimps that emit loud noises that frighten off cnidarian-eating fish. Some anemones, such as *Telmatactis* (Isophelliidae), are carried about as tools by crabs using them to pick up food or sting enemies. *Adamsia* and *Calliactis* (Hormathiidae) occur on snail shells carried about by *Dardanus* and *Petrochirus* hermit crabs.

Many Pacific sea anemones are hosts to clown anemonefishes such as Amphiprion ocellaris.

Condylactis gigantea, *a common Caribbean sea anemone, tends to wander about the reef tank.*

Quite a few anemones are clownfish hosts. *Entacmaea*, the bubble-tip anemone (Actiniidae), is a fast grower that multiplies in captivity after first retreating to a dark area, shrinking its tentacles, and subsequently dividing to form two daughter anemones; it may be the hardiest clownfish host anemone available. *Stichodactyla* and *Heteractis* (Stichodactylidae) are carpet anemones requiring bright light, including actinic light for their symbiotic zooxanthellae. *Stichodactyla* can kill and eat fish other than its host clownfish, and even prey on other anemones. The Stoichactidae (*Stoichactis, Homostichanthus, Radianthus, Gyrostoma*) carpet anemones also require bright light. *Cryptodendrum adhesivum* is the only member of the Thalassianthidae that is host to a clownfish, *Amphiprion clarkii.* Its two kinds of tentacles are different colors and shapes, but despite this attractiveness, it does poorly in captivity.

Other anemones are nuisances in a reef tank. *Aiptasia* (Aiptasiidae) is a small, rapidly multiplying species that stings other cnidarians unable to get out of the way. The Sagartiidae (*Actinothoe, Anthothoe, Sagartia, Sagartiogeton, Cereus*) can have a powerful sting and must be handled with rubber gloves or in a net.

Corallimorpharia

The Order Corallimorpharia comprises the mostly hermatypic mushroom anemones, not true sea anemones but false (soft) corals. Many species come from lagoons or shallow nearshore habitats enriched with nutrients. These species need only minimal light and current, and may safely be kept in very small (10-gallon) aquariums with low-wattage actinic units and daylight fluorescent bulbs and an outside power filter. In larger reef tanks, place these mushroom anemones away from strong currents, as they easily tear. Many produce potent toxins, so don't place them near other corals. Some of the large elephant ears will eat small fish, but supplemental feeding isn't required.

Most popular are *Corynactis* (Family Corallimorphiidae), and the Actinodiscidae genera *Actinodiscus, Amplexidiscus, Rhodactis* (having protuberances with small points) and *Ricordia* (with rounded protuberances and sold as colonies on live rock called Florida mushroom rock). *Actinodiscus* are inexpensive, often blue, brown, or reddish, and usually sold in groups with many individuals to a "mushroom rock." *Actinodiscus* reproduce by budding at the edges or dividing at the base, faster under brighter light. You can transfer a small budded mushroom anemone recently separated from its parent to another rock, where it might start another colony. You can also propagate the species by cuttings. Mushroom anemones eat fish, and can be fed dead guppies, mollies, or small minnows at the end of a pointed section of rigid airline tubing. Corallimorphs also absorb nutrients from the water (doing especially well in heavily fed tanks containing fish), and many are hermatypic.

Zoanthinaria

The Order Zoanthinaria (= Zoanthidea) or sea mats are hardy, fast-growing, usually inexpensive colonial anemones forming clusters on rocks, shells, sponges, mangroves, brown algae stalks, and other firm substrata, even overgrowing filamentous algae. Many sea mats have green, red, yellow, or rust-colored pigments. A few have powerful toxins (*Palythoa* palytoxin) to protect them from predation.

Sea mats are common on coral rubble; sea mat rock is a commercial name for zooanthid-encrusted live rock sold in the hobby. The two families are the Epizoanthidae, with *Epizoanthus* and *Parazoanthus*,

Actinodiscus *species are common, hardy, inexpensive mushroom anemones that need occasional feedings of meat.*

Actinodiscus nummiformis *is one of the more beautiful mushroom anemones.*

Rhodactis, *a mushroom anemone, requires occasional feedings of a small fish or piece of seafood.*

Zoanthus pulchellus *of the Caribbean is often for sale as sea mat rock.*

and the Zoanthidae, with *Palythoa* and *Zoanthus*. Some sea mats cannot live away from the sponges upon which they are found in nature, and the sponges cannot yet be kept alive in minireef aquariums. Individual polyps are not connected except during gemmation (dividing near the base), so damage to one polyp does not spread through the colony. Hermatypic or ahermatypic, all do better fed live brine shrimp nauplii, frozen adult brine shrimp or bloodworms, and macerated shellfish. Native to nearshore or reeftop habitats, sometimes exposed at low tide, they do best in minireef

Parazoanthus gracilus *multiply by gemmation, but the polyps quickly break off to assume independent lives within the colony.*

aquariums under strong light close to the surface with moderate to strong currents.

Propagation: You can turn to good use the fact that they reproduce by dividing near the base (gemmation). A small rock or shell placed against a colony will eventually be overgrown, and you can then cut the connections at the base with a razor blade to move the overgrown rock elsewhere. For large-scale propagation, chisel the colony into fragments with a substantial rocky base to protect the runners, and glue the fragments to new locations with cyanoacrylate (Super Glue) or other adhesive.

Scleractinia—Stony Corals

The Order Scleractinia comprises the major stony corals. Most are reef-builders, others free-living but contributing to rubble when they die. Most are colonial, their massive exoskeletons a honeycomb of calcareous cups with sharp ridges pressing in from the sides, and thin plates below walling off chambers of the colony's earlier polyps. The majority are light-loving hermatypic corals with symbiotic zooxanthellae; others are ahermatypic denizens of caverns and shaded ledges, feeding by stinging or sticking plankters from the passing currents.

Shallow-water stony corals often exposed to the sun at low tide must possess protective substances to prevent the zooxanthellae and coral tissues from burning under the sun's ionizing UV and hot IR irradiation.

Corals of the blue depths sport supplemental pigments of unknown function. Perhaps they shift the energy of shortwave blue light to the red longer waves that drive zooxanthellae photosynthesis. Red algae of great depths may use minute amounts of radiant energy in their photosynthesis.

About half the stony corals and a few other invertebrate groups of the Great Barrier Reef, and undoubtedly elsewhere in

SPS Corals

The small polyp stony corals (SPS corals) are fast-growing hermatypic species with branches often tipped with red, blue, or purple pigments that are produced in response to intense light in nature and in the aquarium. The pigments are unrelated to UV, and not UV-protective. Maintain calcium at or above 400 mg/L, alkalinity at 7–12 dKH or 2.5–4.5 meq/L, use strontium and iodine supplements, aragonite as a base, powerful surging currents, and carbon filtration plus skimming to keep dissolved organic concentrations low. Because the small polyps are easily damaged, new specimens should be transported submerged under a styrofoam float. These corals ideally should have their own all-SPS tank.

SPS corals are at considerable risk when placed with soft corals. Damaged SPS corals take a long time to recover, if they recover at all, the wounds becoming foci of infections and polyp recedence. *Acropora* especially is vulnerable to protozoan infections from which it rarely recovers. Algal grazers (snails, tangs, pygmy angelfish) help prevent overgrowth. Artificial moonlight (timed lighting on a 30-day cycle) and temperature oscillation may induce spawning of the coral.

Some manufacturers claim that SPS corals will keep their colors best under "their" brand of 10,000 K or 20,000 K metal halide lamp. A number of minireef aquarists have switched from standard 6,500 K metal halides to these newer lamps based on the claims, but the jury is still out.

Montipora digitata (left) branches profusely.

December. This lunar and temperature periodicity is being replicated by some aquarists in hopes of inducing spawning in reef aquariums using artificial moonlight and temperature oscillation controlled by 30-day timers.

Almost all species within the four families making up the Suborder Astrocoeniina are hermatypic and hermaphroditic, releasing into the water sperm that is taken up to internally fertilize the eggs; the zygotes are then brooded well into the planula larval stage. This brooding is unique among scleractinian stony corals. All four families have small polyp stony (SPS) corals.

Pocilloporidae

The Family Pocilloporidae (*Pocillopora, Seriatopora, Stylophora, Palauastrea*) are mostly corals of shallow upper-reef slopes. *Madracis*, with hermatypic and ahermatypic species, contains deepwater species.

Easiest of all for the hobbyist is *Pocillopora damicornis*. A fast grower, it can be induced to spawn with an artificial lunar and temperature cycle. This causes bursts of planula larvae every one or two months; these larvae settle on the glass to begin new colonies. Also fast growers, *Stylophora* can be propagated by cutting off

the Pacific Ocean below the equator, shed gametes into the sea during the night approximately two to five days after the full moon in October, November, and/or

Pocillopora verrucosa *(left), shares a tank* *with* **Montipora digitata.**

Varying in body form by species and with depth, this bulky **Montipora** *will adapt to powerful surges.*

Thin **Acropora** *branches break in violent storms and contribute to the coral rubble at the base of the reef.*

branches, the fragments doubling in size in three months. The red-polyped *Pocilloporida* species are not recommended for beginners.

Acroporidae

The closely related Family Acroporidae (*Acropora, Montipora, Anacropora,* and *Astreopora*) require intense light (VHO or metal halide), strong alternating currents to wash particles from the polyps restricted to the stiff corallum, strong protein skimming, carbon filtration, and constant, dripwise addition of rapidly depleted calcium and strontium solutions. Feed supplementary *Artemia* nauplii sparingly, if at all. Acroporids can be kept in the same long aquarium with soft corals, but far apart to avoid terpenes and smothering by extruded mucus. Acroporids may get important nutrition from the dissolved organic compounds (DOC) secreted by soft corals. *Acropora,* under excellent conditions of light and water quality, has sexually reproduced in reef aquariums.

The most abundant of reef-building corals, the Acroporids can be branching, encrusting, massively boulderlike, fingerlike, or tablelike. Many dominate shallows at the crest of the reef where, battered by waves and storms, their fast-growing branches break off and become substrata for hard and soft corals at all depths. *Acropora* is the largest genus of all corals, with some 400 species. Atlantic snorkelers are familiar with abundant staghorn coral (*A. cervicornis*) and elkhorn coral (*A. palmata*) at Caribbean resort islands, but the Indo-Pacific has most of the species. *Acropora formosa* is a spectacularly fast grower. Cuttings originating with Dieter Steuber are widely distributed in the hobby. *Acropora* must be trimmed back to keep them from spreading over the entire water surface, where they shade the remaining corals.

Acropora digitifera *is a Pacific species of this large genus.*

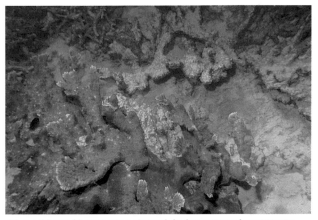

Live elkhorn (Acropora palmata) *in foreground contrasts with rubble of staghorn coral* (Acropora cervicornis) *on a Caribbean beach.*

Montipora is the second largest genus with 211 "species" named by 1986 but probably consisting of fewer than 100 valid species. *Astreopora* has 15–30 species with colonies mostly appearing as platelike or toadstoollike incrustations. The half dozen *Anacropora* are small corals not associated with reefs.

Agariciidae

The Family Agariciidae are a mixed group from sheltered areas, some hermaphroditic, others with separate sexes, some brooding eggs to planula larvae, others not. The colonies are leaflike, platelike, massive, or club- or finger-shaped. *Pavona* (cactus coral) are leaflike (foliar) or platelike and easily broken. Some colonies resemble toadstools and others mimic hammer corals. *Leptoseris* are delicately leaflike colonial corals of protected waters, some forming overlapping plates with complex ridges and whorls. *Pachyseris* has two species, typically leafy, forming massive colonies that can cover vast segments of deep reefs. *Gardineroseris* is massive or encrusting with two widespread species.

There is only one massive species making up *Coeloseris*. *Agaracia* is strictly Atlantic with seven species of leaflike or encrusting platelike colonies, horizontal or vertical, mostly in protected waters, sometimes 80 meters (250 feet) deep. Members of the family require moderate to gentle currents and strong light provided by metal halides and VHO lamps, but do not need supplemental plankton.

Some forms of cactus coral, Pavona, *are leaflike and easily broken by falling live rock.*

Siderastreidae

The Family Siderastreidae are hermatypic corals requiring metal halide or VHO lighting and calcium and strontium supplements. Colonies, which consist of a single sex, are dome-shaped, fingerlike, encrusting, or platelike. *Psammocora* (27 species usually massive or fingerlike) and *Coscinaraea* (six species usually platelike) dominate the family. *Coscinaria* extends into temperate regions and is cold-tolerant. *Siderastrea*, with one or two species, has the most widespread of all corals with *S. radians* in the Atlantic and Indo-Pacific, including the Red Sea. *Pseudosiderastrea* has only one species, *S.tayami*, which ranges from Asia to northern Australia. *Anomastrea* and *Horastrea* are in the western Indian Ocean.

Fungiidae

The Family Fungiidae or mushroom corals are distinctive in their radial symmetry and stand-alone habit. Some are elongate; most are circular and rather flat. They are entirely Indo-Pacific, and have only one

Psammocora contigua *requires metal halide or intense VHO light, and calcium and strontium supplements.*

Making Cuttings of Hard Corals

Fast-growing branching corals like *Acropora*, popular Caryophylliidae like *Plerogyra* (bubble coral), and even massive brain corals like *Favia* can be snapped, cut, or broken and the fragments moved to another location. Cuts of broad-base brain corals should be done with a diamond-edged power saw blade and then smoothed with the saw blade. Cutting with heavy stainless steel shears or simply snapping will suffice for thin branches; make the break or cut as close to the base of the branch as possible. Branch coral cuts should be quick, not slowly squeezed. Caryophylliids can also be placed on their sides in a basin underwater and broken at a narrow point with a broad-bladed screwdriver struck hard with a hammer. The exposed end of the fragment is smeared with cyanoacrylate (Super Glue) or other underwater adhesive and pressed against a rock or shell until it holds; complete hardening will take more than a day. The fragment should not be moved to another aquarium until some recovery is evident and even, in the case of branching corals, some growth, which can take a month or more. Fragments not affixed, but allowed to rest on shell hash or rubble, will attach to something by themselves over time.

ahermatypic genus (*Fungiacyathus*). These free-living, mostly non-reef-building stony corals usually consist of a giant polyp on its own large corallite; those with several mouth openings are considered colonial. Despite massive size, many can upright themselves if tumbled by a storm or can climb out of the sand if buried. Moving like sea anemones, fungiids travel across sandy areas by gliding on ciliary hairs below or inflating and pulling forward with the tentacles above.

Sexes are almost always separate, the females brooding or not. They can also multiply asexually by budding or dividing. Minute juveniles called acanthocauli develop from planula larvae or by budding off a buried or damaged parent. The acanthocaulus is a small stalked polyp that develops its calcareous plate at the end of the basal stalk, the skeleton forming from within the polyp rather than secreted from its base.

Fungia has 16 species, each furrowed platelike skeleton a single animal. *Cycloseris*, with a dozen species, is similar, but has a concave bottom. *Diaseris* has distinctive radial fractures signifying ongoing fragmentation, this mode of asexual reproduction often producing large aggregations on hard or quiet bottoms. *Halomitra pilaeus* is the Neptune's cap coral, its helmet-shaped colony plastered with longitudinally grooved platelets. *Sandalolitha* is similar, but the two species have more or less curved grooves and the platelets are more flattened than stacked. *Herpolitha, Polyphyllia,* and *Herpetoglossa* are colonial (more than one mouth), more often longer than round. *Herpolitha* has two species, one angular at the tips (*H. weberi*), the other rounded at the tips (*H. limax*). They are often massive, the heaviest of the Fungiidae. Of the four species of slipper corals, *Polyphyllia*, with three species, has long tentacles providing a shaggy appearance, whereas the similar *Herpetoglossa simplex* differs in skeletal structure.

With its long, white-tipped tentacles, *Heliofungia actiniformis* looks like a sea anemone until you discover its stony, *Fungia*-like skeleton below and notice that it doesn't have symbiotic clownfish or damsels among its tentacles. The largest of all coral polyps can be 20 inches across with a mouth over an inch wide. It may be

Plate corals, represented by Fungia, *are not reef-builders. When fully expanded, the tentacles may mask the corallum plate so that the animal resembles a sea anemone.*

the only hermaphroditic fungiid. Because it moves around, it is easily damaged and may suffer infections leading to death.

Most unfungiid, the leaflike colonial reef-building forms include *Lithophyllon* and *Podabacia*. The two species of *Lithophyllon* are rare to uncommon. The monotypic *Podabacia crustacea* is similar in habit, but its grooved platelets are recurved back at the ends as if withdrawing.

Fungiids should be placed on aragonite sand with room to move about and feed on supplemental detritus and microbes gathered from the sand and water. Fungiids require little current, but in most tanks their zooxanthellae need intense light from metal halides and VHO bulbs capable of delivering energy to the bottom. In small or shallow aquariums, less light suffices, but fungiids are then vulnerable to shock from oscillating water quality.

Poritidae

The Family Poritidae are hermatypic and with separate sexes. Sperm released into the water is gathered by female colonies

Colonies of yellow porous coral, **Porites astreoides,** *on rock at St. John, U.S. Virgin Islands.*

Flowerpot corals, **Goniopora,** *long-tentacled members of the Poritidea, are often isolated.*

Blue polychaetes colonize a cavity within a **Porites lobata.**

and the eggs are retained and brooded through the planula stage.

The predominant genera are *Porites* (with 12 short tentacles) and *Goniopora* (with 24 elongate tentacles).

Goniopora, the flowerpot corals (*stokesi, stutchburyi,* and *fructicosa*) have polyps and tentacles long enough to sting other corals and maintain large territories. Perhaps as a result, *Goniopora* neither has nor needs sweeper tentacles. *Goniopora* tend to waste away after a few months, and are not recommended for beginners. They need intense light (metal halide and VHO) and moderately slow current. Their requirement for supplemental large zooplankton (especially frozen euphausid shrimp) and sensitivity to water quality make them difficult to manage in all but the largest aquariums with stable water quality.

Porites are usually massive and lobed, but can be fingerlike, branched or not. *Stylaraea,* with one species, is probably a sub-genus of *Porites.*

Alveopora, with eight species, has some of the largest polyps known among colonial corals, those of *A. gigas* up to 10 cm long and 2 cm thick when fully extended. Reproduction is not known, and if their offspring differ from what has been described for the family, they may have to be removed from the Poritidae.

Faviidae

Hermatypic with a great demand for intense light, the faviid brain corals all require metal halides supplemented with VHO actinic fluorescents and any other light you can make available; most of all, keep them close to the light source. Almost all are massive forms that do well in either moderate or strong currents. Supplemental plankton are not necessary, but basting the tank daily with *Artemia* nauplii just before turning on the lights may be beneficial to

Rose coral (Mancinia), *with its meandroid valleys, is flanked by two colonies of* Porites *in St. John, U.S. Virgin Islands.*

Moon coral (Favia), *here with polyps extended, are most common on shallow back reefs.*

Montastrea *species are boulder corals of the Faviidae.*

Corallites of the seven species of Favites *share common ridges.*

these nocturnally active corals. A thin film of mucus indicates a healthy specimen. A few types need larger foods such as pieces of oyster or mussel, placed at their tentacles just before dark.

Colonial and very social hermaphrodites, the Pacific species shed eggs and sperm into the water during the night some five days after the full moon in October, November, and December, in synchrony with spawnings of many other lunar-triggered corals.

Newly imported faviid corals may not survive after transfer to a store or home aquarium. The reason may be shipping damage from heat on the tarmac or in the hold, bouncing against container sides, or ammonia toxicity from too much time in the bag (the ammonia cannot be used by the coral's symbiotic algae in the dark package). In aquariums, faviid corals need supplemental strontium without which they

Goniastraea paluensis *is one of the massive honeycomb corals of the Faviidae.*

Caulastrea furcata *has tall conical corallites. Only four species are placed in this genus of the Faviidae.*

Trachyphyllia *species are the open brain or sand corals of the Faviidae.*

cannot build new skeletal compartments for descendant polyps.

Of any hard coral family, Faviidae has the most genera and the second largest number of species. The vast majority are massive brain or boulder corals with multiple high-ridged corallites packed close together with circular, subcircular, or elongate meandrine corallites. A few faviids are platelike or foliaceous, others arborescent or branched, and one is termed phaceloid (having very tall corallites).

The Atlantic genera are *Diploria, Colpophyllia, Solenastrea, Cladocora*, and *Manicinia. Montastrea* and *Favia* have species in both the Atlantic and Pacific. All other genera are strictly Indo-Pacific.

Diploria, Colpophyllia, and *Manicinia areolata* (rose coral) form massive colonies with meandroid ridges and valleys. *Favia, Favites* (closed brain coral), *Cladocora, Solenastrea, Plesiastrea, Leptastrea, Diploastrea*, and *Montastrea* (star and boulder corals) have elevated and circular corallites. *Caulastrea* (four species) is unique in its very tall and conical corallites that jut from the massive corallum; its thick fleshy polyps extend even further and may be smooth, ridged, rounded, or branched. *Barabattoia* (three species) are shorter versions, with very massive tubular rather than conical corallites.

Favia, with at least 14 species, occurs mostly on shallow back reefs where staghorns do not dominate. Its conical corallites and rounded, massive corallum are typical of brain corals of the Faviidae. The very colorful *Favites*, with seven species, is superficially similar, but the corallites share common ridges and these corals might occur anywhere.

The seven or eight species of *Goniastrea* (honeycomb corals) are typically massive, the corallites with single centers (monocentric) or multiple centers (polycentric), rounded or curved (meandroid). *Goni-*

astrea occur in estuaries, on reef tops, in full-strength seawater or out of it at low tide, on rocks, corals, sand, and mud. Captions of photographs of brilliant green specimens sometimes fail to mention that brilliant colors are exceptional rather than the rule. Among the hardiest of corals, *Goniastrea* are ideal for beginner minireef tanks with intense metal halide and VHO actinic light.

Similarly variable yet more beautiful are the five species of *Platygyra* (squiggle brain coral) with corallites usually meandroid, sometimes rounded; *P. daedalea* and *P. verweyi* are the only common species, the former with a meandroid pattern and the latter between meandroid and circular. The three species of *Oulophyllia* are equally varied. *Leptoria phrygia*, with meandroid channels, is massive and often elevated rather than broadly rounded; it is the only species in its genus (monotypic). *Cyphastrea* has protruding circular corallites, and may occur in massive branching forms.

Echinopora is usually leaflike, but can be encrusting, or even tubular or branching.

Most striking of all faviids is the monotypic *Moseleya latistellata* of muddy inshore bottoms; the sharply angular corallites of the species have six or seven straight walls resembling a honeycomb instead of rounded or meandroid ridges.

Two other monotypic genera, *Trachyphyllia* (sand coral or open brain coral) and *Wellsophyllia*, are sometimes placed in a separate family Trachyphyllidae, but their close relationship to *Moseleya* supports inclusion in the Faviidae. *Trachyphyllia geoffroyi* when alive resembles *Cataphyllia* (elegance coral) or *Lobophyllia* (tooth coral or open brain coral), with very large, contorted, meandrine valleys surrounding one to three mouths, and colorful fleshy polyps extended at night. *Trachyphyllia* is free-living on soft bottoms, and predaceous on small fish. With supplemental feedings of meat and strong metal halide and VHO

Trachyphyllia geoffroyi *is distinguished by very colorful fleshy polyps.*

light, it does well. *Wellsophyllia radiata* is known only from a few small museum specimens with great similarity to *Trachyphyllia*, and the name may not be valid.

Faviid corals are susceptible in nature to black-band disease, an infection with the cyanobacterium *Phormidium corallyticum*. The infection follows an injury, is not highly contagious, and is self-limiting in cool water. Faviids cut by sharp rocks in reef tanks or in shipping may succumb to Gram-negative bacterial infections or invasive protozoa feeding in the wounds.

Oculinidae

The Family Oculinidae form single species colonies. They may be hermatypic, thickly branched, and fast-growing in clear shallow water or ahermatypic, thin-branched, and slow-growing at great depths where no light penetrates. In different areas oculinids are either hermaphroditic or female brooders.

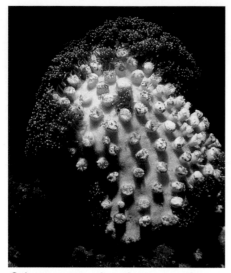

Galaxea **commonly make up an entire fringing reef in shallow, turbid water.**

Galaxea consists of tubular corallites extending from massive or platelike basal skeletons, sometimes making up the sole species on a fringing reef, most common in turbid water. In all five species of *Galaxea* the very beautiful, large, colorful polyps extend from the tips of the widely spaced

One way the Oculinidae may become the sole corals on the reef is by aggressive use of digestive tentacles as seen protruding from this Galaxea astreata.

tubular skeletons to feed in the surrounding plankton, and in shallow water are also (but not exclusively) hermatypic. The monotypic *Acrhelia horrescens* is a shallow hermatypic coral of outer reefs in the western Pacific with great masses of branches supporting elongate corallites whose polyps only come out at night. *Archohelia* and *Cyathelia* are also hermatypic oculinids of shallow Indo-Pacific waters.

Oculina diffusa and *O. valenciennesi* are bushy Atlantic corals with widely spaced corallites along thin branches. In shallow waters off the Bahamas, ivory bush coral, *O. varicosa*, is hermatypic and occurs mixed with other corals. At lightless depths of 200–300 feet along a ninety-mile stretch off eastern Florida, 4–5 foot high individual colonies of ahermatypic ivory bush corals cap hundred-foot high hills of rubble and sediments, the sole species of coral on these banks. These 400–500 year old single-species reefs formed when a solitary coral settled on a rocky outcrop and began to grow at just 16 mm/year, living solely on captured plankton and sediments snared from the strong surrounding currents. With time, the sediments and rubble accumulated to form huge mounds, strengthened by dead branching coral within, capped by live coral bushes above. Today, the Oculina Banks off Florida are protected. The range of their associated fauna is staggering. From 41 coral colonies examined, scientists recovered 230 species of molluscs, 50 species of crabs and shrimps, 21 species of echinoderms, and 47 kinds of amphipods. Oddly, the massive sponges and gorgonians common on other deep reefs are uncommon on Oculina Banks.

Meandrinidae

Among the Meandrinidae, *Dendrogyra* are pillar corals, and *Meandrina* a brain coral. *Dichocoenia* is also in this family.

Merulinidae

The Family Merulinidae are herma-typic, colonial hermaphrodites of the Indo-Pacific with every conceivable body plan imaginable, but distinguished by high ridges or mounds (hydnophores) formed where adjacent corallite walls fuse, most prominent in *Hydnophora*. Picture a collection of dominoes placed flat side to flat side and extending a great distance, and you'll understand the shape of the ridges characterizing the family. The forms in the following descriptions may not always occur. It is likely that the early settling larvae form encrusting plates that only later arise to form leaves, or grow protuberances that develop into stubby branches, with a couple of species specialized into highly branched, reduced plate forms.

Merulina has two leafy species of spectacular brown or bright pink corals with flaring or concentric plates decorated with rows of prominent high ridges perpendicular to the ridge lines. The monotypic *Scapophyllia cylindrica* has stubby branches arising from a flat plate, and characteristic elevated ridges of perpendicularly fused corallite walls.

The five species of *Hydnophora* are either staghornlike branched (*H. rigida*), platelike or with stubby branching (*H. pilosa, H. exesa*), or massive (*H. microconos*). *Hydnophora* are brittle, but grow well under bright light. The monotypic *Paraclavarina triangularis* is also highly branched, but the branches are not sharply angular and the white polyps provide a soft surface appearance.

Merulinids are hermatypic corals requiring intense light provided by metal halides and VHO fluorescents, and supplementary *Artemia* nauplii. Place merulinids in a moderate flow out of the direct path of a powerhead effluent. Activated carbon filtration

The Merulinidae, here represented by **Hydnophora exesa,** *have fused corallite ridges, stacking up like leaning dominoes.*

helps protect other corals from noxious merulinid aromatic secretions.

Pectinidae

Massive, encrusting or leaflike, the pectinids are hermatypic, with colorful, thick polyps that come out only at night. The five

Polyps of the hermatypic **Hydnophora exesa** *should be fed supplementary brine shrimp nauplii.*

The five species of Echinophyllia *form lumpy encrusting colonies with well-spaced protruding corallites.*

The two species of Mycedium *occur as encrusting colonies with angular corallites.*

The leaflike Pectinia *is Pacific elkhorn coral, not to be confused with Caribbean elkhorn of the Acroporidae.*

species of *Echinophyllia* have lumpy encrusting colonies, each polyp within a moderately spaced, large, protruding corallite with almost beaded, longitudinal ridges. *Mycedium* has two species of encrusting corals with protruding and angular corallites, each resembling a bent nose with a single nostril extending off the plate. *Oxypora* contains two species of leaflike plates covered with widely spaced corallites appearing as blisters on the hard, thin base. The coral can be encrusting or the flat plates raised in a whorl to resemble a head of leaf lettuce. *Pectinia* (elkhorn corals, not to be confused with *Acropora* elkhorn) is fully leaflike. It contains the hibiscus and carnation corals, seven species with closely packed upright plates that may be smooth, lumpy, or even branched, and brown, green, or (most beautiful) red. The plates can resemble a smooth-edged or rough-edged head of lettuce, the closely packed petals of a flower, or clumps of branches arising from a diffuse base (thickly knobbed modified leaves). Based on its leafy appearance the monotypic *Physophyllia ayleni* may be a form of *Pectinia*.

Mussidae

Among the most distinctive and popular corals in the hobby, the Family Mussidae includes twelve genera of green and brown corals with polyps sometimes more than an inch wide. All are hermatypic but also eat zooplankton. Some are solitary and resemble fungiids while others with multiple centers resemble brain corals. At least some are hermaphrodites with external fertilization.

Scolymia is a solitary (monocentric or single center) form with two Indo-Pacific and two Atlantic species, the only mussid genus in both basins. (The Indo-Pacific *Lithophyllia vitiensis* has been moved to *Scolymia*.) *Cynarina* (meat polyp) is a deli-

Scolymia vitiensis *is one of five members of the Mussidae, a family with both Atlantic and Pacific species.*

Lobophyllia hemprichii *is a Mussid with colonies having elongated, abutting centers.*

cate monocentric species of the Indo-Pacific, its polyps swollen with water and translucent during the day when tentacles are withdrawn, shrunken at night when extended. *Cynarina* lives on rocks or soft bottoms, just like fungiids. Tolerant of many water conditions, the one or two species of *Cynarina* are good selections for minireef tanks.

Blastomussa is polycentric, Indo-Pacific, with three species that may be red, brown, green, or purple, with contrasting centers. The similar *Mussa* of the Atlantic may be solitary when young, but more often is polycentric; *M. angulosa* is the large flower coral of the minireef hobby. The six species of *Acanthastrea*, all Indo-Pacific encrusting corals, are also polycentric (each center with its own distinct rim) and variably colored. The monotypic *Australomussa rowleyensis* of the Indo-Pacific has rims coalescing into what isn't quite a meandroid pattern.

With fewer than half a dozen species, the Indo-Pacific *Lobophyllia* can have rounded centers abutting one another (*L. corymbosa, L. diminuta*), elongated abutting centers (*L. hemprichii*), or meandroid arrangements of the polycentric colonies (*L. hataii*) in green, yellow, or red.

The Indo-Pacific Cynarina lacrymalis *polyps swell with water during the day while its tentacles are withdrawn.*

Symphyllia valenciennesii *is in a small Mussid genus having the largest and deepest valleys of all meandroid corals.*

The five species of Indo-Pacific *Symphyllia* (modern brain coral) are fully meandroid, with prominent fused ridges and the largest, widest, and deepest valleys of all corals, much deeper than in the meandroid faviids. *Symphyllia* are often markedly circular rather than uneven in outline as in the related *Lobophyllia*. In the rare *S. valenciennesii*, the meanders radiate from a central point.

With its hammer-shaped tips, Euphyllia ancora *is among the most recognizable of corals.*

Strictly Atlantic genera are *Mussismillia, Mycetophyllia, Isophyllastrea,* and *Isophyllia. Isophyllia* is meandroid; *Mycetophyllia* is meandroid but with very low ridges and shallow valleys, so that it appears almost encrusting.

Caryophylliidae

Probably the hardiest of the stony corals, Caryophylliidae collected from shallow shores—with variable light, turbidity, and temperatures—adapt well to minireefs. Those collected from deep water may be more difficult to keep. Most do well with a combination of metal halide and VHO actinic and full-spectrum lights, moderate indirect currents, regular additions of calcium, strontium, and iodine, and daily supplemental feedings of zooplankton or weekly feedings of seafood meats or small dead forage fish (you can buy smelt or silversides and "popcorn" shrimp at a seafood market). *Caryophylliidae* may starve and decline without supplemental foods. All require intense metal halide and VHO light, and carbon filtration and water changes to deal with the abundant TOC metabolites resulting from heavy feeding and to replace trace elements and dilute nitrates.

Euphyllia contains the popular hammer (C-shaped tip) and frog's spawn (rounded tip) corals from the Pacific. *Euphyllia ancora* and *E. fimbriata* are called hammer corals, *E. cristata, E. divisa,* and *E. glabrescens,* frog's spawn corals. If just two of these names are valid, then the frog's spawn is *E. divisa,* and hammer is *E. ancora.* From a stony base, elongate tan or white wormlike polyps with inflated rounded or hammer-shaped, white or green tips roll back and forth with the currents, exposing their symbiotic zooxanthellae to the light. Given sufficiently strong current, a healthy colony extends elongate sweeper tentacles resem-

Some Euphyllia *may simply be variants of bubble or frogs spawn coral, but that issue hasn't been settled.*

Euphyllia glabrescens *or frogs spawn coral has round-tipped tentacles.*

bling very long polyps far out from the colony, seeking to digest competitors.

The hermatypic *Euphyllia* require metal halides or VHO lighting, but can survive in a shallow tank under abundant actinic and daylight fluorescent wattage. *Euphyllia* need supplementary animal prey, which they don't sting, but capture with adhesive mucus. They then deliver the prey to the mouths with cilia, so the polyps never scrunch up during the day unless the coral is sick. Sexes are separate, but not distinguishable. *Euphyllia* can be propagated by breaking the stony base below with wire pliers or a hammer and chisel and separating the daughter colonies. Some colonies form little buds at the edge that can be cut off with scissors and attached elsewhere with epoxy or acrylic cement.

The monotypic *Cataphyllia jardinei* (elegance coral) is among the largest and most beautiful of daytime corals, swelling to great size to capture light for its zooxanthellae, shrinking body and tentacles during the night. Hermatypic, it also captures small

prey by stinging, and does better with supplementary feeding. It needs metal halide or strong VHO lighting and enough current to wash away metabolites, doing poorly in nutrient-rich tanks. Several mouth areas dot the large central portion, and the entire colony is ringed with prominent, sometimes pink-tipped tentacles that fluoresce green at the base. Not a reef builder, elegance coral frequents diverse habitats, most often on murky mud or silt bottoms where it can inflate above the substratum like several mobile sea anemones. It has a sting strong enough to kill *Aiptasia* anemones but is easily handled, feeling merely sticky to the touch. You can kill *Aiptasia* by picking up elegance coral by its base and pressing its soft tissue against the nuisance *Aiptasia*.

Sexes are separate. Elegance coral reproduces by gradual fragmentation from within. The vast fleshy body produces new skeletal material inside, to be eventually extruded; the weight of the flesh and skeleton (accompanied by water current pressure on the mass) assists the separation of

Elegance coral, Catalaphyllia jardinei, *ranges from white to brown, but is almost always green in the center.*

Some individuals of Catalaphyllia jardinei *have colorful tips on the tentacles.*

the masses. Elegance coral often divides this way in tanks. You can propagate elegance corals by cutting through a break in the corallum.

Physogyra and *Plerogyra* are the bubble corals or grape corals, half a dozen her-

matypic species with dual-phase polyps. During the day, the polyps inflate vesicles with water to vastly expand surface area for zooxanthellar photosynthesis, the vesicles reaching the diameter of a grape in some species. The stinging tentacles are located

Fox coral (Nemenzophyllia) *alone among the Caryophylliidae, resembles the unrelated mushroom anemones.*

Plerogyra sinuosa *has inflatable tentacles with minute tips at the end, like a balloon not quite fully blown up.*

Underwater Cements

Epoxies are harmless to marine animals, completely inert after they react, and wonderful for adhering live animals to rocks, or rocks to one another. Underwater epoxies (Devcon, SeaRepair, AquaStik, Z-Spar, Holdfast) form inert, rock-hard products from the reaction between the amine of a polyamide resin and the epoxide group of an epoxy resin. Hot-melt glue sticks are good for joining rocks, but must be used above water and allowed to dry before immersion. Super Glue cyanoacrylate adhesive is effective in air or water, on rocks or live animals, but I find the bond between heavy rocks to be fragile. Don't worry about the "cyano" in cyanoacrylate. It is not toxic like potassium cyanide.

below the vesicle and obscured. At night, the vesicles largely deflate, and tentacles are extended to sting and capture plankton and small fish. The genera differ in details of skeletal structure; the species differ in details of the vesicles. The nonretractable *Plerogyra sinuosa* bubbles are opalescent with clear, longitudinal streaks. *Physogyra* vesicles are smaller, pimply tipped, and somewhat retractable. Colonies bud from the edges, and the thin, stalked, stony plates can be broken off for transplantation elsewhere. *Plerogyra* needs strong light, a moderate current, and supplemental feeding with fresh meats of clam, mussel, or fish. *Plerogyra* has a strong sting. Under good conditions, bubble corals will reproduce sexually in reef aquariums. When *Plerogyra* tissue recedes, showing the teeth of the corallum, it is declining from poor water quality, stings of other corals, or predation.

Eusmilia fastigiata, flower coral, the only caryophylliid in the Atlantic, is small with short, thick, yellow-to-tan branches and an oval cup at the end. It is commonly found at the base of brain coral (*Colpophyllia, Diploria, Meandrina*) and boulder coral (*Montastrea*) in the Caribbean.

Nemenzophyllia turbida (fox coral) from the western Indian Ocean and western Pacific is closely related to *Plerogyra* but looks like a green or brown mushroom anemone. Fox coral has broad, flat plates with thin, white, longitudinal streaks, but no bubbles and apparently no obvious tentacles. The trade name is fox coral, probably because an importer who listened to "...phyllia species" on the telephone heard "fox." (In the same way, the tropical fish *Rasbora kalachroma* was first imported into the hobby as *Rasbora* "*kodachrome*," a name that has stuck.)

Dendrophylliidae

The Family Dendrophylliidae contains *Astroides, Balanophyllia, Turbinaria* (yellow scroll, plate, or pagoda coral), *Tubastrea*

Tubastrea aurea *is one of many Indo-Pacific species of planktivorous, ahermatypic orange cup corals.*

Plate coral becomes an obvious name for Turbinaria *when observed with its polyps withdrawn.*

The common name pagoda coral seems appropriate for Turbinaria *with its polyps extended.*

(orange cup coral), *Leptopsammia, Heteropsammia, Dendrophyllia*, and *Enallopsammia*.

Turbinaria are hermatypic and need light. They do well in moderate to gentle currents with supplemental feedings of *Artemia* nauplii and the small organisms disrupted from the gravel surface with a powerhead flow. Note that *Turbinaria* is a generic name for both a coral and an alga.

Tubastrea is an abundant, ahermatypic bright orange-to-yellow coral common in shaded waters on reef slopes or in caves. This coral is indifferent to light, and does well in strong alternating surges that mimic wave action. *Tubastrea* should be fed copiously with live or frozen adult brine shrimp, frozen mysid shrimp, or shredded mussel or clam meat placed onto the tentacles; if the food doesn't stick, disconnect the powerhead, but restart the strong current after feeding. Carbon filtration is important to

deal with wastes. With lots of food and strong current, *Tubastrea* will sexually reproduce in aquariums, releasing planula larvae that settle on the glass. Stick your *Tubastrea* in a strong current close to the surface where you can reach it for hand feeding; light doesn't hurt.

The Evolution of Corals

Coral relationships are difficult to figure out. On the one hand, there seems to be little difference between corals of the Caribbean and those of eastern South America. Yet the corals of western South America are very different from those of the rest of the Pacific Ocean. How can that be?

Equally improbable is the great constancy of corals all across the Indian Ocean and the Pacific Ocean. They differ only in the extreme north and extreme

Orange cup, Tubastrea coccinea *grows among fire coral,* Millepora, *at Bonaire, Dutch West Indies. Note the blue tang,* Acanthurus coeruleus *and the yellowtail damsel or jewelfish,* Microspathedon chrysurus—*the latter almost always found in fire coral.*

Galaxea *are sometimes the only corals of a fringing reef in turbid water.*

south, where the water is colder. And even that's not true when the cold region is invaded by a warm current. Most confusing of all is that, at least in the laboratory, corals that look nothing alike, from vast distances apart, can form fertile hybrids. Does that mean they are the same species?

J.E.N. Veron (Veron, 1995, *Corals in Space and Time*) proposed that coral evolution has been controlled through the millenia by sea level changes associated with ice ages, themselves induced by periodic alterations in the planet's orientation to the sun (up to 100 million-year Malenkovitch cycles), plate tectonics (the riding of the continents on a liquid rock interior), and alterations in the paths of warm-water oceanic currents such as the Gulf Stream

in the North Atlantic and the Kuroshio Current in the North Pacific.

Many of us are familiar with the uplifting of the Central American isthmus to cut off the connection between the Atlantic and Pacific Oceans. That also broke up a continuous coral community, so that today, the corals of the Pacific coast of South America have their closest relatives in the Caribbean. There was also a connection at one time between the Indian and Atlantic Oceans, known as the Tethys Sea. Its remnants today are the modern-day western arm (the Mediterranean Sea) and its eastern fragment, the Persian Gulf. Only the frigid cold of the Mediterranean has interrupted continuity between corals of the Indian Ocean and that of the eastern Atlantic.

The ages of the closing of the Tethys Sea, the uplifting of the Isthmus of Panama, and the fossil record of reefs all help to explain modern coral family distributions.

What had not been explained (before Veron's analysis) is the even diversity of corals over wide expanses of the central Indo-Pacific, the variation in forms associated more with depth than distance, the repetition of species and diversity across great distances, the slow rate of evolution (as shown in the fossil record), and the ability of so many corals to form hybrids even among species that look nothing alike.

Corals frequently release their eggs and sperm into the water on the same day. That a single species might synchronously spawn makes sense for an attached species that exists over a large area. But why would many apparently unrelated species over wide ranges of ocean spawn on the same day of the year? Does this mean that despite the differences, they are the same species? If corals can (a) hybridize in the lab and (b) have an opportunity to hybridize in nature through synchronous spawning, Veron argues, then what can happen must in fact happen eventually.

Thus, the ability of many corals to hybridize, changing ocean currents, the stability of ocean temperatures between ice ages, the opportunities to reconnect their genetic makeups following catastrophes—all these facts lead Veron to conclude that most of the hermatypic corals of the Indo-Pacific exist as species complexes called syngamions. Individuals and populations of syngamions may look different from one another, but genetically they can and do interbreed.

Not all corals exist as syngamions or species complexes. Many coral species are readily identified and do not hybridize. In the aquarium, corals only infrequently release eggs and sperm; they seldom all spawn synchronously, and they reproduce mostly asexually.

Chapter Fourteen
Diseases of Corals

Introduction

Corals are subject to many stressors, including parasites, infectious diseases, and extreme environmental changes. They often respond with loss of zooxanthellae, tissue necrosis, abnormal growths, and diebacks. Around the world, large-scale loss of scleractinian corals is associated with many biological and physical causes.

Variations in weather may damage corals. Heat, excessive ultraviolet radiation exposure during calm winds or at low spring tides, or unusual tidal events that expose near-surface corals are all stressors capable of killing corals at some level of exposure. When combined with other stressors (salinity changes, pollutants, turbidity, sedimentation), the lethal threshold is reduced and coral populations decline. Hurricanes primarily destroy macroalgae, and to a lesser extent the hard corals. In many deteriorating reef systems, storm-damaged corals do not appear to be recovering.

Changes in predator-prey relationships can dramatically reduce coral populations. Population explosions of the crown-of-thorns starfish devastated coral colonies widely in the Pacific. In the Atlantic, die-offs (from unknown causes) of *Diadema* and other algal-grazing sea urchins resulted in loss of algal control. Overfishing of tangs and parrotfish removes algal control on the reef.

With fewer herbivores cropping macroalgae, settling sites for larval corals become rarer and recruitment of new coral colonies declines. The very young coral colonies that do get a foothold are subjected to abrasion and shading from adjacent macroalgae. This slows their growth, exposes bare calcareous rock that the algae invade, and confines the young cnidarians so that they have no basal space in which to expand. The reef becomes macroalgal-dominated rather than coral-dominated.

A few coral diseases are of special interest.

Coral Reef Bleaching

Bleaching, the loss of color in corals and other invertebrates, is dramatic in branching or massive stony corals that lose their brown or pastel hues and become milky white as the corallum skeleton shows through the translucent tissue layer. Bleaching also affects brightly colored soft corals, *Millepora* fire corals, sea anemones, sponges, and other invertebrates.

Bleaching is the result of expulsion of symbiotic zooxanthellae from host corals and/or the loss of accessory pigments (chlorophyll *c,* peridinin, diadinoxanthin) in symbionts not expelled.

Bleaching is neither contagious nor infectious, but can affect all the corals in a large area. Occurring worldwide, bleaching is often a response to prolonged, elevated seawater temperatures such as occur off the Pacific coast of South America during midsummer in El Nino years. The combination of calm seas that allow increased exposure to UV radiation and of

The bleaching of this Montastrea annularis *is a response to protracted high temperatures.*

Palythoa caribbea *showing coral bleaching, the expulsion of symbiotic algae.*

prolonged midsummer water temperatures only 2°C above normal may trigger the response.

Corals adjust to the normal high temperatures of their region. Corals from the Florida Keys can tolerate maximum temperatures much lower than the maximum temperatures tolerated by corals from more tropical locales. The interaction—of temperature and time for a specific region sufficient to induce bleaching—can be calculated. A formula in degrees heating weeks (DHW) developed for Belize and Jamaica predicted that 26 DHW would induce mass bleaching.

Cold upwellings and reduced salinities can also induce localized bleaching, indicating that it is a general stress response. Bleaching develops in a few days but may go on for weeks or months. The longer the event, the less likely the colony will recover and avoid succumbing to infectious disease or other stressors. Mortality rates of 95 per-

cent of coral colonies have been recorded following mass bleaching, with whole reefs lost in the eastern Pacific.

Montastrea and other corals frequently recover from a few days or weeks of bleaching, but long-term bleaching (over a month) can cause death of corals that cannot survive without their symbiotic zooxanthellae. Some partial, short-term bleaching is not unusual; the increasing frequency and severity of bleaching has been attributed by some to global climate change.

Bleaching in noncoral hosts results from the loss of symbiotic algae or cyanobacteria or the explosive multiplication of symbiotic fungi. It is not uncommon throughout the animal kingdom to eliminate symbionts during periods of stress, but some symbionts are more important to the host than others.

Corals often fade or change color in reef aquariums, sometimes as a response to a different light regime rather than temperature; that is not bleaching. In other cases, corals seem to undergo bleaching identical with what occurs in nature during long hot spells. If fading occurs, the temperature should be measured; if over 80°F, corrective action should be taken to gradually reduce it to about 72°F. Presumably, high temperature-induced rapid fading of color in home aquariums is no different from coral bleaching in nature. However, because it is a stress response, other stressors may also induce fading, including those (such as a strong chemical excretion from one of the invertebrates) that do not cause bleaching in nature.

White-band Disease

White-band disease may follow a recent hurricane or occur for no discernible reason. The polyp tissues die and slough off from the base to the very tips of the branches in acroporids (elkhorn and staghorn corals), leaving the bleached white skeleton of the corallum exposed. Primarily affecting acroporids, the disease has also been seen in other corals where it has been termed white plague or white death. White-band diseased corals contain bacterial colonies in the calicoblastic epithelium, the layer of tissue that secretes the skeleton, but it is not known if the bacterial colonies are a cause or a result of the disease.

Stress-related Necrosis

A similar sloughing of tissue has been observed in acroporids, faviids, and poritid corals, where no bacteria are apparent. This condition has been termed stress-related necrosis (SRN). White-band disease and SRN may be manifestations of the identical disease, the intratissue bacteria only opportunistic invaders of tissue already dying from some other cause. Tissue sloughing in captive hard corals is

Meandrina meandrites *bleached by high temperatures in the Caribbean.*

sometimes reversible by moving the coral to another aquarium.

Black-band Disease

Black-band disease is an infection of faviid scleractinian corals and certain gorgonians; the cause is the pathogenic cyanobacterium *Phormidium corallyticum* and other bacteria. Often beginning at the site of an injury, the tissue is destroyed and disappears from the coral skeleton at a few millimeters a day, the advancing margin marked by a thin black line or band of *Phormidium*. The role of accessory microbes, including fungi, is not clear. Black-band disease causes severe damage in the summer or when the water is warmer than usual, but stops with the onset of cold.

Platygyra and *Goniastrea* are most often affected, but the disease is also known in *Montastrea, Siderastrea, Diploria*, and *Colpophyllia*. Diseased faviids are often

A dark line of Phormidium *blue-green algae marks the advance of black-band disease on this colony of Caribbean* Diploria.

sometimes survive if polyps are separate. Tissue tears can become deadly when invaded by opportunistic pathogenic bacteria. Under the microscope, these bacteria are usually Gram-negative, short rods that may be susceptible to 10 mg/L of nitrofurazone. Treatment should always be in a separate aquarium, because many antimicrobial drugs, especially neomycin (250 mg/gallon), Chloromycetin (80 mg/L for 25 hours), and erythromycin (any dose) may kill nontarget nitrogen cycle bacteria, red algae, and cyanobacteria.

The bacteria identified so far in coral diseases are not short Gram-negative rods, but members of different groups that use sulfur products. *Beggiatoa* is a member of the gliders, sulfide-oxidizing filamentous bacteria that live in sediments at the interface of anoxic and aerobic zones. *Desulfovibrio* is an anaerobic sulfate reducer shaped as a curved rod, sometimes a spiral. *Beggiatoa* and *Desulfovibrio* have been found in corals, but whether they are primary or secondary invaders is not always clear.

widely separated on the same reef, with adjacent faviids uninfected. However, a recent outbreak in the Florida Keys showed many simultaneous infections of adjacent corals. Work at the University of Puerto Rico indicates that the disease may be transferred by infected pieces of coral carried elsewhere by currents. The gorgonians *Pseudopterogorgia* in Florida and *Gorgonia* in Costa Rica have also been found infected with *Phormidium corallyticum* and other bacteria.

Phormidium is susceptible to antibiotics and intolerant of cold. Outbreaks in a minireef aquarium are rare. Try removing the infected coral to a separate, 70°F aquarium and treating the water with 10 mg/L of oxytetracycline hydrochloride, with a new dose in new water every two days until the disease clears.

Bacteria

Corals injured by rocks, crabs, fish bites, boring snails, or rough handling often die if the polyps are interconnected, but

Growths and Tumors

True tumors or neoplasms are known from acroporid corals, and can be seen as raised, white calcarous nodules. The tissues producing the calcareous deposits overgrow the polyps. As the tumors enlarge, the covering tissue loses its mucus secretory cells and the tumor eventually becomes ulcerated. The skeleton becomes exposed and can be invaded by filamentous algae or other organisms. This neoplasm or true cancerous condition is called calicoblastic epithelioma. The cause of calicoblastic epitheliomas is unknown. Other skeletal anomalies in corals are the result of overgrowth of a foreign invader.

Just as parasites or sand grains can induce nodule formation such as pearls in oysters, some endoparasitic algae can irritate corals sufficiently to wall them off. A parasitic trematode, *Plagioporus* or a relative, whose host is the coral-eating butterfly fish, *Chaetodon multicinctus*, has an encysting larval form that penetrates *Porites* corals and induces nodule formation. These nodules are then selectively eaten by the host fish.

Gorgonians parasitized by algae also develop tumorlike nodules. A filamentous green alga, *Entocladia endozoica*, is an endoparasite of the gorgonians *Pseudoplexaura* and *Pseudopterogorgia*. Its algal filaments irritate coral tissues, which subsequently wall them off. Another endosymbiont of (usually) stony corals (probably the alga *Ostreobium*), induces hyperplasia (cell multiplication), followed by walling off with gorgonin when the alga infects the sea fan, *Gorgonia*.

Minute motile algae and rotifers cultured to feed larval fishes are sufficient food for a few common sponges, but wild plankton are a better food.

Chapter Fifteen
Sponges

Introduction

The Phylum Porifera consists of 10,000 species of mostly marine animals at the lowest level of multicellular organization, without any kind of organs. They are primitive, but not simple. Some form elongate tubes off the bottom, others beautiful branching tree forms, some latticed clumps, and still others huge bowls. Many grow as beautiful encrusting growths such as the bright red patches on Gulf of Mexico live rock. Many fishes, shrimps, crabs, and lesser-known invertebrates live within the cavities of sponges in a commensal (beneficial, but not obligatory) symbiosis. Sponges are food for some angelfish, sea turtles, and gastropods.

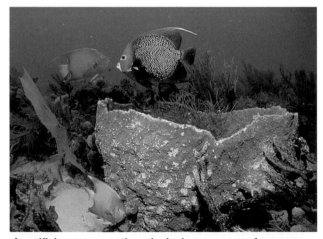

Angelfish are among the principal consumers of sponges like this vase sponge at Belize in the southern Caribbean.

Sponges contain a cellular epithelium or skin on the inside and outside, and in between a mostly acellular layer called the mesohyl. The basic body plan looks like a punctured vase, with water containing microplanktonic food entering holes in specialized skin cells (porocytes) and leaving through the open top of the vase (osculum). Inside is a hollow space (spongocoel) lined with flagellated cells (choanocytes) that create the in-through-the pores-out-through-the-osculum current. The choanocytes, in a manner not yet understood, capture microscopic-sized particles in the current, such as bacteria, minute phytoplankton, and other particles too small to be identified with an ordinary microscope. Brightly pigmented amoeboid cells (archaeocytes) then engulf and digest this food. The mesohyl layer below the epithelium consists of loosely spaced cells separated by secretions of proteinaceous collagen (sometimes fibrin) and other cells specialized to secrete silicious or calcareous spicules.

Most sponges are more than a simple vase. The insides are often convoluted or subdivided, increasing surface for chaonocytes and amoeboid feeding cells. Like corals, sponges adapt to surrounding surges: those growing in strong currents often are squat or rounded to expose minimal surface area. Sponges in quiet water are often elongate, extending well off the bottom, even branching. No matter how complex the sponge, it usually has just one osculum.

Most sponges are hermaphrodites that expel gametes through the osculum, the egg fertilized in the surrounding ocean, and then developing into a ciliated or flagellated larva. The larva settles on an appropriate substratum and develops into a vase-shaped sponge at first, then into its more complex structure.

Demospongia

There are four groups. Some 90 percent (9,500 species) are in the Class Demospongia, with gelatinous interiors developed from fibers of spongin, silica, both, or neither and with bodies that are simple, encrusting, or branched. Some large members of the family Spongidae were collected for bath sponges before our switch to synthetics. The Family Clionidae are borers, with special brightly colored amoeboid cells that etch holes in shells or corals. Several species are bright yellow and are common on live rock.

Calcarea

The Class Calcarea, about 50 species, have well separated 3- or 4-pronged carbonate spicules and no spongin in their gelatinous mesohyl.

Sclerospongea

The Class Sclerospongea are cavern dwellers with a gelatinous mesohyl containing

Keeping and Breeding Sponges

A few sponges have photosynthetic symbionts, and all of them require the finest of foods. Daily feedings of green water (unicellular algae) or liquid suspensions used to feed corals may support further growth of sponges introduced on live rock. Sponges may grow in a reef tank when adequate phytoplankton, microzooplankton, and/or particulate nutrients are provided either as a supplement or through the biological activity of the other reef aquarium inhabitants. Sponges often cover most of the hard surfaces in fish-only marine aquariums that get heavy feedings of blended fish and shellfish meats and fluids.

Sponges can be propagated by cutting into small pieces and moving them to another part of the aquarium, or even by fragmenting in a blender and pouring the slurry into the tank. The particles include specialized amoeboid cells that start new sponges wherever they settle, provided that adequate food is available.

The central excurrent opening of sponges is apparent in this underwater photo at St. Lucia.

calcium carbonate, silica, and spongin in a complex arrangement. The Class Hyalospongiae or glass sponges (450 species) don't have a gelatinous mesohyl, but rather a loose arrangement of six-pointed silicious spicules arranged in long fibers, the spicules even penetrating the outer skin.

The skin and lattice work are so loose that water flows through with little need for choanocytes. These colorless but complex sponges resemble crystals.

Some attractive sponges for reef tanks are *Haliclona permollis*, *Verongula* sp., *Clathrina coriacea*, *Siphonochalina* sp., *Raspailia hispida*, *Cliona* spp., *Hippospongia* sp., *Tethya, Suberites*, and *Pseudsuberites* spp., *Lotrochata purpurea*, and *Spirastrella cunctatrix*. Trade or common names aren't standardized, and not very useful to a buyer.

Some sponges offered by collectors, such as purple vase and orange-red clump types, can be difficult to maintain without supplemental feedings, yet those same feedings can induce nuisance algae blooms. Beautiful sponges are often available but can be difficult to maintain. Yellow and brown sponges that arrive on live rock often take hold and occasionally spread.

Unidentified sponges from live rock glow with the pastel colors of their amoeboid feeding cells.

Chapter Sixteen
Molluscs

Introduction

The 150,000 species of the Phylum Mollusca include turbo and astraea snails and tridacnid clams popular with reef tank aquarists, nudibranchs and octopuses familiar to snorkelers, and much more.

Most are aquatic, about 10,000 species terrestrial. They all have a large organ called the foot that is used for locomotion (snails) or anchoring (clams), and a membrane enveloping the viscera called the mantle that secretes calcium carbonate and proteinaceous shell material. Many molluscs have a rasping band of tissue in the mouth called a radula. In some this is a movable belt armed with tiny hooks. The blood system is based on copper at the center of the heme molecule instead of iron, making the blood blue instead of red; molluscs are also quickly killed by copper.

Molluscs can be male, female, or hermaphroditic, but always reproduce sexually to produce miniature juveniles (as in freshwater snails) or a planktonic larva. If the planktonic form is an early-stage ciliated larva it is called trochophore. In most species, a later-stage larva called a veliger is produced.

Malacologists (mollusc scientists) divide the phylum into seven classes. The Gastropoda, Bivalvia, and Cephalopoda all have species important to marine aquarists. The Polyplacophora or chitons commonly arrive on live rock and multiply in reef tanks. The remaining three classes of negligible interest to reef aquarists include the deepwater Monoplacophora, the Aplachophora with wormlike forms, including some living on cnidarians, and the Scaphopoda or burrowing tusk shells.

Gastropoda

The Class Gastropoda (*gastro-poda* = stomach foot) contains the 125,000 known species of snails. These mobile animals extrude mucus from the foot bottom to assist in gliding and pulling themselves forward over any hard surface. The slime can be instantly liquified for ciliary gliding (common in smaller snails) and just as quickly gelled for muscular pulling. Larger snails use waves of muscular contractions to pull themselves forward.

The radula within the mouth can be mounted on a cartilaginous rod like the base plate of a sander. The radula can be used to scrape like a strip of sandpaper, in some snails in a rotary motion, in others, back and forth. The radula can be everted onto the food source (algae, dead plants and animals, live animals, including other molluscs). Oyster drills have an accessory boring organ that applies a chemical secretion to chelate calcium, separating it from its carbonate; the radula is then inserted into the hole to grind up prey soft tissues.

Some marine snails produce masses of fertilized eggs that develop directly into miniatures of the adult, while most snails produce planktonic veliger larvae.

The three groups of gastropods are the prosobranchs, opisthobranchs, and pulmonates. The pulmonates are mostly freshwater and land forms of no interest to marine aquarists.

Prosobranchs

The three groups of prosobranchs are archaeogastropods, mesogastropods, and neogastropods.

Archaeogastropods The archaeogastropods include limpets, abalones, and topshells, all mostly herbivorous grazers on diatoms and soft algae. Keyhole limpets may also graze on sponges and some corals. All have external fertilization, and thus the male has no need for a penis. The most important archaeogastropods for reef tanks are the herbivorous grazing topshells, turbans, and starshells of the superfamily Trochacea, especially *Turbo, Clanculus, Margarites, Gibbula, Astraea*, and *Calliostoma*. Every minireef aquarium should have one or two trochid snails per ten gallons to control diatoms and soft algae on glass and rock. Several species are better than one to accommodate pref-

Juveniles of the Florida conch, Strombus gigas, *are excellent algae-eaters.*

erences; *Astraea*, for example, feed mostly on diatoms while *Turbo* feed mostly on hair algae. Most *Astraea* in the hobby are collected from the Caribbean, the *Trochea* from the Sea of Cortez.

Trochaceans shed eggs in a gelatinous mass that adheres to rocks or plants. Sperm shed into the surrounding water find and penetrate the mass to fertilize the eggs, which hatch to release planktonic larvae. Keyhole limpets and the trochids *Turbo* and *Astraea* often spawn in reef tanks during the summer. Prosobranchs can be induced to shed gametes by placing them in a ten-gallon aquarium at high temperature (80°F), draining most of the tank, and adding cold (60°F) water. Alternatively, place a snail upside down in a small container with warm water, then decant and replace with cold water. Some will emit sperm and others egg masses. Add the sperm water to the egg container and then watch the eggs develop into swimming larvae.

Mesogastropods The mesogastropods (*meso* = intermediate) include myriad snails from grazing herbivores to carnivores with an elongated proboscis that can capture and engulf prey. Aquacultured baby queen conchs (*Strombus gigas*), available to reef aquarists, are excellent detritus and algal feeders for tanks with aragonite gravel; wild specimens are protected and may not be collected. Most mesogastropods are colorful nuisances, such as the Ovulidae that graze on live soft coral, the Cassidids or helmet shells that prey on echinoderms and some molluscs, and the Cypraeidae or cowries that eat almost anything. Some cowries eat sponges, but egg cowries (which differ in the radular teeth) feed on soft corals, especially gorgonians, and even mimic their prey. Other cowries feed on black corals. Those cowries and their nudibranch mimics that are toxic to mollusc-eating fishes often carry aposematic (warning) colors or patterns. Cowries in reef tanks will eat sponges and soft corals in addition to algae and detritus, and should be limited to fish-only marine aquariums.

Cerithium are valuable algal grazers readily collected from south Florida sea walls and bridge stanchions, and are common on Atlantic and Pacific live rock. *Vermetus* are sessile, with elongate, wormlike shells cemented together in large colonies on rocks, and are often confused with worm tubes. Lacking a planktonic stage, *Vermetus* rapidly multiply in reef tanks. Both types are popular with reef tank aquarists.

Neogastropods The neogastropoda (*neo* – new) include the whelks, tulips, volutes, olives, and oyster drills. Most neogastropods are predators, the cone shells (*Conus* spp.) among the most venomous marine animals known. In some, a protrusive proboscis has a modified radula enlarged into a hollow harpoon that anchors in flesh and injects a neurotoxic venom. Specialized feeders on invertebrates and bottom fish, *Conus* inject, instantly paralyze, and consume the prey whole. Some predators on fish (*C. striatus, C. geographus*, others) have venoms lethal to humans. Cone shells have occasionally been exported to the hobby by collectors who didn't recognize the risk; all should be avoided as potentially dangerous.

Opisthobranchs

The major groups of the 5,000 species of nonparasitic opisthobranchs are the sea hares (with lateral respiratory parapodia), nudibranchs or sea slugs (many with a circle of gills appended at the rear), bubble snails, notaspids, sacoglossans, shelled sea butterflies, and naked sea butterflies.

The sluglike opisthobranch body has a pair of oral tentacles in front and secondary tentacles called rhinophores immediately behind. Some have a normal shell. In oth-

This Atlantic cowry, **Cypraea cervus,** *will prey on other reef invertebrates.*

ers, a reduced shell is hidden by the mantle or lost entirely, while in a very few, the body is encased by a pair of shells resembling a clam wrapped on a snail's body. Some

Fasciolaria tulipa, *the Florida tulip, may prey on clams.*

Chromodoris quadricolor *from the Pacific.*

This **Nembrotha** *nudibranch was seen in the Philippines.*

opisthobranchs have a gill inside a respiratory cavity, in others the gill is located on the top rear of the body, and in others still, beautiful mantle outgrowths called cerata take care of gas exchange. Many opisthobranchs travel on plants, rocks, or corals on a broad, undulating foot, while others have expanded the foot edges into swimming wings. Hermaphrodites, the opisthobranchs deposit strings or masses of fertilized eggs that produce planktonic larvae; these are often not difficult to raise.

Nudibranchs: Nudibranchs often come in on live rock and manage to live and grow well in reef tanks, finding their requirements in the diverse communities. The predatory habits of nudibranchs are often within acceptable bounds, considering their beauty.

Feeding may be generalized or specialized. *Sacoglossa,* the Anaspidea, and some Cephalaspidea are herbivores, but may be specialized on certain algae. The herbivorous sea hares (*Aplysia*) and sacoglossans (*Tridachia*) have a planktonic stage of

weeks or even months. The larvae require antibiotics to protect them from bacterial attack and droplets of alcohol in their culture containers to keep them from sticking to surface film. The larvae become abnormal with inadequate strontium and must be fed cultured microalgae. Thus, home aquarium propagation is possible but time-consuming.

The most brightly colored of the nudibranchs, the Doridacea, recognized by a ring of retractable gills around the anus, are mostly highly specific predators on sponges, sea squirts, corals, crustaceans, bryozoans, or anemones; in the reef tank Doridacea eventually starve because their specific food is not available. Common genera are *Chromodoris, Phyllidia, Glossodoris, Gymnodoris, Casella, Tambja, Peltodoris, Platydoris, Polycera, Spurilla,* and *Pteraeolidia.*

Dirona albolineata, the white-lined nudibranch, is a generalized feeder from the northeastern Pacific that will eat tissues of some cold-water reef tank inhabitants, but die if the temperature exceeds 15°C (59°F).

Pacific nudibranch species occur in a rainbow of colors.

Another Pacific nudibranch roams over the rocks.

Some nudibranchs have a toothed radula, but a few (*Melibe, Dendrodoris, Doriopsilla*) eat their prey whole. Aeolids have very few radular teeth and use them to cut, rather than rasp, chunks of tissue from their prey. Sacoglossans have long, hollow, sharp-tipped teeth that puncture prey and suck out symbiotic algal cells.

Some nudibranchs that feed on cnidarians transport unfired cnidocysts to their

Chromodoris *species, a Pacific nudibranch.*

Hermisenda crassicornis *is the cold water opalescent nudibranch from the northwestern Atlantic.*

Offensive Nudibranchs

Many opisthobranchs use chemical weapons. Some species of *Hexabranchus* feed only on the sponge *Halichondria*, concentrating the sponge's metabolic product dihydrohalichondramide to deter predation. The same nudibranchs concentrate toxins called uapualides in their egg masses, protecting the eggs from all predators except for some species of the nudibranch, *Favorinus*, which are immune. *Phyllidia varicosa* concentrates isocyanopupkeanane, a predation inhibitor, from its sponge prey. *Chromidoris* concentrates the cytotoxin laulimalide from its sponge prey, *Hyattella*. The sea hare *Stylocheilus longicauda* concentrates the tumor promotor aplysiatoxin from blue-green cyanobacteria. The nudibranch *Phestilla melanobrachia* feeds only on the ahermatypic coral *Tubastrea coccinea*, selectively concentrating some of its chemicals and producing a toxic alkaloid the coral doesn't have.

own skin to be used for protection. Some algal feeders save and transport chloroplasts to their own skin where they photosynthesize and provide nutrients to the nudibranch just as do zooxanthellae of hermatypic corals.

Bivalvia (Pelycepoda)

Clams, mussels, and oysters are sessile aquatic molluscs of rivers, lakes, estuaries, and oceans. Some attach to hard structures by burrowing into a small space and growing to imprison themselves, by secreting silky byssus threads to withstand surge and crashing waves, or by secreting a calcareous cement. Some do not attach at all, remaining not only free of the bottom, but capable of rapid escapes by flapping their valves to create jets of water.

Many unattached bivalves move by extending the muscular foot forward into the sand or mud, pumping blood to swell the tip into an anchor, and then pulling themselves forward by retracting the muscle. Scallops (*Pectin, Aequipectin, Caribachlamys, Nodipectin, Argopectin*) can open and then shut their valves suddenly to leap forward or upward, jet propelled; they often have light-sensitive eyes on the rim of the mantle that can form images and detect predators.

Bivalves may be hermaphroditic or have separate sexes. Most shed gametes into the water, but in some species the sperm are taken in with filtrate water and the fertilized eggs brooded until hatching. The larva is a ciliated trochophore, which transforms into a veliger larva that, by chemical cues, seeks out a suitable substratum for settling. Many bivalves can be induced to shed gametes by injection with the hormone serotonin or with 0.1 N potassium hydroxide, both available from laboratory supply houses.

The bivalves can be divided into seven subclasses. Two are important to marine aquarists.

Flame scallops (Lima scabra) *have eyes at the tips of their numerous tentacles lining the mantle, and can leap out of danger by jet propulsion.*

The Subclass Pteriomorphia: This group contains bivalves that live on the surface, usually attached by cement or byssus threads. It includes the mussels (*Mytilus, Modiolus*), scallops (*Pecten, Argopecten, Aequipecten*), ark shells (*Arca*), pen shells (*Pinna*), file shells or flame scallops (*Lima*), and oysters (*Ostrea, Crassostrea, Spondylus*). *Lithophaga* is a mussel that bores into corals.

The Subclass Heterodonta: This group contains bivalves with siphons and without a shiny nacre layer. It includes the common edible clams (*Venus, Mercenaria*), cockles (*Cardium, Dinocardium*), razor clams (*Ensis*), coquinas (*Donax, Tellina*), exotic zebra mussels (*Dreissena*), exotic Asian clams (*Corbicula*), rock-borers (*Petricola*), wood-borers (*Teredo, Martesia, Xylophaga*), and Indo-Pacific giant clams (*Tridacna*).

Tridacnid Clams

Indo-Pacific clams of the Family Tridacnidae live in shallow, often intertidal, well-lit tropical waters where they are adapted to high levels of sunlight, ultraviolet light, desiccation, infrared heating, and nutrient-poor water. The giant clams *Tridacna gigas* and *T. derasa* are common in exposed reef tops where they may reach more than a yard across and over 400 pounds. *Tridacna, Hippopus*, and certain cockles are the only clams known to harbor symbiotic algae. Tridacnid veliger larvae, already containing symbiotic *Symbiodinium (Gymnodinium) microadriaticum* zooxanthellae, settle on coral rocks where they soon attach with byssus threads and eventually burrow into the coral rock by excreting acids. They filter the water for plankton, but get most of their nutrients from symbiotic zooxanthellae. The zooxanthellae in tridacnids are extracellular, lining the outer edge of the mantle and digestive tract where they are exposed to sunlight. Tridacnids provide the zooxanthellae with waste phosphate and ammonia and a platform awash in seawater and sunlight. In turn, the algae provide the clam with amino acids and carbohydrates. The clams are capable of harvesting and swallowing excess populations of algae, which have been found deep in their digestive tract and in their wastes. Even though lacking the enzyme cellulase, the clams are able to digest algal cells because the cellulose cell walls of these algae are leaky.

Tridacnid clams have exquisite fluorescent pigments that possibly protect them from ultraviolet radiation. Situate the clam near the tank surface but with enough distance from a metal halide lamp to prevent UV burn; VHO lamps are not such strong UV-emitters.

Tridacnids have valuable functions in a reef aquarium. They absorb ammonia and nitrates, and are a simpler alternative to the complex and labor-intensive algal scrubber.

As with hermatypic corals (those containing symbiotic algae), tridacnid clams

Tridacna gigas *is one of several giant clams, all requiring metal halide light.*

Hippopus porcellanus *is another giant clam suitable for reef tanks.*

should be provided calcium for their shells, iodine for their algae, and intense light (preferably metal halide, but VHO may be sufficient) close to the animal and not fewer than six hours a day.

Tridacnid clams propagated in captivity include *Tridacna derasa, T. gigas, T. squamosa, T. crocea, T. maxima, Hippopus hippopus*, and *H. porcellanus*. The clams are induced to shed gametes, and two days later the veliger larvae collected, transferred, and exposed to zooxanthellae. Later, the pediveliger settles on the bottom for growth in raceways. Growth is accelerated by supplementary ammonia or nitrate, especially in daylight; nitrate is taken up only as ammonia is depleted, and all uptake activity is depressed after dark. Young clams are sold to food farmers for a three year grow-out period to five or six inches market size. Called vasua in Fiji, they are propagated throughout the Indo-Pacific for sushi, sashimi, cooking in coconut milk, or salt-

dried. The aquarium market is a recent but important development.

The smallest and most beautiful species is *T. crocea* with its blue iridiophores, but the other tridacnids with green or yellow pigments are also quite beautiful and only rarely might some outgrow an aquarium. The narrow end is open and vulnerable to predatory crabs, so crabs should not be kept in a reef tank with tridacnids. This narrow end produces the byssal attachment threads and chemicals that erode rock to give the clam a tight fit.

Mark Gervis, Manager of the ICLARM Coastal Aquaculture Center in the Solomon Islands, had these recommendations for minireef aquarists:

"Purchase a clam that isn't gaping, with a mantle nicely spread out over the shell edge and not torn. In *T. maxima, T. crocea*, and *T. squamosa* the byssal gland should be visible. Reject clams with flatworms or the small white snails that look like sand grains and near the byssus or in the scutes of the shell. Make sure there are no dead organisms attached to the shell. Place the clam horizontal, not vertical, on a hard surface, and shorten the metal halide exposure from the normal 8–10 hours down to just 2–4 hours until the clam adjusts to the light level. In fact, small clams don't need so many hours of metal halide light, doing just fine as long as they get 12 hours of fluorescent. Small clams need less light than large clams. Tridacnids also like warmer water than corals, so place them high up where they'll be warmed by the metal halide light. They do best at close to 27°C (80.6°F), pH 8.3, calcium 400-480 mg/L, and salinity 32–35 ppt. High-quality skimming is essential for water quality. Don't place the clam directly in a strong current. Tridacnids don't do well in heavily fed tanks and should not themselves be fed."

Because they occur in tropical shallows, tridacnids do not require actinic (420 nm) light but do require strong light. Thus, they may thrive under aged 5,500–6,500 K lamps that have color shifted but retained most of their intensity. The same is true for VHO lamps. Ordinary fluorescent lamps have insufficient intensity for tridacnids.

The very colorful tridacnids sometimes lose their bright pigments in a home reef tank, the mantle becoming brown. The problem is caused by excessive light and nutrients, resulting in overgrowth of zooxanthellae in the clams, which then mask the iridescent pigments. The solution is to cut back on feeding. Tridacnids retain their colors in reef tanks kept nutrient-starved.

Tridacnids are susceptible to boring molluscs (*Cymatium*, Pyramidellids), predaceous polychaetes, many shrimps and crabs, and some fishes that will pick at the mantle. Tridacnids have few defenses beyond inserting themselves deeply into a rock, and that takes considerable time.

Chemicals can also affect them. Strontium supplements for hard corals may be toxic to tridacnid clams, and should be avoided.

Manuals on tridacnid clam aquaculture (Monograph 15 by Braley, Monograph 16 by Calumpong) are available from Bibliotech, Australian National University, Canberra ACT 0200, Australia (fax 61-6-257 5088); at 38 and 32 Australian dollars ($AUD) each. Mark Gervis advises, however, that the techniques are not directly applicable to aquarium culture. Other publications describe anatomy and histology of clams (48 $AUD) and the economics of clam culture in the Pacific (45 $AUD), which might interest aquaculturists in the United States.

The remaining five subclasses of the Bivalvia (the Palaeotaxodonta, Palaeoheterodonta, Analodesmata, Cryptodonta, and Solemyoida) are small groups of little interest.

Chapter Seventeen
Crustaceans

Introduction

The predominant land arthropods are insects (750,000 species), while those most important in the sea are crustaceans (38,000 species). Marine crustaceans include crabs, shrimps, lobsters, barnacles, and copepods. Copepods, the most important zooplankton, may be the most abundant animals on earth.

Crustaceans have an outer skeleton composed of chitin, a mucopolysaccharide (complex carbohydrate combined with a peptide). Crustaceans possess two pairs of antennae. As they increase in size and advance in development, crustaceans molt, swell with water and salts, and form a new cuticle to protect the soft body. A crustacean has several larval stages, each accompanied by a molt before maturity; the creature molts again to breed. Many crustaceans mate only during the brief period before the new cuticle hardens. Molting (ecdysis) is under hormonal control.

The body has 15 segments apportioned among a cephalothorax (eight), abdomen (six), and telson (one). The front of the cephalothorax carries appendages for sensing and filtering (antennae) or feeding (chelipeds or claw-bearers); behind these appendages are others modified for chewing (maxillipeds); the remaining appendages are used for locomotion. The abdominal appendages (pleopods) are used for swimming, respiration, carrying the eggs, copulation, and even digging into the sediments. At the end of the abdomen, the telson or tail (a single segment) may be covered by narrow or flattened abdominal appendages.

Crustaceans feed by filtration, grazing, or predation. Copepods, cladocerans (daphniae), barnacles, and anacostracans (brine and fairy shrimps) use bristles on their antennae to sweep drifting algae, protozoa, and other zooplankton from the water. Crabs and shrimps use additional modified appendages behind the antennae to macerate detritus, algae, leaves, and

1. telson
2. abdomen
3. cephalo-
   thorax
4. antennae
5. cheliped
6. pleopods
7. uropods

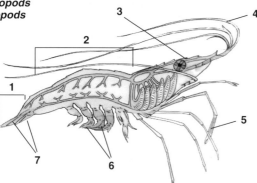

Typical decapod crustaceans, shrimp and prawns are divided into three body areas, the cephalothorax in front, the abdomen in the middle, and the telson or tail area. The cephalothorax appendages are modified into sensory antennae, chewing mouthparts, and sometimes grasping appendages. The abdomen has appendages for walking, swimming, and delivery of sex products (eggs and sperm). The tail has a fanlike array of flattened uropods for simple flipperlike swimming.

other animals, placing the macerated food into the mouth opening.

Some crustaceans feed on corals. A few crustaceans can be propagated as live food (brine shrimp, copepods). Others are ideal tank inhabitants that can be collected or propagated.

Barnacles

The Cirripedia are bizarre modified crustaceans living inside a double shell or carapace reinforced with calcareous deposits. Many are free-living and abundant on rocky shores (*Balanus*) or attached to drifting flotsam and seaweeds (*Lepas*); others are parasitic on crabs (*Sacculina*) or other animals (*Lernaeodiscus*). *Balanus* frequently occur on live rock, *Lepas* on sargassum weed and driftwood. *Lepas* is sometimes sold in aquarium shops. Feed barnacles copious amounts of brine shrimp nauplii, which they will filter from the water by waving and withdrawing their antennaelike legs.

Copepods

Harpacticoids and cyclopoids are the most abundant copepods in the ocean. The harpacticoid *Euterpina acutifrons* is easily cultured and rich in essential fatty acids. Copepods have been cultured on the same algae used to grow rotifers, such as the green algae *Chaetoceros, Tetraselmis, Isochrysis, Nannochloropsis*, and the dinoflagellate *Gymnodinium*. The copepod goes through six naupliar and five juvenile copepodite stages, and then the adult stage. The nauplii are within the size range of rotifers, but have a different motion that attracts larval fishes. Copepods are cultured in screened cages (37 micron mesh Nitex) suspended in water enhanced with algae, and the smallest larvae are harvested from outside the screens. The

breeder copepods must be fed new algae culture daily. A good substitute for cultured algae is a resuspension in seawater of concentrated algal paste available from Innovative Aquatic Products, Vancouver, B.C. (fax 1-604-755-9531). The nutritive value of any cultured copepod, brine shrimp, or rotifer can be increased by treatment with omega 3 highly unsaturated fatty acids (HUFA). Commercial HUFA preparations include Super Selco (Florida Aqua Farms,

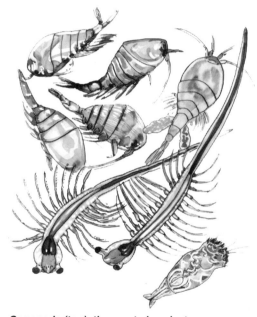

Copepods (top), the most abundant planktonic animals in the sea, are the principal nutrition for almost all fishes and larger sea creatures at early ages. Brine shrimp, (center), are salt pond variants of a freshwater group of crustaceans. The nauplii or larvae are ideal for aquaculture and feeding marine fishes and invertebrates. Rotifers such as the brackish water Brachionus plicatilus, (lower right and not to scale), are cultured to feed marine fish babies too small to eat brine shrimp nauplii.

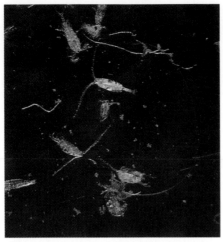

Microscopic view of calanoid copepods.

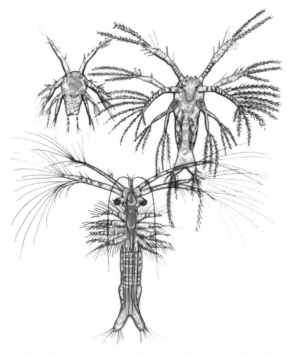

Larvae of shrimp, prawns, and copepods may go through stages called copepodid, naupliar, zoea, and mysid.

fax 904-567-3742) and Selcon (American Marine, fax 914-763-5367).

Many kinds of large parasitic copepods occur on marine fishes. The most common types are described in Chapter 23.

Crabs

Small hermit crabs of the genera *Paguristes, Clibanarius, Phimochirus,* and *Calcinus* are harmless to corals and may consume algae and detritus; very popular are blue-legged and red-legged hermits (*Clibanarius tricolor, Paguristes cadenati*). Sally lightfoot crabs (*Grapsus, Hemigrapsus*) of mangrove forests are excellent algae eaters. Small reef crabs such as *Stenorhynchus, Percnon, Melybia, Neopetrolisthes, Lybia, Carpilius, Mithrax,* and *Peresphona* even help control bristleworms. Porcelain crabs (*Porcellana, Pachycheles*) are free-living or symbionts of corals, anemones, and hermit crabs unlikely to damage corals. However, other tiny symbiotic crabs found in *Acropora* coral sometimes induce stress, indicated by bleaching, during shipping. Sponge crabs (*Dromidia, Macrocoeloma*) are attractive when small, but untrustworthy when more than an inch in carapace (upper shell) width. Crabs can be propagated in the same manner as shrimp.

Crabs to avoid: These include the spectacular shamefaced and box crabs *(Calappa)* and coral crabs (*Carpilius*), which eat anything they can catch, including sleeping fish. Large hermit crabs (*Pagurus, Dardanus, Petrochirus*) may graze corals. All swimming crabs (*Portunus, Arenaeus, Callinectes*) are predators to be avoided. The rock and mud crabs (*Carcinus, Menippe, Panopeus, Rhithropanopeus*) are omnivores difficult to remove from rock cavities. Fiddler crabs (*Uca*) often climb out of the aquarium.

Red hermit crab.

Trizopagurus strigatus, *an Indo-Pacific hermit crab.*

The Caribbean arrow crab, Stenorhynchus seti-cornis, *is common in shallows of the Bahamas.*

A porcelain crab symbiotic in a sea anemone waves its plankton-straining rakers.

Neopetrolisthes maculatus *is an anemone-inhabiting Pacific porcelain crab.*

Calappa flammea, *the flame-streaked box crab of the southern United States, will pry open clams and graze on other invertebrates.*

The shamefaced crab, Hepatus epheliticus, *is a southern United States box crab.*

Molting in Crustaceans

Crustaceans increase in size by shedding the chitinous exoskeleton that confines the soft body, and then growing into a new and larger exoskeleton. The molt is called ecdysis, and appears identical in crustaceans and insects. The inactive form of the hormone controlling molting is called ecdysone, secreted by the crustacean Y-organ. Other tissues in the body change a single hydrogen (–H) on the ecdysone molecule to a hydroxy group (OH), altering the molecule to 20-hydroxyecdysone, the active form that initiates ecdysis.

The eyestalk of crustaceans contains a bundle of secretory neurons called the X-organ producing a molt-inhibiting peptide stored in a nearby sinus or cavity. You can see it in lobsters as a 1 mm light blue spot on the top side of the stalk. When this peptide is released from the sinus into the circulatory system (hemolymph), the Y-organ slows its formation of ecdysone.

The rare Portunus sebae, *like all members of the Portunidae, have rear legs modified into swimming paddles and front claws that are swift, razor-sharp weapons.*

Shrimp

Recommended reef-tank shrimp are the small, colorful, or symbiotic *Periclimenes, Stenopus, Lysmata, Gnathophyllum, Hippolysmata, Hymenocera, Stegopontonia, Pontonia, Pinctada, Conchodytes, Rhynchocinetes, Saron, Tozeuma,* and some colorful species of *Palaeomon.* Some are symbionts or predators specifically requiring cnidarians, sponges, gobies, starfish, sea urchins, and clams. *Lysmata wurdemanni,* the peppermint shrimp, normally a symbiont of sponges, does not require them, and will eat anything, including stinging anemones, *Aiptasia.* Snapping or pistol shrimps (*Alpheus, Synalpheus*) may prey on other shrimp, although some are symbiotic with burrowing gobies and do well in tanks with deep gravel and a goby partner. Snapping shrimp do wonderfully with goby partners, and often accept any goby willing to share its burrow. Mantis shrimp (*Squilla, Gonodactylus, Odontodacytlus, Lysosquilla*) are capable of slicing a fish, a soft coral, or an aquarist's finger with the efficiency of a razor blade, and should never be placed in a reef tank.

Periclimenes and its relatives should be provided with their host cnidarians in a reef tank. Reef tanks with decorative shrimp should not have large tangs or pygmy angelfish, which sometimes forget their mostly herbivorous habits.

Breeding Shrimp

Lysmata amboinensis, L. rathbuni, L. wurdemanni, L. seticauda, and *Stenopus hispidus* have all been bred in aquariums. *Lysmata* are hermaphroditic for much of their lives, and almost any two will behave as a breeding pair. Within hours of a molt, one shrimp delivers a packet of sperm to another before its cuticle hardens, the latter shrimp then carrying the fertilized eggs attached to abdominal appendages or

Periclimenes yucatanicus *lives in sea anemones of the Caribbean.*

Golden coral shrimp on red sponge.

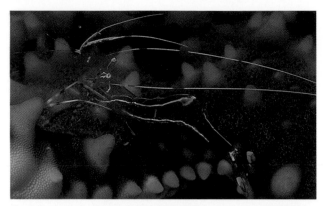
Periclimenes pedersoni *on a sea star.*

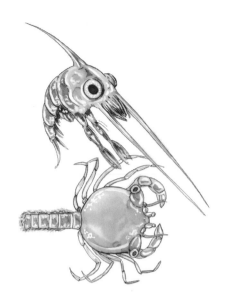
The sharp spine at the top indicates a zoea crab larva. A later stage, the megalops, looks like a baby crab before its abdomen has wrapped around its lower body.

Lysmata wurdemanni, *the peppermint shrimp, will eat* Aiptasia *anemones.*

Lysmata grabhami *is a ready spawner in captivity.*

pleopods. While carrying its own fertilized eggs, this shrimp can also deliver a sperm packet to the other shrimp when the latter molts.

Either capture an egg-laden shrimp from the reef tank for removal to a hatching tank or devote a small tank to breeding. Place one egg-laden shrimp or two or more nonovigerous shrimp in a well-illuminated ten-gallon aquarium with a sponge filter, aragonite sand for pH control, and live rock with good macroalgal growth or nitrate control. The shrimp mate after a molt induced by heavy feeding. It takes two weeks from fertilization until the eggs are ready to hatch, and they hatch at night. The zoea larvae are slightly larger than brine shrimp nauplii, move with very slow up-and-down jerks, and congregate toward light.

The symbiotic Lima *shrimp occurs on flame scallops.*

The coral banded shrimp, Stenopus hispidus, *is common on pier pilings in the Bahamas.*

Hymenocera picta, *the harlequin shrimp, feeding on a starfish.*

Lysmata debelius, *the fire shrimp, only breeds occasionally.*

After hatching, remove the adults, turn off all aeration so the water is perfectly still, and add rotifers or brine shrimp nauplii, preferably enriched by immersion in algal culture or HUFA preparation. Most zoea die within days, perhaps from competition, predation, or ammonia buildup. The larval shrimp and the live food aggregate toward the light in the absence of current. That makes feeding them easier, and requires less food, which reduces the risk of pollution and ammonia buildup.

In *Lysmata* it takes 2–9 weeks to get to the quarter-inch long juvenile stage. The adults continue to produce clutches every 10–12 days.

Lysmata amboinensis and *L. debelius* larvae are large at hatching, while *L. wurdemanni* are very small, yet *L. wurdemanni* have been raised quite often and *L. debelius* (with the largest larvae of the three) not at all as yet.

Lobsters

The rock lobsters (*Panulirus, Enoplometopus*) and slipper lobsters (*Evibacus, Scyllarides, Scyllarus*) have beautiful species very attractive when small. All are carnivores that may attack tridacnid clams, tubeworms, and even resting fish at night.

Chapter Eighteen
Echinoderms

Introduction

Sea stars, brittle stars, sea urchins, crinoids, and sea cucumbers live on the bottom of all the seas in the world. Of almost 6,000 species, a few are desirable in minireef aquariums because they graze algae, clean the gravel, or multiply in captivity. Most are unsuitable for minireef aquariums because they're too large, require frigid water, or kill other reef animals. All are intolerant of variations in seawater salinity, and some cannot tolerate exposure to trapped air. The Atlantic coast of the United States has relatively few species, the cold Pacific northwest many more. The greatest diversity of echinoderms occurs in the tropical Indo-Pacific. An outstanding photographic collection of tropical Indo-Pacific species appears in *Coral Reef Animals of the Indo-Pacific* by Gosliner et al., available from Sea Challengers, 4 Sommerset Rise, Monterey, CA 93940.

The unusual water vascular system is used not for rigidity but for respiration, excretion, mobility, and delivery of nutrients throughout the body. The vascular system contains a seawaterlike body fluid often with a small amount of hemoglobin. This fluid enables echinoderms to move by filling and depleting tiny sacs arranged in five rows around the body. These sacs continue into tiny extensions on the bottom of the animal called tube feet. Fluid pumped into the tube feet causes them to elongate.

These tube feet are used for motility, capturing food, or cleaning the skin.

Echinoderm skin contains particles or ossicles of calcium and magnesium carbonate. These ossicles can be loosely connected (sea stars, brittle stars), fused to form a rigid covering, or test (sea urchins, sand dollars), or minute and almost irrelevant (sea cucumbers).

Most remarkable is the ability of echinoderms to transform from watery limpness to rock-hard rigidity. In this way, an urchin can lock itself into a crevice, a sea cucumber can instantly change from limp to solid, or a sea star can exert incredible force to wrench open the valves of a clam. Echinoderms accomplish this change from limp to turgid (which can be generalized throughout the body or localized) by forming calcium ion bridges among specialized macromolecules in their connective tissue. The calcium bridge, turned off, can instantly liquify tissue connecting an arm or part of the intestine or respiratory system, breaking off a body part. In the same way, sea cucumbers are able to break off and release pieces of their intestinal tracts or respiratory systems, sometimes to eliminate unneeded tissue, sometimes to smother or (in some species) to poison a predator.

Echinoderms are then able to regenerate the lost part. New England oystermen years ago discovered to their dismay that cutting up predatory sea stars in order to kill them only resulted in even more sea stars when the parts grew into whole new animals.

Similarly strange chemistry is employed by the tube feet of sea stars. Although tube feet touching an aquarist's hand may feel like suction cups, in fact the sea star secretes an instantly bonding adhesive, and just as instantly can secrete a chemical that dissolves the bond.

Echinoderms are usually male or female, shedding eggs or sperm into the water that hatch into a bilaterally symmetrical, ciliated larva. The swimming larva eventually settles on the bottom to form the new echinoderm. In some species, the fertilized egg is brooded, and a completely formed juvenile is released from the mother.

Feather Stars

Feather stars (Crinoidea) are frequently offered for sale through mail-order suppliers, but don't ship well. If handled, they harden their connective tissues and may break. Feather stars have the basic complement of 5 parts divided into 10, 20, or even 200 arms. The arms have comblike teeth and sticky tube feet that capture suspended planktonic tintinnid protozoa, bacteria, and detritus, wiping off the collected food with cilia and rolling the food into small packets carried to the upward-facing mouth. Feather stars begin life attached to the bottom with a stalk, but soon break off and move about on their mobile arms; some can even flap the arms to swim. A single large group, the Order Comatulida, is of recent origin and is radiating out of the tropics. Many live on or below live or dead coral, on or under rocks and rubble, and a few associate with gorgonians. Most are active after dark. I've found them frequently in the Caribbean in deep cracks and holes in shallow water rock walls (from which they were impossible to extricate). *Comatula, Comaster, Comissa, Comanthina, Comantheria, Amphimetra, Heterometra, Himerometra, Oligometra, Oxycomanthus, Oxymetra, Pilometra, Stephanometra, Petasometra, Liparometra,* and *Lamprometra* are Indo-Pacific; *Analcidometra* and *Nemaster* are Caribbean.

In minireefs, tropical feather stars will eat blended fish-shrimp particles or brine shrimp squirted onto the arms with a food baster. Few aquarists report success keeping crinoids, and I don't recommend them for beginners.

Holothuroids

The Order Holothuroidea (sea cucumbers) contains 900 species of elongate echinoderms with very reduced ossicles resulting in a rubbery or leathery skin. The minute ossicles have distinctive shapes useful for identification. Sea cucumbers range from an inch to three feet or more in length, and from squat to wormlike in shape. Of five rows of tube feet along the body, two on top are reduced to bare eruptions, and three on the flattened lower side provide mobility. There are no arms; tube feet around the mouth are enlarged as feeder tentacles that gather food and stuff it

Red feather star, **Himerometra robustipinna.**

into the pharynx. The pharynx then contracts around the tentacles to remove the food.

There is no circulatory system, and a rather odd respiratory arrangement. Sea cucumbers swallow water at the cloaca, pump it through the body into blind compartments making up a respiratory tree, and then discharge it back at the cloaca. During starvation or when attacked by a predator, the sea cucumber can activate calcium ion loss in the rear connective tissue macromolecules, liquifying the connections to its gut and respiratory viscera, and then expel the offal from its cloaca to distract the predator. Expelled vicera are regenerated in a matter of weeks. Some sea cucumbers have converted defense to offense, special sticky white strings (Cuvier's tubules) of the expelled respiratory tree adhering to and strangling the predator; in still others the tubules contain the toxic saponin, *holothurin*. This toxin also occurs in the sea cucumber's skin. Crushed sea cucumbers are used as a natural poison to kill food fish trapped in tidal pools in Asia. Other sea cucumbers are harvested and prepared as delicacies in China and elsewhere.

Sexes are mostly separate, the single gonad expelling eggs or sperm into the water. A few sea cucumbers brood fertilized eggs, releasing fully formed juveniles. Breeding can be induced by putting groups of at least a dozen individuals together on a deep sand bottom and rapidly changing water temperature. Sea cucumbers with small eggs may require a month or two of planktonic care, including feeding with algal culture; sea cucumbers with large eggs often don't need feeding, and settle out of the plankton in less than two weeks.

Sea cucumbers are valuable scavengers, detritus feeders, and grazers in minireefs with aragonite sand or gravel, less useful and less likely to find adequate detritus in bare-bottom tanks. The burrowers churn gravel, recycle detritus, and control infaunal worms and crustaceans. Other sea cucumbers sweep detritus from the surface, and still others collect material from the water column. In most cases, particles are collected by a sticky substance on the tentacles, and the sea cucumber then wipes the tentacles off in its mouth, as though licking its fingers of candy. Most sea cucumbers require no special foods, but should be introduced only to well-established aquariums several months old with considerable accumulated detritus in the sand. Using a powerhead to blast accumulated detritus into the water column is beneficial to many sea cucumbers, and much of the uneaten detritus will then be captured by a mechanical filter or the protein skimmer.

The Caribbean five-toothed cucumbers (*Actinopyga floridana, A. agassizi*) have teeth around the cloaca through which enter and exit pearl fish (Carapidae) that live in the cucumber's respiratory tree. *Holothuria* and *Stichopus* occur in both the Atlantic and Indo-Pacific. Atlantic genera

---

Cold-water Echinoderms

Echinoderms of the Pacific northwest are as diverse as they are beautiful, and popular display animals in public aquariums. They do well in refrigerated minireef aquariums with live rock and less intense light than tropical reef aquariums. One longtime source is Pacific Coldwater Marine (503-625-2314). Among the most popular species are the sea cucumbers *Parastichopus californicus* and *Cucumaria miniata*, the urchin *Strongylocentrotus franciscanus*, and the spectacular sea stars *Pycnopodia helianthoides, Solaster stimpsoni*, and *Pteraster tesselatus*.

Some spectacular sea cucumbers rely on poster coloration to ward off predators.

mals within. Others sweep surface detritus. Some sticky species live among rocks (*Euapta, Synapta*), grazing attached algae and other marine life, and a few are plankton feeders. Still others are surface forms always out and about, either plain (*Stichopus, Astichopus, Actinopyga, Holothuria, Isostichopus*) or beautifully colored (*Brandtothuria*, and the sea apples, *Pseudocholochirus*). The brightly colored surface forms are most likely to contain holothurin, but seem to be perfectly safe for most minireef and marine fish aquariums, because it takes considerable trauma to generate a release of toxin.

Echinoids

The Class Echinoidea (sand dollars, sea urchins, heart urchins) lack arms, and the ossicles are tightly joined providing a solid case or test. The lower body has tube feet, enabling them to move freely over rocky surfaces. Sea urchins have two sets (occasionally one set) of elongate movable spines used for defense and movement. The spines are connected through holes in the test with mesenchyme, and can lock the body tightly in place when the macromolecules are stimulated to form calcium bridges. Some urchins also have barbs and irritants on their spines. Pedicillariae, tiny jawlike structures on short stalks located all over the body, are used for catching small particles or cleansing the skin. Sand dollars and heart urchins have tiny spines and burrow through sand, feeding on deposits of detritus. Sea urchins have a powerful five-part calcareous jaw structure (Aristotle's lantern) that scrapes algae and other incrustations from rocks and coral. One species grinds out a personal cave, then becomes sessile and captures planktonic algae for food. The majority of echinoids are grazers. Grazing urchins are among the most important algal controls on the

include *Actinopyga, Euapta, Astichopus, Isostichopus, Pentacta,* and *Parathyone. Ceto, Neothyonidium, Psolidium, Synapta, Synaptula, Cucumaria, Cholochirus, Pseudocholochirus, Thelenota, Bohadschia,* and *Opheodesoma* are Indo-Pacific genera. The most popular minireef sea cucumber is the purple *Pseudocholochirus violaceus* from the Philippines and elsewhere. The recently discovered *Thelonota rubrolineata,* a spectacular red and white striped cucumber from deep water in Indonesia and the Solomon Islands, is sure to be a hit when it arrives.

A few swimming species (*Pelagothuria*) occur in deep Atlantic waters from the surface to the bottom. Many (*Cucumaria, Actinopyga, Thyone*) burrow, swallowing sand and digesting the small benthic ani-

coral reef. When an epidemic almost wiped out sea urchins in the Caribbean a few years ago, algal overgrowth severely damaged coral reefs from Florida to South America, and recovery is still incomplete.

Most echinoids have separate males and females that release gametes into the seawater; a few are brooding species. Sea urchins can be kept sexually ripe with a summerlike 18 hour light/6 hour dark photoperiod, and induced to shed gametes by touching the shell with electrodes connected to a 12-volt transformer for 30 seconds, injecting 0.1 M acetylcholine, or injecting 0.3–0.5 ml of 0.5 M potassium chloride (dissolve 9.32 grams of granular KCl in 250 ml of distilled water to make a 0.5 M solution). Urchins are stimulated while upside down on a beaker of seawater, the red eggs and white sperm mixed, and the zygotes allowed to develop into swimming larvae. Aquaculturists can use the minute echinopluteus larvae as live food for marine fish larvae that won't accept rotifers.

The common pink, black, and purple long and short spine or pencil urchins (*Arbacia, Colobocentrotus, Lytechinus, Echinometra, Eucidaris, Diadema, Strongylocentrotus, Heterocentrotus*) are good algal grazers in reef tanks, but large ones may knock over rocks and even small ones may eat right through everything. Watch for bald patches where the coralline algae have been eaten down to the rock; in that case, you have too many or they're too large. Sea urchins are generally useful glass cleaners for marine tanks.

Note: Sea urchins are best transferred under water to avoid getting air inside the test, which might oxidize their exposed tissues and kill them. Avoid *Toxopneustes* and *Asthenosoma*, whose poisonous spines are painful or even lethal if they penetrate human skin.

Sand dollars and heart urchins are deposit feeders. Heart urchins like *Culcita*

Diadema antillarum *of the Caribbean is making a comeback from a serious recent widespread mortality.*

and *Echinoneus* are attractive but clumsy, and they tend to hide. Sand dollars (*Clypeaster, Echinodiscus, Encope*) are valuable subterranean gravel stirrers, and don't need to be attractive.

The Atlantic slate or pencil urchin, **Eucidaris tribuloides.**

Ophiurioids

The brittle stars and basket stars are the most successful echinoderms, with 2,000 species occurring in every conceivable habitat, from muddy estuaries to deep ocean trenches.

Brittle stars: These are abundant in holes within rocks, avoiding light during the day, coming out to forage at night or when-

Ophiocoma echinata, *a brittle star of Florida and the Caribbean.*

Ophiothrix spiculata, *an Atlantic brittle star.*

ever they smell food in an aquarium. They'll eat almost anything small, and some are planktivores that come out at night. Brittle stars are harmless to corals, and do a great job of cleaning beneath rocks and within gravel. Five very long, thin, and mobile arms radiate from a distinct central disk. Any arm can coil snakelike to lay out a loop and rapidly pull the body forward; tube feet are hardly used. Each arm has a single row of articulated ossicles, providing incredible mobility in certain planes, like a vertebral column. The mobile and even prehensile arms encircle food and carry it to the jaws, dig in sediments, climb rocks and tank walls, and wrap around structures that provide stability in current. The arms can immediately stiffen (calcium bridges among macromolecules in the mesenchyme) and break off when attacked, but soon regenerate. Most brittle stars release gametes into the water where fertilization takes place and a swimming ophiopluteus larva develops, but female brooding of retained embryos to fully formed juveniles is also common, and brittle star multiplication in reef tanks is not unusual. Some of the prettiest species are in the genera *Conocladus, Ophiomyxa, Ophioderma, Ophiomaza, Ophiolepis, Ophioactis, Ophiomastix, Ophiocoma,* and *Ophiothrix,* but it's hard to find a brittle star with a bad reputation.

Basket stars: These are a very small family (Gorgonocephalidae) with divided arms and large disks requiring considerable food. Basket stars are carnivores and planktivores of moderately deep reefs that climb up onto a structure and capture small crustaceans and worms drifting by, trapping them with both mucus and microscopic hooks on the highly branched arms for delivery to the endlessly hungry jaws. Basket stars probably shouldn't be kept in the same aquariums with small colorful shrimps or crabs. The common tropical reef genera are *Astroboa* from the Indo-Pacific and the very hardy *Astrophyton* of the Caribbean. Basket stars require daily feedings of frozen adult brine shrimps, shredded fish or shrimps, or frozen euphausids. Basket stars climb air lines and tubes to the top of the water, going where they wish. They emit gametes that develop into ophiopluteus larvae that drift through the ocean; they finally sense and settle on adult basket stars. At one time these newly settled larvae were thought to be the adult basket star's brooded offspring. There is no information on whether they can be propagated by fragmentation of arms.

Asteroidea

With 1,500 species from the tropics to the polar regions, from rocky shores to the silty abyss, the sea stars (starfish) are almost as numerous as brittle stars, and more prominent. One of the richest areas in the world for sea stars is the Pacific northwest coast of the United States, with 70 species. Far more, of course, occur in the tropical Indo-Pacific, and far fewer in the Atlantic.

Sea stars usually have five large stiff arms, but can have more. The arms have little mobility except at the tips. Sea stars glide over any surface by first sticking to that surface with an adhesive from myriad tube feet beneath each arm, and then dissolving that adhesive with a second secretion. The arms continue into the central portion of the body, with no demarcation setting off a separate disk.

Creatures of grass beds, sand flats, rocks, and reefs, the sea stars are major predators of clams, whose shells they force open ever so slightly by crawling over them and suddenly freezing their arms solidly in place (the mechanism is the chemical formation of calcium bridges connecting the macromolecules in the mesenchyme) to maintain a viselike grip that prevents the

Many kinds of longspined sea urchins occur in the tropical Atlantic.

clam from closing. The sea star then extrudes its stomach and inserts it into the gap between the valves and onto the flesh of the unfortunate clam or oyster. Sea stars eat other animals as well.

Astropecten articulatus is the abundant royal sea star of the southern Atlantic states.

Starfish with everted stomach digesting a sea urchin.

Indo-Pacific genera include, in part, *Acanthaster, Archaster, Iconaster, Stellaster, Pentagonaster, Tosia, Bothriaster, Choriaster, Culcita, Halityle, Mithrodia, Monachaster, Pentaceraster, Pentaster, Pateriella, Protoreaster, Radiaster, Euretaster, Ferdina, Fromia, Gomophia, Leiaster, Nardoa, Neoferdina, Ophidiaster, Tamaria,* and *Thromidia.* Atlantic sea star genera are less extensive, but include species of *Coscinasterias, Hacelia, Ceramaster,* and *Oreaster.* Genera common to both the Atlantic and Indo-Pacific include *Asterina, Astropecten, Echinaster, Luidia,* and *Linckia.*

Sea stars can divide through the disk to form two individuals from one, but normal reproduction requires shedding gametes into the water where they meet and develop into bipinnaria and then brachiolaria larvae that later become juveniles. One group attaches eggs to rocks. The Mediterranean *Echinaster sepositus* lays fertilized eggs that develop completely into baby starfish at hatching, bypassing a free-swimming larval stage. A *Henricia* species may have similar reproduction. Smooth-skinned sea stars have a reputation for safety in reef aquariums. That may be true regarding predation on corals, but the generality is risky in aquariums containing $75 tridacnid clams and a sea star that hasn't eaten in a few days. In tanks without clams, sea stars can be attractive additions. Blue and red species of *Linckia*, especially, are popular with minireef aquarists.

The Pacific crown-of-thorns starfish, *Acanthaster*, a predator on scleractinian corals, has undergone a population explosion over parts of its range, leaving some reefs practically bald of living hard corals. This is due in large measure to the harvest of a predatory snail for the tourist trade in shells.

Chapter Nineteen
Annelids

The Phylum Annelida contains 14,000 species of segmented worms with a blood circulatory system based on hemoglobin or a similar substance, a coelom or fluid-filled body cavity with additional respiratory and some excretory functions, a straight gut, complex nervous system, and great diversity in habitats. The major groups are the oligochaetes, leeches, and polychaetes.

Oligochaetes: These species are mostly terrestrial (earthworms, white worms, grindal worms) or freshwater aquatic (red tubifex, blackworms) hermaphrodites that lay their eggs in capsules called cocoons.

Leeches: Leeches are parasitic on marine, estuarine, and freshwater vertebrates, and also are hermaphrodites that lay eggs in cocoons.

Polychaetes: In this group the sexes are usually separate. Males and females shed eggs and sperm through pores or by splitting the body wall, and the developing trochophore larva swims or crawls on the bottom. A few polychaetes store eggs until the larva is advanced in development or transformed into a juvenile.

Polychaetes can be motile and roaming (errant) or sedentary. Each body segment has a branched lateral tissue extension called a parapodium that looks like a tiny oar or lump, and each branch of each parapodium is armed with stinging bristles (setae) used for respiration and defense. The setae in the sea mouse cover the entire body, while in nonerrant worms living in tubes, setae are reduced. The parapodia (*para-podium* = accessory foot) are used for purchase to push the body forward; the setae provide additional traction, like cleats on a golf shoe. In the brightly colored predatory fireworms (Family Amphinomidae), the calcified toxic bristles easily break off and imbed in any fish foolish enough to attack. Polychaetes also move by sequentially inflating the coelom in each segment and then pulling themselves forward

Sabellid polychaete worm.

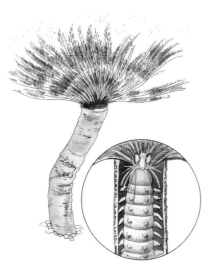

Polychaete marine worms often have complex jaws or other mouthparts in front, or they may have mouthparts modified to function as both gills and planktonic filters. The sides of the body have numerous appendages modified for movement and sometimes to assist in respiration.

through sand or mud, or by extending the pharynx, everting the jaws to grab onto something, then retracting the pharynx and pulling the body forward. Polychaetes, like snakes, can also sinuously twist their bodies for rapid traverse.

The polychaete head is modified for filter-feeding, predation, deposit-feeding, or grazing. Four or more eyes detect light and shadows, but one pelagic form, with fully formed eyes—lens and cornea—and a head reminiscent of E.T., can see complete images. The mouth cavity leads to a protrusive pharynx armed with four, six, or eight pincerlike jaws that have drawn blood from more than one fisherman trying to put a bloodworm (*Glycera*) on a hook.

Pincers aren't always a sign of a raptorial (catching) predator. Significant coral predators are the amphinomid fireworms; the far more abundant nereids mostly eat detritus and algae and occasionally take a nip of a coral, but usually scavenge dead tissue and macroalgae. Errant nereids are among the most abundant and important of

Epitokal Reproduction

Palolo worms of the Indo-Pacific live within coral reefs, and swarm at the same time in great masses of individuals. The nonreproductive worm in the coral is called an atoke. With the reproductive moon approaching, the rear worm segments change into a series of short but complete worms with modified heads, enhanced swimming appendages, and a coelom packed with eggs or sperm. This string of dwarf reproductive worms or epitokes break off and swarm at the surface during one particular night, the male epitokes seeking out female epitokes. Each epitoke releases gametes upon sensing gametes of the opposite sex. The swarming epitokes emit bursts of phosphorescent light, and the sea is illuminated with myriad blue-green sparks as if millions of fireflies were mating just beneath the glassy surface. Epitokal reproduction occurs in many other kinds of polychaete worms. Epitokes can form by multiple division of the atoke's original body or the growing of additional epitokal individuals from the rear of the atoke. Polychaetes, including epitokal species, are common in live rock. Search your reef tank with a flashlight after dark, and you may see an occasional half-inch long epitoke arching and flapping its short body this way and that as it swims in the upper reaches of the aquarium seeking a mate.

The Caribbean Christmas tree or plume worm, Spirobranchus giganteus, *lives in corals.*

Sabellastarte *may occupy holes in corals.*

live sand infauna, working oxygen and water through the sand as they consume and recycle detritus.

The nonerrant polychaetes are mostly filter feeders or deposit feeders. The deposit feeders (*Terebella, Amphitrite*) live in holes in rock or sediment and thrust out very long, thin, white tentacles that adhere to selected food particles on the surface, then bring them to the mouth where they are wiped off the tentacles like a kid licking an ice-cream stick.

The most beautiful filter feeders of the coral reef are the sabellid, sabellarid, and spirorbid Christmas tree worms, feather duster worms, and fanworms (*Sabella, Sabellaria, Sabellastarte, Hydroides*). These beauties may be red, blue, orange, or yellow. Their clusters of filaments at the head end are arranged in helical vortices,

their bodies buried in the rock or extending above it in a sand tube or calcareous tube. The vortices of filaments are modified for both gas exchange and for filtering plankton from the water, just as many fish have cartilaginous rakers to capture plankton arising from opposite ends of the same gill arch carrying the respiratory tissue. Captured plankton and other particles are delivered down the vortex to the mouth. Here the catch is sorted into food, waste, and moderate-sized sand grains to be mixed with mucus and laid down around the top of an ever-growing protective sand tube (in sabellariid and pectinariid worms). In those fanworms with a calcareous tube (spirorbids) the sand is discarded. Fanworms have primitive photoreceptors to detect passing shadows of predators and can instantly withdraw into their tubes,

Sabellastarte *is a large feather duster worm.*

The sabellid and sabellarid Christmas tree worms and other fanworms require zooplankton, and should be fed daily with live *Artemia* nauplii. These worms are picked on by many pygmy angels, some shrimps, and most wrasses, and do best in a hard coral tank devoid of all fish other than tangs.

Some species are easily overgrown by macroalgae and need shade for protection, while others do quite well in brilliant light. In St. Johns, Virgin Islands, I noted that the blue forms were in shade below rock ledges, the orange forms in full sun on top of the same rocks.

Most polychaetes, including fanworms, can reproduce by fragmentation, each fragment developing into a complete worm. Several polychaetes that fragment, or that brood eggs and hatch late stage crawling trochophore larvae or even juveniles may suddenly populate an entire reef tank.

closing the walls of the tube to protect the head, or capping the tube with a snail-like opercular lid.

Chapter Twenty
Urochordata

The higher animals make up the 50,000 species of the Phylum Chordata. That phylum today contains three subphyla, the Urochordata, Cephalochordata, and Vertebrata. Fish are in the last subphylum, along with humans and all other animals with backbones.

A fourth group, the Hemichordata, contain the common marine acorn worms and less prominent pterobranchs. The hemichordates were recently removed from the Chordata and placed in their own phylum. Because they are not suitable as reef tank animals, they will not be covered in this book.

Cephalochordates are known to biology students as lancelets. The most common genus used in school laboratories is *Amphioxis*, but other genera include *Branchiostoma, Epigonichthys*, and *Asymmetron*. All are small translucent animals that live mostly in or under the sand, filtering small particles and microbes, passing water through gill slits. Lancelets are recognized as chordates in part by the embryonic steps in development of gill slits in a pharynx, the straight gut, the form of the circulatory system, and mostly by the developmental steps that result in a notochord adjacent to a dorsal hollow nerve cord. These adjacent elements, and how they develop, are thought to represent the primitive central nervous system associated with a backbone. Lancelets are great teaching animals, but rarely seen by most people. One tropical species, *Branchiostoma caribaeum*, might survive in a reef aquarium devoid of fish or large hermit crabs.

The Urochordata are divided into three groups, the Ascidia (tunicates), Larvacea (larvaceans), and Thaliacea (salps and their relatives). The larvaceans and salps are transparent, planktonic or drifting marine animals occurring singly, in chains, or in massive clusters. They are not suitable for reef tanks and not considered further.

The tunicates are sessile, attached to any nearshore hard structure. The body wall contains a very tough substance called tunicin, a celluloselike carbohydrate bound with protein. Most familiar is the pudgy greenish brown *Ciona intestinalis* (sea grape, sea liver) of rock jetties and pier pilings in cold climates around the world. Many species have symbiotic shrimp, are preyed upon by specialized nudibranchs, or require symbiotic prokaryotic algae.

Sea squirts can be solitary or colonial, each animal or zooid typically ranging in size from a walnut to a pea. Often, the larger the colony, the smaller the zooids. Often, much of the tunicin-based body is shared by the colony in a common test (structure) reinforced with calcareous spicules.

An inhalent siphon protrudes from the rounded body of each zooid, drawing in enormous volumes of seawater. Plankton and drifting detritus passing through meshlike slits in the pharynx are captured by a sticky exudate for passage down the gut, where it is digested. The filtered wastewater is excreted through an exhalent siphon or, rarely, through a common siphon shared by a group with a common test. The worldwide *Pyrosoma atlanticum* forms giant colonies with one exhalent siphon large enough to insert your arm or leg.

Most sea squirts are hermaphrodites that release sperm, fertilized eggs, or fully formed tadpole-shaped larvae into the surrounding water. The swimming larva locates a suitable site to settle down, then attaches by its head and grows into an adult tunicate. Sea squirts also reproduce asexually by budding (blastozooid formation) from a specialized reproducing zooid called an oozooid, or even from the larval stage. Some colonies of cloned siblings number in the hundreds.

Many tropical tunicates are brilliantly colored in ice blue, lime green, or shades of red and orange. Many live beneath ledges where they are protected from sunlight, while others thrive in full sun. Green tunicates often have symbiotic algae, and transport these algae from generation to generation through the tadpolelike larva.

About 1,250 species of tunicates occur around the world, a considerable number not restricted to any one ocean. The most recent classification breaks them into three orders: the Aplousobranchia with 14 families, Phlebobranchia with five families, and Stolidobranchia with four families.

Among the most important tropical families in Aplousobranchia are the Clavelinidae (*Clavelina, Oxycorynia, Neptheus, Sycozoa*), and Didemnidae (*Didemnum, Lissoclinum, Diplosoma, Trididemnum*). *Clavelina* is especially rich in species around the world, many of them quite beautiful and in various colors. Visitors to the Caribbean will find colonies of beautiful ice blue *Clavelina* mostly beneath ledges in shallow water, other green or white types coating dead boulder coral surfaces. *Didemnum* is also rich in species, often brilliant red, yellow, or orange. *Sycozoa* and *Oxycorynia* resemble green macroalgae, with colonies of zooids growing at the end of a stemlike common stalk.

Important members of the Phlebobranchia are the Corellidae (*Corella, Rhodosoma*). The Diazonidae, containing the delicate lacelike *Diazona* and the spectacular blue *Rhopalaea* are sometimes included in the Phlebobranchia (Gosliner et al., 1996) and sometimes the Aplousobranchia (Mather and Bennett, 1994).

Prominent among the Stolidobranchia are the Styelidae (*Botryllus, Botrylloides, Eusynstyella, Polycarpa, Cnemidocarpa*) and Pyuridae (*Pyura, Herdmania, Microcosmus*). *Pyura* is peach-colored or lavender-colored and grows as a clump at the end of a stalk that can be two feet tall. It has sharp calcareous spicules in the body wall. Photographs in Gosliner et al. (1996) illustrate the spectacular species.

Sea squirts are tough-skinned and transport easily, but should have large volumes of both shipping water and oxygen (not air). Feed sea squirts daily with suspensions of particulate foods such as unicellular algae, rotifers, brine shrimp nauplii, and commercial nutrient suspensions based on egg yolk. Iodine is extracted rapidly from water and must be supplemented as though you were providing for an aquarium filled with soft corals. Calcium levels should be maintained as for hard corals.

Colonies will grow at different rates depending on species, light, supplemental iodine dosing, regularity and volume of feeding, and predation. A few herbivorous snails (*Turbo*) and many nudibranchs graze on tunicates, but otherwise they have few enemies in a reef tank. The potential combinations of grazers and tunicates from around the world is astronomical. Use trial, error, and cost to determine which of the available tunicates will thrive in your reef tank.

Chapter Twenty-one
Fishes: Foods and Feeding

Hermatypic corals can get all their nutrient requirements from symbiotic algae and the minute invertebrates in the water, rock, and gravel. At least once a week, use a hand-held powerhead to blow upon the gravel and live rock, dislodging and sweeping the surface microorganisms into the water column where they can be harvested by coral polyps. This invisible life consists of myriad protozoa, gastrotrichs, rotifers, annelids, roundworms, flatworms, bacteria, minute crustaceans, fungal and algal cells, and other life midway between microbes and visible invertebrates. An important food source in reef tanks, these microorganisms are beneficial to many hermatypic corals, essential to ahermatypes. A side benefit is that noxious biofilms and encrustations of cyanobacteria and fungi on gravel are disrupted, regenerating the free exchange of gas and nutrients between gravel and water.

Ahermatypic corals need additional feedings of prepared or, preferably, live foods. Fishes in the reef aquarium, even tangs and pygmy angels, also benefit from supplementary frozen and live foods.

Propagation of marine fishes and crustaceans usually requires special foods such as newly hatched brine shrimp nauplii, rotifers, and copepods.

Brine Shrimp

Brine shrimp (*Artemia*) are the salt pond representatives of fairy shrimp (*Stephano-lepis*) crustaceans (Branchiopoda: Anostraca) that occur around the world in temporary, ephemeral, and vernal fish-free pools and ponds. The species whose eggs are most commonly sold in the United States is *A. franciscana* from California and Utah; it is also widespread through introductions around the world. Another species, *A. monica*, occurs in Mono Lake, California, but is not in commercial play. Other species around the world include *A. tunisiana, A. urminiana*, and *A. salina*. *Artemia franciscana* live adults are netted and sold from salt ponds in California, but the bulk of the American supply is cultured indoors and sold by a company in Florida.

Brine shrimp reproduce both parthenogenetically and sexually, the dark brown eggs gathered from windblown shores of large saline lakes for sale to the aquaculture industry. The aquarium hobby uses less than 5 percent of production, the bulk of the harvest shipped to Asian aquaculture facilities for the production of shrimp and fish.

Brine shrimp eggs are available from pet stores in small quantities, but the packages are seldom airtight, and hatches are poor. Brine shrimp eggs should be purchased in sealed 15-ounce cans. Open the can by puncturing with a can opener, pour a small amount into a covered jar for use over a two-week period, and cover again with a tight-fitting plastic lid before storage in a freezer. Exposure to water vapor in air damages eggs and reduces the hatch, while storage in a freezer prolongs useful life by pulling water vapor out of the air.

Most containers provide hatching instructions using uniodized salt in tap water. Brine shrimp hatches are better using 1 level teaspoonful of shrimp eggs per gallon in normal strength synthetic seawater, at room temperature, in the presence of 12 hours of bright light, and with vigorous to violent aeration. This is a good use for wastewater removed from the reef tank during regular partial water replacements.

The hatchlings from the eggs are called nauplii, and richest in essential fatty acids for the first 24 hours, when they are smallest. Beyond 24 hours, the nutritive value of *Artemia* nauplii drops off markedly as they use up their fatty acids, and their usefulness as live food for the smallest larval fish and invertebrates declines as the nauplii double in size.

After 24 hours, pour the hatch water through a brine shrimp net and invert the retained shells and nauplii into a pitcher of cold tap water. Within 15 minutes, the nauplii sink to the bottom and the empty shells remain floating. Decant the shells and excess cold water, wipe the remaining shells from the pitcher walls with your finger, and refill the container with tap water or seawater. The cleaned nauplii can now be fed to fish and corals. Used hatch water can be recycled by mixing into a larger volume (30-gallon barrel, aerated, filtered, and darkened), but not used immediately for a second hatch.

To grow adult brine shrimp, fill a large shallow container with used seawater or brine shrimp hatch water, add vigorous aeration and intense overhead light, and inoculate the water with hatched nauplii (not eggs). Feed lightly with an aged suspension of baker's yeast in water once a week; dry yeast will sink and cause bacterial blooms. Unicellular algae (green water) are

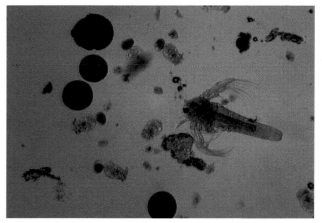

Brine shrimp nauplii are most nutritious before the first molt.

a better food, and need not be marine species, as all green algal suspensions are consumed rapidly. Excess juvenile and adult brine shrimp are wonderful foods for marine fish and filter feeders.

Brine Cladocerans

Some species of *Diaphanosoma, Moina,* and other cladocerans live in hypersaline brine ponds and alkaline soda (salt) lakes from the American west to Australia. These *Daphnia*-like species are not yet cultured for the aquarium hobby. Starter cultures and recommendations should be sought from local invertebrate zoologists and physiologists at state university zoology or biology departments in the desert states. A local expert who is not culturing them can still probably direct you to a professor or graduate student elsewhere currently working on one of these species.

Live Fish

Most reef tank invertebrates and fishes will find all their nutritive needs in the aquarium and need no supplementary feeding. Carnivorous fishes (hawkfish, scorpion fish, lionfish, groupers) are popular in reef tanks because they ignore corals and clams; they will, however, take unwary shrimp (even cleaners) and crabs. Carnivores can be fed mollies or killifish, which survive indefinitely in marine water, or goldfish, guppies, and minnows, whose short survival time simplifies capture by sedentary predators.

Prepared Foods

Fish, shrimp, sea stars, and crabs can smell, see, and find nonliving foods, but such foods should be delivered to sessile invertebrates with a baster, straw, or tweezer. Frozen, thawed, and finely ground uncooked ocean fish fillets, shelled shrimp, and clams are excellent foods. Packaged seafoods are available in pet stores and the raw products from supermarkets. Fresh raw mussel (open the shell with a blade, not by cooking) will help capture polychaetes and noxious crabs at night for removal from the aquarium.

A paste food combining many animal and vegetable ingredients can be made by combining uncooked and unshelled popcorn shrimp, shelled larger shrimp, fresh tuna fillet, squid entrails (the mantle is too tough), Japanese seaweed soaked in water to soften, cooked fresh (not canned) spinach, brewer's yeast, and a powdered or liquid multivitamin. The ingredients should be blended in a food processor with enough cool water to make a thick paste, then stored in thinly packed zip-lock bags in a freezer. As needed, a portion of the paste is broken off, thawed, and hand-fed to the inhabitants.

An alternative approach is to cook the mix with gelatin to keep particles and juices from escaping, but the cooking heat degrades essential nutrients.

Flake, pelleted, and freeze-dried foods and liquified preparations and suspensions release juices or dust-fine particles that cannot be used by the inhabitants. These residuals can feed bacterial and cyanobacterial blooms, resulting in a loss of alkalinity and oxidation-reduction potential, a depressed pH, and in stressed ammonia-sensitive and pH-sensitive animals.

Only advanced reef-keepers with an eye for water quality and coral health should use liquified supplements. These supplements are commercially available, or you can make your own with blended raw clam, mussel, shrimp, fish fillet, fish liver (ask at your seafood dealer), yeast dissolved in water (not particles), and blended cooked spinach. Do not heat. Filter through 300–500 micron nytex or a plastic coffee filter, stir in liquid multivitamin mix, and freeze in one-ounce packets, thawing as needed. The particles retained by the filter are good for *Xenia* and other planktivorous corals, many fish, and decorative shrimp and crabs.

Prepared foods for larval fish and shrimp are used by commercial aquaculture farms, yielding improved growth and survival and decreasing dependence on expensive and sometimes unreliable supplies of brine shrimp eggs. Larva "Z" diet (Zeigler Brothers, Gardners, Pennsylvania, tel. 800-841-6800) has a high content of cholesterol, phospholipids, xanthophylls, and 5 percent by weight of HUFA. The components enhance growth of edible (penaeid) shrimp by promoting molting (ecdysis). This diet should work on decorative aquarium shrimp and crabs and other invertebrates and larval fish once the correct particle size for each stage of each species of shrimp larva is determined by trial and error. It has also been used successfully by Florida Aqua-Farms as a supplement for growing clownfish. Feeds are packaged in semibuoyant microparticle sizes of <100 through >450 μ in 50 μ intervals.

Macroalgae

Many minireef aquarium fishes (*Centropyge* angelfish, Moorish idols, yellow and kole tangs) consume nuisance macroalgae or reduce desirable macroalgae to acceptable levels. If the tank becomes depleted, the fish require supplementary feedings. Potter's angel (*Centropyge potteri*) is obligately herbivorous and dies of starvation after depleting the tank of algae.

Vegetables

Some fishes will accept cooked leaf lettuce (not iceberg, which is nutrient-poor) or iron-rich spinach. These foods are deficient in iodine and the complex carbohydrates provided by marine algae. Many red and brown marine algae from the Indo-Pacific are dried for the Oriental food trade; nori is a general term for these dried seaweeds. Nori sheets should be separated or fragmented, then soaked in cold water (do not cook) until rubbery and limber. In this form, nori is highly nutritious and acceptable to some herbivores. Other herbivores cannot deal with the texture; for them, cook the nori until it falls apart. The variety, flavors, and textures of these products differ, so try several to determine those accepted by your various fish.

Chapter Twenty-two
Fishes: Care and Breeding

Reef tanks benefit from fishes that consume algae, break up and mix the aragonite sand/gravel substratrum, or control noxious polychaetes. Some very attractive forms are difficult to accommodate because they eat coral polyps (Chaetodontidae) or sponges (Pomacanthidae), or produce excessive waste products (Antennariidae, Serranidae). Bursts of wastes induce blooms of organic decomposing (heterotrophic) bacteria that disrupt populations of ammonia-oxidizing and nitrite-oxidizing (autotrophic) bacteria. Some Pomacentridae (damselfish) kill corals in order to cultivate algal turfs upon which they feed. Other fishes are so predaceous on other fishes and crustaceans (Balistidae, Ostraciidae, Tetraodontidae) as to be incompatible with diverse captive reef fauna. (In nature, cnidarians are also eaten by sea turtles, sea mammals, and sea birds.)

Guidelines for Keeping Marine Fishes in Reef Tanks

What a fish does in nature is the product of adaptation over the eons (evolution) and during each fish's lifetime (experience). Evolution may have adapted a fish's teeth to crop algae, and competition with other species on the reef may restrict it to that food source. From a very early age a fish learns what food it can get and which foods it cannot. In short, competition trains that fish to become specialized to a particular food, while evolution has prepared it to be efficient at this activity.

When an older fish (one already trained by experience) is placed in a new environment, two outcomes are possible. The first is that the fish will search only for the food it has learned to eat; failing that the fish will waste away and die. The second possible outcome is that it will learn from watching the other tank inhabitants and adapt to the available foods, even though they are new and different. This applies both to tank-raised and wild fish.

Examples abound. Before coral mini-reefs, marine aquarists had little success with most butterfly fish (Chaetodontidae), because they are generally adapted to feeding upon corals and worms extracted from crevices, and they are poor learners. However, if a butterfly fish is captured when very young, its capacity for learning is very great. It happens even in the wild. In Hawaii, for example, swimmers on beaches feed the local butterfly fish frozen peas and canned synthetic cheese spread. It is likely that these fish have virtually given up feeding on corals.

Any fish in any tank might behave differently from before, or be induced to behave differently, by watching its cohabitants. With this caution in mind, be aware that a fish believed to combine safely with corals may, in fact, learn to be a terror, while another reputed to be a fierce predator may, in fact, be a pussycat.

You will frequently see a large (trophy) marine fish in a shop at a remarkably low price. It was likely not imported, but brought back by someone whose aquarium or good graces it had outgrown. As with used cars, consider that you may be buying someone else's headache.

A safer approach is to select only young fish so that they may be trained under your care. Older fish are risky for the bad habits they may have learned, or their inability to change.

By all means, select reef tank fishes with good reputations and be wary of those not recommended. Just remember that any fish can turn aggressively territorial or predaceous, may learn to pick on corals and eventually feed on them, or otherwise disrupt the harmony of a reef tank. Watch your fish. They don't read books.

Acanthuridae

Some tangs or surgeonfish (named for the razor sharp bone on either side of the caudal peduncle) are essential for the control of algae in a reef aquarium. In the absence of those fish, filamentous and other macroalgae growth would overgrow the live rock faster than pygmy angelfish and other algal feeders could consume it. Several tang species on the reef will have different food preferences (called resource partitioning), reflected by different kinds of teeth. Preferences dissolve in captivity where availability determines what is eaten and, tooth structure notwithstanding, tangs become more flexible than their anatomy indicates.

However, not all tangs are herbivores. Some feed primarily on zooplankton in the water column (*Paracanthurus hepatus*) and very little on fleshy algae. Many are both herbivorous and coprophagous, eating the feces of other fish, and providing another circuit of digestion before the waste frag-

Paracanthurus hepatus *requires brine shrimp and won't keep algae under control.*

ments sink to the invertebrate detritus feeders and deposit feeders (e.g., worms, sea cucumbers).

The herbivorous tangs control algal succession on the reef, and tang populations in turn are limited by the reef's production of (mostly blue-green) algae and fleshy red microalgae. Where tangs (and parrotfish)

Zebrasoma flavescens *is the best tang to control algae in a reef tank.*

Acanthurus pyroferus, *is a Pacific yellow tang, (better known for protective coloration mimicing a yellow pygmy angelfish) than for controlling algae.*

Zebrasoma scopas *prefers fleshy red algae in nature, but will eat fleshy and filamentous reds and greens in a reef tank.*

are harvested as food, algal overgrowth of reefs is a problem.

Herbivorous tangs are divided by ecologists into *browsers* that crop algae (in the way cattle crop grass by biting it off above the dirt and root zone) and *grazers* that

Ctenochaetus hawaiiensis, *the Hawaii chevron tang, will also recycle sediment, detritus, and fecal wastes of other fishes.*

scrape algae along with the underlying calcareous rock. In common with parrotfish (Scaridae), tangs metabolize about 11 percent of the algae and pass 89 percent through the gut as fragments that become the organic detritus and calcareous sand of the reef. Tangs feed mostly on surface algae, whereas parrotfish specialize in algae growing inside limestone cavities, especially in the rubble zone, but both groups can leave distinctive tooth marks on rock and scraped coral.

The most popular reef tank herbivore is the inexpensive yellow tang (*Zebrasoma flavescens*). The more expensive sailfin tangs (*Zebrasoma veliferum, Z. desjardinii*) eat fleshy red and green algae in nature, but in the reef tank, both control green and red fleshy and filamentous algae. *Ctenochaetus striatus* and *C. strigosus* (kole or yellow-eye tang and chevron tang) feed heavily on sediment and detritus in nature, but are good algae eaters in reef tanks.

Acanthurus nigrofuscus and A. striatus eat mostly fleshy red microalgae in nature; A. triostegus eats various fleshy microalgae. Zebrasoma scopas prefers small fleshy red algae. Many tangs are too large or expensive and not recommended for reef aquariums algal control (Acanthurus achilles, A. olivaceous, A. aliala, A. leucosternon, A. guttatus, Naso spp.).

Many tangs benefit by supplemental feedings of frozen brine shrimp and parboiled or microwaved lettuce or spinach leaves.

Tangs spawn by rising into the water column. Some breed in pairs, others in groups, some daily or periodically, others in conjunction with moon phases. There are no reports of aquarium spawnings.

Zanclidae and Siganidae

Moorish idols (Zanclus canescens = Z. cornutus) and foxface (Lo vulpinus) previously considered difficult by marine aquarists unaware of their natural diet of algae and sponges are excellent herbivores for reef tanks, harmless to cnidarians. Given a tank of live rock, Zanclus and Lo do just fine. Moorish idols have been bred in the United States in a large tank with abundant live rock for grazing, but the young have not been raised. The long-lasting pelagic acronurus larval stage (similar to the larva of tangs) must attain more than two inches before transformation to adult form. Captive-bred Moorish idols once advertised by a South African company have, in fact, not been produced commercially. Siganids other than Lo are commonly cultivated in fish ponds in the Middle East.

Pomacentridae

The 350 species of pomacentrids, better known as damselfish, include the gregories, dascyllus, jewelfish, sergeant major, and popular clownfish or anemonefish. They take any foods, from flakes to meats, yet are rarely predaceous on other fish or moblie reef tank invertebrates, and except those attaining large adult size, they seldom fight. Pomacentrids are among the easiest fish to keep, and frequently spawn in captivity.

Not all are recommended. Sergeant majors, jewelfish (yellowtail damsels), and gregories get much too large (over three inches), aggressive, and become gray-black as adults. They should be enjoyed in the wild, but do not belong in a minireef tank or any other kind of home marine aquarium.

Other damsels make excellent reef tank inhabitants. Stately dascyllus, some growing to a large size as adults and losing some of their pretty black-and-white contrast, nonetheless remain social with one another and seldom bother corals. Small yellowtail and orange-bellied blue damsels remain small (under two inches) and hold their bright colors into adulthood. One or two will adapt well to a reef tank, but may damage some polyps within the very small area adopted as a breeding territory. A few damsels, in the wild, cultivate an algal turf food supply by killing polyps on a branch of hard coral, but this behavior is rare in captivity. All damsels with lyre-shaped tails should be considered innocuous midwater plankton-feeders that will do best in groups. By far the most popular pomacentrids are the clown anemonefish, all of which adapt well to reef tanks.

Except for the strictly Indo-Pacific clown anemonefish and some dascyllus species, damsels tend to have many hundreds or thousands of minute fry too small for rotifers and seldom raised even with sifted plankton or green water; the larval period is long, averaging three weeks. The clown anemonefish have a small batch of perhaps 100–200 eggs, and a short larval

Amphiprion clarkii *caring for patch of benthic eggs.*

period (two weeks or less). All clownfish species propagated to date have been raised on rotifers followed by brine shrimp nauplii. The pomacentrids have separate sexes determined at birth, with no sex reversal. In clown anemonefish, sex is not determined at birth. A group settles on a protective anemone, and the largest individual becomes a functional female, the second largest fish a functional male. Should the female be removed, the male becomes a female and the next largest indeterminate fish matures to a male. Thus, any group of small fish will yield a pair, but purchasing two large fish is certain to result in two determined females.

Spawning behavior depends on at least a 14-hour photoperiod. In a reef tank, two or more clownfish will take over a suitable host anemone or other type of cnidarian, but will set up housekeeping even if no cnidarian is available, and may also accept an Atlantic sea anemone. A pair selects and scrapes a hard surface often in the shade of an anemone. The smaller male displays to the larger female by arching and trembling as though in tetanus. Spawning is then cichlid-style on any hard surface, usually horizontal but sometimes ver-

tical. The oblong eggs adhere by filaments; time till hatching may be a few days (most damsels) to two weeks (clownfish). Typically hatching occurs within an hour after dark. The pelagic fry are attracted to light, and can be retrieved near the surface if the pumps are turned off. Harvest the fry with a clear plastic cup or ladle, as a siphon or baster may cause damage.

The fry cannot capture food if the water is moving. Keep them in an unaerated container with dim light and a dark bottom. Feed rotifers starting on the second day for at least 10 days. In the absence of aeration, the rotifers aggregate at the oxygen-rich surface where the nearsighted fry easily locate and capture them. Even gentle aeration disperses the rotifers so the fry starve. Brine shrimp nauplii can be started on day three. Do daily water changes. The bottom should be siphoned to remove dead fry and food every day, and a good portion of the water replaced with reef tank (not newly made) water. Losses the first three days are high, but after that you should raise the remainder. By day 10 the fry have usually transformed and are wagging on the bottom, and aeration can be started. Continue daily water changes. The fry can be transferred to a grow-out tank when not less than a half inch long. Use a clear cup. Netting can induce a fatal panic reaction in which the juveniles go into tetanus.

Dascyllus species are also easily raised on rotifers. In nature, dascyllus can smell a preferred hard coral species during the night when the larvae most often settle out of the plankton. The Hawaiian endemic *D. albisella* usually settles on *Pocillopora meandrina*. Neither clownfish nor dascyllus species require a host cnidarian in captivity.

Pomacanthidae

The eighty-plus species of marine angelfish are highly specialized invertebrate feeders and algal grazers, with few types suitable for reef tanks. All the larger angelfish (*Pygoplites, Pomacanthus, Apolemichthys, Holacanthus*) consume large amounts of sponges, sometimes only particular species, and are unsuitable for reef tanks specifically and some for captivity in general. The intermediate-sized species of *Chaetodontoplus* tend to be omnivorous; they must have a varied diet that includes vegetation supplemented with fat-soluble vitamins. *Genicanthus* species are planktivorous (note the forked tails, a dead giveaway), difficult to feed adequately and maintain in good health. The sole group suitable for reef tanks are the pygmy angels in the genus *Centropyge* with about two dozen species. *Centropyge* species are primarily algal browsers and grazers, but some individuals may pick on coral polyps (rarely doing damage) in the absence of adequate fare. Larger species such as *C. bicolor* have poor captive survival records that may indicate a more complex diet, perhaps including sponges or other animal fare. The large *C. potteri* is a strict herbivore that starves to death after consuming all available green algae. It will not feed on cyanobacteria and rarely adapts to spinach or lettuce. Intermediate-sized species (*C. bispinosus, C. ferrugatus, C. loriculus*) are omnivorous on algae and small crustaceans, readily adapting to an aquarium diet when filamentous macroalgae are allowed to flourish. The smallest species, represented by *C. argi, C. acanthops*, and *C. shepardi*, are easiest to keep because of the small amounts of food required and their receptivity to filamentous algae and other meaty foods. They do not bother corals.

All angelfish are territorial. A group (harem) of one species should be introduced at one time. Species can be mixed, but not if they have similar patterns.

Centropyge, in common with other angelfish, are sequential hermaphrodites. They mature as females first (protogynous), and (usually) the largest member of a distinct group (of as few as two fish) develops subsequently into a male. Harem spawning is the rule, with one male controlling a territory that contains one to several females. Just before sunset, a pair rushes upward into the water column for spawning, the small, floating eggs sometimes recoverable by placing a net over the tank's outflow. The male will spawn with different females on different upward rushes or on different days. *Centropyge* fry have not been raised on cultured rotifers, which may be too small or have the wrong motion. They might be raised on the larvae of oysters or sea urchins, and that is being studied now. *Pomacanthus* fry have been raised from stripped eggs and sperm, and feeding with screened natural plankton as a first food, followed by rotifers and then brine shrimp nauplii.

Gobiidae and Eleotridae

More than 2,000 species of gobies and hundreds of their close relatives, the sleepers, occur worldwide in nearshore ocean waters on sand, coral, rocks, pilings, and in grass beds, a few entering freshwater. In gobies, the pelvics are fused into an adhesive disk with which they adhere to solid surfaces even in strong current. If the pelvics are not fully fused, then the fish is a sleeper in the Family Eleotridae. Although most sleepers are bottom dwellers resembling gobies, the most popular sleepers in the marine hobby are the midwater firefish.

All gobies and sleepers are carnivorous on zooplankton and small benthic invertebrates, and are harmless to corals. They associate with crevices in rock or burrows in sand, sometimes shared with symbiotic snapping shrimp and sometimes another

Nemateleotris magnifica, *the purple firefish, spawns under rocks or in a PVC tube.*

Among the easiest fishes to breed, female gobies and sleepers deposit adhesive eggs inside a burrow, crevice, or shell defended by the male. For aquarium breeding, use a PVC tube that can then be removed for aeration after the eyes appear in the eggs. The pelagic, planktonic larvae of neon and other gobies require rotifers as a first food, but many other gobies and sleepers have fry too small even for rotifers; a HUFA-enriched powdered dry food might be effective. The pelagic stage lasts days to weeks. Upon settling out of the plankton, the larvae are difficult to see among the gravel and rocks. Keep feeding baby brine shrimp on faith, and you'll eventually be rewarded when the cryptic young make themselves visible. Hovering sleepers metamorphose at a very large size (about an inch), and take up their off-bottom habit right away. Hovering sleepers are elongate and resemble food to many other kinds of fish; they should never be kept with larger predators.

species of fish. Bottom-living gobies and sleepers are solitary or occur in pairs throughout suitable habitat. The firefish and related sleepers (*Nemateleotris, Oxymetopon, Parioglossus*, and *Ptereleotris*) are planktivorous and hover in the water column, but retreat to a home crevice, burrow, or cave when threatened. Hovering sleepers often form dense aggregations, a common defense strategy of planktivorous fishes.

The neon goby (*Gobiosoma oceanops*) and its relatives are produced commercially. Green, blue-spotted, and yellow *Gobiodon citrinellus*, *G. histrio*, and *G. rivulatus* are small, stubby fish that typically live outside crevices but spawn inside. Many gobies are new in the reef hobby, including the yellow *Quisquilius* from Hawaii, *Ctenogobius* with rusty spots, and the colorfully spotted *Oplopomus* of the Philippines.

Grammatidae and Pseudochromidae

The Atlantic grammas and Indo-Pacific dottybacks are small (2–4-inch), colorful fishes that feed on large zooplankton, small crustaceans, and minute fishes. In aquariums, they'll take brine shrimp, bloodworms, blackworms, finely ground shellfish meats, and baby guppies and mollies. Protogynous hermaphrodites, any two will develop

Gramma melacara *is the deepwater blackcap basslet of the Atlantic.*

into a pair if you start with very small specimens and lots of room. Grammas and dottybacks require a cave, PVC tube, or hollow shell for a refuge. Harmless to corals and large shrimps, they are vulnerable to large piscivores.

Grammas are a small group, but the dottybacks consist of many species. Some dottybacks are sexually dichromic, and colors of some species differ among regions. Most are exceptionally aggressive to conspecifics irrespective of sex, and may even kill one another. Several introduced at one time may adapt as they divide territories. Grammas are sexually monochromic but populations differ in coloration, and they are more sociable than dottybacks.

Dottybacks and grammas spawn in PVC tubes or shells in the aquarium. Male grammas may guard unattached eggs of different ages from more than one spawn; dottybacks may do likewise with egg clusters or balls. Eggs can be removed for aeration and hatching in the dark, but hatches are better when the male tends them. The eggs hatch just after dark within a week. The phototropic fry accept rotifers as a first food, but grow better if the food is supplemented with fatty acids. Exceptionally good water quality is critical to survival of the newly hatched fry.

Clinidae, Blenniidae, and Pholidichthyidae

Almost identical to the untrained eye, the clinids, blennies, and engineer fish are elongate bottom-dwellers of vegetated coral rubble, soft sediments near reefs, rocks, or wooden breakwaters. They are tropical and temperate, marine and estuarine, in the Atlantic and throughout the Indo-Pacific. Most graze constantly on macroalgae, but in captivity will rush out to take a treat of brine shrimp or bloodworms. Rarely do they bother decorative shrimp, and they

The bicolor dottyback, Pseudochromis paccagnellae, *is among the most territorial of dottybacks.*

are harmless to corals. Common in the marine hobby are engineer fish (*Pholidichthys*), rockhoppers (*Atrosalarius*), bicolor blennies (*Escenius*), and canary blennies (*Meiacanthus*). Many are spectacularly colorful (*Runula, Aspidontus*), and still others are constantly being introduced to the hobby. They commonly lay eggs in PVC tubes, shells, or burrows in the gravel, and the fry are big enough to take rotifers. The engineer fish has enormous eggs, and large fry capable of taking brine shrimp as first food. J.R. Shute has observed one of a large pair carrying a mass of eggs in its mouth, and I have found a mass of eggs under an undergravel filter plate.

Tripterygiidae and Callionymidae

Triplefins are small, gobylike fish. Only three species occur in U.S. waters, all in the Atlantic, yet triplefins are one of the dominant families in the tropical Indo-Pacific. Most are nearshore fish of rocky

Pterosynchiropis splendidus, *the mandarin fish, is a dragonet of the Callionymidae. It will breed in a reef tank.*

pools, breakwaters, and nearshore coral reefs. The spiny dorsal fin is divided into a forward area of a few long spines and a rear area of many spines. The soft rays are situated in yet a third area to the rear, hence the common name. Dragonets are similar, again with just three species in U.S. waters in the Atlantic, but far more in the Indo-Pacific. The only common species of these two families in reef aquariums are *Synchiropus* (=*Pterosynchiropus*) *splen-*

Synchiropus picturatus, *the false mandarin, is a Callionymid or dragonet that will breed in captivity.*

didus (mandarin) and *S. picturatus* (spotted mandarin). Related species are *S. calauropomus, S. lineolatus, S. ocellatus*, and *Pogonemus pogognathus*. The largest genus is *Callionymus*. Mandarins breed in shells or caves in reef aquariums, and a few fry can be raised on rotifers or live sifted plankton, but not easily. Mandarins are very sensitive to water quality and do not do well in small aquariums.

Apogonidae

Cardinalfish are advanced perciform fish found in all the warm seas of the world, reaching their greatest diversity in the Indo-Pacific. They occur at all depths, some in tide pools or estuaries, and there are even freshwater species. All are mouthbrooders, producing large young that will accept brine shrimp nauplii as a first food. Most cardinalfish are bright scarlet; some are pink or silvery. A spectacular silver and black scalare-like apogonid with young the size of baby mollies was discovered by Gerald Allen just a few years ago at Banggai in the central Indo-Pacific. It is already in the hobby, and easily bred by aquarists. Apogonids in general are catholic feeders that take just about any live, dried, or fresh meat. Giant parasitic isopods in the mouth, gill chambers, chin, or head of wild fish are readily removed with tweezers.

Apogonids avoid light and prefer caves, cracks, and other enclosed areas, including holes beneath rocks. Their large and cavernous mouths use current to wash food inside, and they'll take everything from plankters to moderately large chunks of meat. The conchfish, *Astrapogon stellatus*, lives inside the mantle cavity of the queen conch, *Strombus gigas*. *Phaeoptyx xenus*, the sponge cardinalfish, lives inside sponges of the genera *Verongia* and *Callyspongia*. Common in the hobby is *Sphaeramia orbicularis*, a social form.

Wood's siphon-fish, *Siphamia cephalotes*, occurs in low-salinity estuaries, an ecological equivalent of a stickleback. *Mionurus bombonensis* lives in Lake Taal (Bombon Lagoon) in the Philippines.

Spawning follows side-by-side trembling. The female lays 30 or more eggs up to 4.5 millimeters in diameter in a single mass connected by threads or enclosed in a sac, and the eggs are picked up by the male for brooding. In *Sphaeramia*, the eggs are smaller than a millimeter in diameter, but number 6,000 to over 11,000. In the Banggai cardinalfish, spawns number 15–40 eggs and the molly-sized young aggregate loosely in midwater, resembling a school of young freshwater angelfish.

In nature, cardinalfish breed twice a month, usually during high tide. In captivity, they may spawn repeatedly and within days of releasing the last brood. Brooding fish should be isolated and undisturbed, without outside filtration. The large fry do well on newly hatched brine shrimp nauplii cleaned of shells and other debris. Premature releases of yolk-sac larvae are common. These premature fry rest on the bottom until the yolk is resorbed and the fish are able to swim up into the water column. Dealers receiving cardinalfish in bags should check each bag for fish with swollen jaws, released eggs (they're too large to miss), or fry.

Plesiopidae

In nature, most plesiopids attach adhesive eggs to the floor of a cave. The comet "grouper" or marine "betta" *Calloplesiops altivelis* is a popular, spectacular reef-tank fish of modest temperament, unusual resistance to disease, and an omnivorous appetite that threatens only the smallest of decorative shrimps. Because plesiopids are expensive, few aquarists keep more than one. That's too bad, because

The Banggai cardinalfish, Pterapogon kauderni, *comes from the Banggai Islands off Sulawesi in Indonesia. It breeds readily and the fry are as easy to raise as mollies or guppies.*

they are peaceful and have even spawned in aquariums.

The genus *Assessor* contains three beautiful species (*flavissimus, meleagris, macneilli*) now known to be mouthbrooders. They are among the most appealing, durable, and peaceful of fish for the mini-reef aquarium.

Other plesiopid genera include *Plesiops* (longfins), *Belonepterygion* (spiny basslets), and *Trachinops* (hulafish).

Antennariidae

The frogfish are a large family of anglerfish found in all the warm seas of the world. These baglike, soft-bodied, seemingly cumbersome predators motionlessly await passing prey, or slowly stalk it. Equipped with a fishing lure on the end of a stalk on the snout, their taxonomy is partly based on the structure of the rod-and-lure structure called an illicium. The lure, if fleshy and enlarged, is called an esca. Different species have one or two illisciums, with or without escas.

Abundant in sargassum weed, Histrio histrio *will breed in captivity if fed enough live food to keep it from consuming its mate.*

There are 23 species of *Antennarius. Histrio, Kuiterichthys, Allenichthys, Lophiocharon, Nudiantennarius, Echino-phryne, Trichophryne, Histiophryne, Phyl-lophryne, Tathicarpus,* and *Rhycherus* have usually just one, at most two, species each.

Predators all, antennariids feed on crabs, shrimps, other invertebrates, and

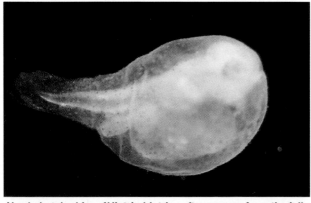

Newly-hatched fry of Histrio histrio, *after escape from the jelly mass of eggs, looks like a white tadpole in a clear vessel.*

fishes, including other antennariids. A stalking frogfish resembles a cat creeping up on a bird, the pectoral fins used as hands to pull the fish along. They use these little "hands" to push away and even to "brush" a partially engulfed meal in the same way a toad or frog brushes its food to align it for swallowing. Feed all frogfish with live minnows, guppies, or mollies, or a strip of cut fish on a thin rod. Frogfish will eat all the other fishes and motile invertebrates in the tank, even up to their own size.

As spawning time approaches, the female swells enormously and changes color, breathing with apparent difficulty. The male turns darker and mouths the vent of the female. They lumber about the bottom for a time, then suddenly dart upward, simultaneously expelling sperm and (usually) an egg raft. The female loses balance and tumbles down, but will recover and feed the next day. The male recovers right away.

Histrio contains only the sargassumfish, *Histrio histrio*, the only antennariid that lives in floating sargassum weed. Since the sargassumfish creeps up on its prey, a wiggling esca is not necessary. The eggs are in a huge, jellylike egg raft or scroll rolled up at the ends. I've found sargassumfish babies in plankton samples. They don't look like other baby fish, and not even like many baby *Antennarius.* Those babies have bony plates on the head and were once thought to be a distinct genus (*Kanazawichthys*), but *Histrio* babies look like white tadpoles inside clear balloons.

Antennarius commersoni, instead of shedding an egg raft with a huge number of eggs, produces a few eggs with tiny looping filaments that hook to the skin thorns or to other eggs, the entire mass a brightly conspicuous egg cluster on the flanks of the mother. It's been suggested that piggy-backing the eggs in this way serves the dual purpose of protecting the eggs from predators and attracting prey to mama. *Lophiocharon* and *Histiophryne* also brood eggs on the body or in the angle of the pectoral fin.

Related anglerfish families from abyssal depths may be so modified as to have the male reduced to little more than a parasitic gonadal sac.

Serranidae

And the great fish swallowed Jonah... If you thought that Jonah was a pip to be expectorated by a finicky whale, think again. Biologists, who know about such things, assure us that Jonah was slurped up and spat out by a grouper, a member of the Family Serranidae. Bohlke and Chaplin, in Fishes of the Bahamas, mention an Indo-Pacific grouper that attains twelve feet and a thousand pounds, claiming that this is "the fish responsible for the stories of divers being swallowed alive by giant groupers." J.L.B. Smith concurred, noting that *Promicrops lanceolatus* was reputed to "attack men in the water" (Smith's Sea Fishes). (But was Jonah in the Indian Ocean, the Pacific, the Mediterranean or the Atlantic?) Another great grouper, occurring in the North Atlantic (including the American coast), Mediterranean, and around New Zealand is *Polyprion americanus*, which, at a top size of only seven feet, is puny compared to its Pacific cousin. But does anyone know how big Jonah was?

The 380 serranid species are divided into subfamilies Serraninae, Epinephelinae, Anthiinae, Liopropominae, and a couple of smaller groups. In many ways they're weird.

Take sex. In the Serraninae and Epinephelinae, the average fish begins life as a female, but what you see is not what you get. These fish are protogynous hermaphrodites. Our young female will produce eggs until three to twelve years old, depending on

All of the hamlets (Hypoplectrus) are given different names but may be of the same species. These small groupers are good choices for breeding.

species. Then she undergoes a sex change, turning into a male. A few serranids (*Hypoplectrus, Serranus*) are simultaneous hermaphrodites.

Most groupers gulp down crabs, shrimp, and small fishes. At one time it was believed that groupers fed on small fare, their enormous open maws creating a suction no planktonic prey could resist. Today we know that groupers also use those big mouths to eat big prey animals. Like Jonah.

In the Indo-Pacific region, the Epinephelinae contains *Centrogenys, Cromileptes, Anperodon, Plectropoma, Variola, Aethaloperca, Aulacocephalus, Promicrops, Pogonoperca, Dermatolepis*, and *Ypsigramma*, each with just one or two species. The big genera in the Indian and Pacific Oceans are *Epinephelus* (31 species) and *Cephalopholis* (12 species), not including the species occurring along the Pacific coast of South America or those of the Red Sea.

Epinephelus akaara, E. awoara, E. bleekeri, E. areolatus, E. fuscoguttatus, E. malabaricus, E. polyphekadion, E. coioides,

The western Atlantic coney (Epinephelus fulvus) is a grouper rarely exceeding a foot in length, making it an ideal candidate for breeding.

Epinepheline grouper larvae have distinctive spines. Because many are collected and then raised for the food fish market, they are excellent choices for aquaculture.

E. tauvina, Cromileptus altivelis, Plectropomus leopardus, P. areolatus, and *P. pessuliferus* are all collected in the Indo-Pacific region for the Asian food fish market (mostly Hong Kong, mainland China, and Japan). The bulk of the collecting effort is in the Indonesia-Philippines region, and much of that by cyanide. A lesser effort is expended in the western Pacific, where other forms of fishing predominate. Juveniles of some species (*Cromileptus,* polka-dot grouper) are also provided to the aquarium market.

E. coioides and *E. malabaricus* (epinephalines with giant larvae) have been aquacultured. Typically, the juveniles are collected by fishermen inshore, where the juveniles are attracted to palm fronds placed in shallows. Juvenile groupers can also be found inshore in mid-Atlantic estuaries, where they aggregate wherever sargassum weed grows attached to the bottom.

Small groupers do well in reef tanks with large tangs, but may eat any other fish up to half their size, and particularly relish shrimp and crabs. Small groupers, harmless to corals and other sedentary invertebrates, should be fed live goldfish, guppies, minnows, and mollies.

Labridae

The wrasses are among the most abundant species of reef fishes. The variety of wrasses on any reef is explained by assuming that each type is specialized to feed on certain benthic invertebrates (resource partitioning), a specialization that breaks down in the absence of competition (as in an aquarium). Diverse color phases occur in juveniles, females, males, and supermales of many species. Most wrasses in a population practice group spawning (many males and many females). In wrasse species that have supermales (e.g., the Atlantic bluehead wrasse), one supermale may spawn with one female.

Except for the hogfish, which was spawned in captivity in a laboratory by manipulating day length, wrasses have not been targeted by breeders, in part because they are inexpensive and in part because most of them need very deep tanks for their upward spawning rush through the water column.

Many wrasses sleep under the gravel at night and are good gravel mixers. The flasher wrasses, *Pericheilinus*, are excellent and popular reef-tank fishes. Others that are harmless to corals when young and under four inches long include *Pseudocheilinus*, *Halichoeres* and *Coris*, although they may go after decorative shrimp. *Anampses* are cleaners that pick parasites off other fishes, but might pick at worms and corals.

Many wrasses, popular in marine fish aquariums, are unsafe in reef tanks at any size because of their catholic feeding habits or preferences for corals. These include *Gomphosis* (bird wrasse), *Lienardella*, *Cheilinus*, *Thalassoma*, *Novaculichthys* (dragon wrasse) and *Hemipteronotus* (razorfish). In general, if you see a wrasse in a dealer's coral show tank, it is probably safe for your minireef.

Cirrhitidae

The hawkfish are a small group (35 species) of coral reef ambush predators related to the scorpionfish, but differ in lacking a bone across the cheek. Within species colors vary by habitat rather than sex.

Genera include *Cirrhitus, Cirrhitichthys, Gymnocirrhites, Paracirrhites, Cyprinocirrhites, Cirrhitoidea,* and *Amblycirrhitus. Amblycirrhitus pinos* (red-spotted hawkfish) is common on corals in Florida and the Caribbean. *Paracirrhites arcatus* (arc-eye hawkfish) is widespread in the Indo-Pacific on branches of *Pocillopora meandrina*.

One or a pair of hawkfish will take up station among hard corals to quietly await

Neocirrhites ornatus, *like other hawkfish, are ambush predators peaceful with fishes their own size, but not to be trusted with small shrimp.*

mobile small invertebrates inching to within strike range. Hawkfish eat amphipods and isopods and help control predaceous polychaetes. Adapting quickly to frozen brine shrimp and edible shrimp, hawkfish thrive in reef aquariums but cannot be kept with decorative shrimp.

Cirrhitichthrus falco *is a hawkfish with the ambush predatory habits shared by its group.*

Breeding Reef Fishes

The variety of breeding modes in marine fishes is less than in freshwater fishes, because the habitats are so less varied. Oceanic habitats do not have, for example, areas so quiet or dry as to accommodate bubble nesting or burial of eggs for three or six months. Marine fish breed in surprisingly few ways.

Most reef fishes (tangs, parrotfish, angelfish, wrasses, butterflyfish, snappers, groupers) release floating eggs and sperm high in the water column during a spiraling spawning rush from the bottom to the surface. The eggs are small and numerous, the newly hatched prolarvae incapable of feeding for some days.

Drifting eggs are harvested by placing a fine net over the prefilter or outlet from the tank to the sump, and are then incubated in large containers of high-quality water with gentle aeration. Upon mouth development, the fry are reared on rotifers or sifted wild plankton as a first food, followed by brine shrimp nauplii. This method has been successful with hogfish wrasses, *Pomacanthus* angelfish, jackknife, hi-hat, and spotted drums, porkfish porgies, and cometfish groupers. The fry of *Centropyge* pygmy angelfish have been observed to eat rotifers and copepod nauplii for up to a week, but to date have not been raised.

There are two other principal means of breeding these egg-scattering species. The first is to breed them in bare aquariums, removing the adults after spawning and raising the eggs and fry in situ. The second is gently squeezing ripe adult fish to get eggs and sperm, mixing the gametes, and incubating the zygotes and subsequent larvae in bare containers. The first method has been used with dolphin in a public aquarium and hogfish in small aquariums in Texas, but should work with tangs, Moorish idols, and other herbivores, and with *Cen-tropyge* angelfish. The second method (stripping) has been used to produce young of French and black angelfish and their hybrids, groupers, and many other fishes.

Many others (damsels, gobies, clingfish, grammistids, trypterygiids) are benthic spawners, the eggs attached by adhesive filaments to a hard surface, usually a cave, but sometimes in the open. The eggs may be small and numerous, releasing nonfeeding prolarvae that hatch in a day or two, or the eggs may be large and less numerous, developing over a week or more into advanced larvae capable of feeding almost at once. Pit spawning in gravel is used by triggerfish.

Eggs of benthic spawners have been harvested for hatching in a separate container, or have been allowed to hatch in the breeding aquarium and afterward transferred to a rearing tank. These methods are effective on clownfish and other damsels, skilletfish, clingfish, basslets, dottybacks, grammas, gobies, and callionymiids (mandarin fish). The basslets, dottybacks, and grammas breed almost daily, so the eggs within a nest are of varying ages and require selective removal of those ready for hatching.

A minor form of breeding is mouthbrooding of the fertilized eggs found in the jawfish and apogonids, among others. The eggs are often abundant and small, hatching into prolarvae, but in some species the eggs are large and the fry advanced.

An uncommon breeding mode among reef fishes is live-bearing, but it is quite common otherwise, occurring in almost all elasmobranchs, and among bony fishes in the surfperch, pipefish, and cusk-eels.

Extrusion of a gelatinous egg mass occurs in the popular antennariids or frogfish, and other types of capsules covering the egg mass occur in cardinalfish (Apogonidae) and at least one tilefish (Malacanthidae).

For most marine fish breeding, several principles of care can increase success. Foremost is culturing microalgae and marine rotifers before they are needed, so the skills for production are established in time. Brine shrimp nauplii are suitable first foods for pipefish, but few other species. I have raised a very few clownfish on brine shrimp alone, but my success rate skyrocketed after shifting to rotifers. Both culture and wild collection of copepods also yield a high success rate, but few workers outside of hatcheries, government laboratories, and universities use copepods because they require sifting through Nitex or other fine screening to select the smallest nauplii. Microscopic examination of wild copepods is required to prevent introduction of minute animals that might attack larval fishes.

Refrigerated, concentrated microalgae are useful for feeding rotifers in an emergency, as is yeast suspension (never dry yeast). Powdered flake foods and artificial-plankton-rotifer (APR) have worked for non-aquarium commercial fishery species, but have not worked on reef fish to date. A new refrigerated microparticle product, Larva "Z" Plus, has been used to grow clownfish and edible shrimp in aquaculture farms, but is little known in the aquarium hobby. Both powdered and liquid suspensions can induce bacterial blooms that degrade water quality and kill fry and should be used cautiously, with regular massive water changes between the frequent feedings (more than four times per day).

HUFA

Copepods are the most important larval food in the ocean, primarily because of their high concentration of highly unsaturated omega 3 fatty acids (HUFA). We can collect or culture copepods, but they are difficult to keep on hand in adequate quantity. Good substitutes are rotifers or brine shrimp enriched with synthetic preparations of HUFA.

Artemia nauplii or rotifers enriched with HUFA have greatly increased nutritive value. Commercial preparations (Selco, Super Selco, Selcon) are available from Florida Aqua-Farms and other companies advertising in hobby magazines. The thick pink liquid must be stored in the dark under refrigeration. When the liquid smells rancid, it has oxidized and should be discarded. I add a few drops of HUFA to a gallon jar with brine shrimp nauplii or with rotifers (with vigorous aeration) for a 6–12 hour period of HUFA uptake, then filter out the organisms before feeding them to my larval fish and shrimp.

You can prepare your own HUFA-rich additive by blending menhaden oil, anchovy oil, or cod liver oil with lecithin. These fish oils contain two essential HUFAs, DHA with 20 carbons and five double bonds and EPA with 22 carbons and six double bonds. Cod liver oil is available from pharmacies, anchovy oil from oriental groceries. Menhaden oil is sold in farm supply stores as a poultry feed additive.

Lecithin, a phospholipid powder available at pharmacies, should be dissolved in water, and added drop-by-drop to fish oil in an electric blender until the mixture emulsifies. Before feeding to brine shrimp or rotifers, the emulsion must be broken into microparticles by swirling into absolutely clean seawater in an electric blender. The rotifers or brine shrimp are filtered out of their ordinary culture water, added to the seawater-emulsion mix, and aerated for twelve hours. During this period, the brine shrimp or rotifers feed on the HUFA-enriched food and become little HUFA packages themselves. After twelve hours the rotifers or brine shrimp are filtered out of the suspension and fed to larval fish and shrimp. The wastewater, now a bacterial soup, is discarded.

HUFA at 2 percent by weight is the minimal concentration required for effectiveness; it is commercially available in some dry larval food preparations at 5 percent by weight. Lecithin is used as an emulsifier in making up HUFA-enriched food, but probably has important nutritional benefits itself.

Rotifers

Rotifers are multicellular animals often no larger than protozoa. *Brachionus plicatilus* is commonly cultured as live food for marine fishes and invertebrates. A healthy culture consists of diploid females parthenogenetically producing amictic (unfertilizable) thin-walled eggs that quickly hatch into more diploid females. A deterioration in the environment triggers production of thin-walled mictic (fertilizable) haploid eggs. If the mictic eggs are not fertilized, they hatch into short-lived haploid males. Those males that mate then induce the females to produce thick-walled dormant or resting eggs. These dormant eggs sink to the bottom where they resist pollution and desiccation for days or even years, awaiting another environmental cue, which triggers them to hatch into young parthenogenetic diploid females.

Rotifers are cultured by feeding them motile unicellular microalgae, often in mixed cultures, because unicultures have limited nutritive value. Highly unsaturated fatty acids (HUFA) can be added to the cultures 12 hours before feeding to larvae, but HUFA also stimulates bacterial growth and must be handled with caution.

Green algae (*Dunaliella, Chlorella, Tetraselmus*), golden brown algae (*Isochrysis, Cricosphaera, Monochrysis*), diatoms (*Skeletonema, Phaeodactylum, Thalassiosira, Lauderia, Nitzschia, Navicula, Biddulphia, Rhizosolenia, Coscinodiscus*), and dinoflagellates (*Prorocentrum, Prorocent-*

rum) are grown in 7 tablespoons of marine salt per gallon of tap water with 2 ml/gal of Guillard's F/2 algal fertilizer. The algal cultures are aerated and illuminated with cool white fluorescent light from the top and sides, 24 hours a day. The cultures are subcultured into clean water to produce new algal cultures, and the old, dark green cultures poured into the rotifer container to maintain the rotifers in a light green medium.

The rotifers, also cultured at 7 tablespoons of salt per gallon, appear as fine white specks throughout the aerated container, concentrating at the surface if the air is turned off. *Brachionus* is tolerant of a wide range of salinities up to full strength seawater, but is grown best in brackish water. Rotifers excrete ammonia, and the culture water should not be poured into the larval fish or invertebrate aquarium, because the ammonia may kill sensitive larvae. The chemical stabilizer EDTA is a component of Guillard's F/2 solution, and it is toxic to shrimp larvae at even low concentrations.

Discarding culture water, you should screen the rotifers through a plastic coffee filter, and feed the filtrate to the larvae with a baster. Should the rotifer culture fail, do not discard; the vessel probably contains dormant eggs. Pour off most of the water, and refill with new algal culture water. To store dormant eggs, keep them dark, in full strength seawater, or in the refrigerator. Rotifer cultures, Guillard's fertilizer, HUFA, and instruction manuals can be purchased from Florida Aqua Farms, 5532 Old St. Joe Road, Dade City, FL 33525, or Carolina Biological Supply Company, 2700 York Road, Burlington, NC 27215.

Trochophores

Trochophore larvae are produced by many molluscs, and, because of their small size and movement that is different from rotifers may be useful as a first food for marine fish and crustaceans. A Canadian company sells live trochophore larvae from the Pacific oyster (*Crassostrea gigas*), frozen in liquid nitrogen. When thawed, the larvae resume movement and are used to feed baby marine fishes too small to eat rotifers. Trocohophore larvae do best in laboratory freezers capable of handling liquid nitrogen, as found in a university or hospital. Overall costs of purchase, shipping, and handling preclude ordinary home use. Trochophores may have future use for growing marine angelfish larvae at commercial and research facilities, but no results are yet available.

Copepods

Copepods are the largest component of marine zooplankton, often highly nutritious because of storage of a fat, oil, or wax bodies rich in calories and essential fatty acids. Some copepods swim and others live on or below hard surfaces. Different species feed on phytoplankton, other zooplankton, detritus, and even small fish. Most copepods release free-floating eggs, while others brood. The earliest larvae of copepods are nauplii, followed by immature copepodites, and finally the sexually active adult. The three most common free-living copepods are the mostly benthic harpacticoids, the mostly planktonic calanoids, and the ubiquitous cyclopoids. Only a few species are mass-cultured; starter cultures are often available from coastal universities and fishery laboratories, biological supply houses, and other aquarists. Copepod starter cultures can also be collected from tide pools, or from clownfish tanks after dark. The procedures are the same for the harpacticoids *Tigriopus, Scottolana*, and *Euterpina*. Provide a 10–20 gallon tank with full-strength seawater, a day-night cycle (dark is important for hatching in some species), and the same microalgae used

for rotifers, supplemented with powdered flake food. Aeration keeps the nauplii from adhering to the surface film and aids dispersion of food and waste products. Copepod adults are maintained inside screened containers (plastic milk jugs with the bottom cut out and replaced with 50–60 µ mesh Nitex) through which the nauplii can escape. The nauplii are then harvested as food for larval fish and invertebrates; sweep the nauplii with a 30 µ mesh net or concentrate them at the surface by turning off the aeration. Alternatively, with several 10-gallon aquariums operating, the adult copepods can be swept from the tank with large mesh temporarily, and replaced after harvest of the immatures left behind.

Infusoria

Some marine fish larvae do not take rotifers because they are too large or their movements do not provide visual stimuli. *Centropyge* has been known to take rotifers for about a week but then die, perhaps from a nutritional deficiency. A few mandarin and damselfish fry have been raised with infusoria cultures, and the technique may be applicable to other species. The culture is prepared by collecting wild *Ulva* from the shore and placing it in an aerated bucket of seawater exposed to sunlight. Slow decomposition over a period of weeks yields a variety of copepods and protozoa. Turning off the air causes the minute invertebrates to swarm at the surface, where they are harvested with a plastic coffee filter or food baster. It is likely that the fish larvae that survived were attracted to copepod nauplii, the most common food for fish larvae in the sea.

Note: If fry are to be removed from the spawning aquarium, they should be moved in ladles or clear cups, never by baster or eyedropper. Apparently normal swimming

Dozens of "watchman" gobies, named for their habit of peering out of a burrow, will share quarters with snapping shrimp and even breed in a reef tank.

after baster transfer can be misleading; lethal damage may take hours or days to manifest itself.

Rearing the early-stage larvae in tanks with black sides and bottom is best. Newly hatched larvae not yet able to feed may be inhibited, damaged, or killed by bright light. Even fluorescent light can cause radiation injury or repel larvae. Keep the fry under very dim light for at least the first week of feeding.

Gentle aeration of the fry tank is important to avoid anoxic areas and keep food in suspension. Water quality is maintained by daily partial water changes, preferably by siphoning the bottom. Strong currents interfere with the tendency of plankters (rotifers, brine shrimp) to aggregate in a small area, and with the ability of fry to locate and seize them.

Marine fish larvae grow faster and have higher survival rates if their food is enriched with HUFA. For fastest growth, wean the larvae onto powdered nutritious dry foods just before metamorphosis, and make certain their diet is about 50 percent protein.

Large fry that pass the entire larval stage within the egg, such as Banggai cardinalfish, can take brine shrimp nauplii at once and are as easy to raise as cichlids or live-bearers.

Capture large juveniles for transfer to a grow-out tank using clear plastic or glass jars or cups, and never nets. Netted clownfish juveniles go into shock, body and gill plates rigid, and almost all will die of respiratory failure because the gills do not ventilate. Do not chase the juveniles, but move the cup slowly until the fish swim inside, then lift slowly. Before tipping the cup contents into the grow-out tank, the cup should be floated in the new tank for about 30 minutes to provide temperature equilibration and visual adaptation.

Chapter Twenty-three
Diseases of Fishes

Pet shop books on fish diseases are generally far behind veterinary medicine. Textbooks such as Noga's Fish Disease, Diagnosis and Treatment are more reliable. A few general principles of fish diseases will be covered here. Every marine aquarist should own and regularly consult a fish disease veterinary textbook to aid in making diagnoses and determining the best treatments.

Environmental Stressors

Improper diet and poor water quality frequently cause lowered resistance to environmental and infectious diseases. In nature, fish do not eat soybean-based pellets and flakes and should not receive those foods in captivity. The most nutritious vegetation for herbivores and omnivores is a substantial growth of macroalgae and some filamentous algae. An acceptable substitute for marine macroalgae is slightly cooked spinach or dark green leafy lettuce (not iceberg). Depriving the aquarium of all vegetation will surely induce vitamin deficiency in the fishes. Omnivores and carnivores need a diverse diet that includes worms, crustaceans, fish, and molluscs. Fresh meats are available at supermarkets, and can be fed as frozen scrapings or thawed blends prepared in a food processor. All prepared foods should contain edible shrimp (with the shell) and fish meat, fish gonads (both testes and ovary), and mollusc. The softest molluscs are mussels, readily incorporated into a blend or fed raw by breaking the shell and washing away excess juices. Squid meat is very tough, but entrails (including gonads) are soft and nutritionally rich.

Other valuable foods are frozen bloodworms and adult brine shrimp, and live brine shrimp nauplii, daphniae, mosquito larvae, whiteworms, blackworms, and red tubifex. I cannot overemphasize the importance in the diet of a variety of arthropod shells (proteinaceous and chitinous).

Foods to avoid:
- all liquid and suspension supplements
- flakes
- pellets
- all freeze-dried preparations
- mammalian and bird liver
- beef heart

All can pollute the aquarium and induce bacterial blooms, and the indigestible connective tissue in liver and heart can cause intestinal blockage.

Infectious Diseases

Fish suffering stress have depressed immune systems, allowing even mildly pathogenic bacteria to multiply faster than the leucocytes (white cells) and available antibodies can clear the pathogens from blood and tissues. Fish to be treated with any medication should be removed to a bare hospital aquarium with aeration but not carbon filtration, which adsorbs medicaments.

Bacterial Diseases

Suspect a bacterial infection when there are no white spots on the body and water quality appears normal, yet fish demonstrate bloating, listlessness, abnormal orientation, failure to feed, difficulty in swimming, rapid breathing, reduced mobility of the mouth, loss of color, or stiffly erect fins. Bacterial infections often get started through damaged gills or intestine, or via a wound to the skin. Infections often occur after a fish has been stressed by very low or very high temperature, very low pH, ammonia, or lack of oxygen. The most pathogenic bacteria can attack healthy, unstressed fish.

It is difficult to diagnose an infectious disease without training, access to microscopes, staining procedures, and (for pathogenic bacteria) microbiological culturing equipment. Pet store dealers often consult with a fish-wise veterinarian upon the outbreak of disease; the cost of the visit, diagnosis, and appropriate medication (including prescription drugs not available in pet stores) is typically far less than the eventual losses incurred by failure to treat promptly and properly or, worse, taking action much too late and with the wrong medicament.

Some bacterial infections invade fish through wounds caused by other fishes, or by dashing into sharp objects such as rocks and dead coral skeletons. Wounding by territorial competitors by far is the most common type of skin damage. Ongoing harassment also deprives the fish of security and food, leading to death more often than not. Removing competitors is the best way to correct this risk to fish health. Wounds on large, easily handled fish should also be dabbed with mercurochrome or tincture of iodine.

Antimicrobial Drugs

For bacteria, our arsenal of antimicrobials includes natural antibiotics and synthetic antimicrobials such as the potentiated sulfa drugs and quinolones.

Most of the bacteria infecting marine fishes are Gram-negative curved rods in the genus *Vibrio*. Tetracycline is ineffective on vibrios in seawater because it binds to calcium. Oxolinic acid, nalidixic acid, the synthetic quinolone sarafloxicin, and the potentiated sulfa drug Romet are all effective against some, but not all, vibrios. Treating the water is often useless; the best dose gets inside the fish with food. Some drugs can be taken up by brine shrimp and then, as long as the sick fish is still feeding, delivered at an effective dose. Other drugs, such as oxolinic acid, can be put in flake food to effectively treat bacterial infections in fish. Use flake food only in a hospital tank, not a reef tank.

Another group of pathogens afflicting some marine fish are the acid-fast bacteria (*Mycobacterium*). They cause chronic wasting, with clinical signs of hollow belly, often a bent back, and listlessness, resembling rapid aging. Drug treatment is ineffective,

Several protozoans can produce white spot disease on the skin and gills of marine fishes. Treat with formalin in an isolated hospital tank followed by two weeks of quarantine before returning the recovered fish to a reef tank.

Drug Resistance

Many bacteria are naturally resistant to specific drugs. Gram-positive bacteria, for example, are often unaffected by tetracyclines, while Gram-negative bacteria are unaffected by penicillins and erythromycin. Some bacteria inactivate, block, or fail to take up these drugs, while others excrete it quickly. Some have an alternative pathway for the blocked metabolic product. Some are unaffected by the usual dose, but are susceptible to a higher dose. Most of these attributes are genetically determined. Bacteria with genetic resistance to a drug can become the dominant population when the drug has been given at a low dose, especially over a long time.

The genes for resistance are usually not on the circular bacterial chromosome, but on floating genetic pieces called plasmids. Related bacteria will exchange genes during sexual conjugation. But even unrelated bacteria can transfer mutated genes, conferring drug resistance. One way is by fragmenting at death, the fragments then being absorbed by the unrelated bacteria (transformation). A second way is by transfer of the plasmids by viruses of bacteria (bacteriophages) that incorporate and transmit the drug resistance genes to an unrelated bacterium (transduction) during the next infection.

but the disease is seldom very contagious in aquariums.

Certain antibiotics and antimicrobials sold in the pet industry, such as erythromycin and methylene blue, should not be used in reef tanks. They are ineffective against marine fish diseases, and also kill useful nitrifying bacteria and marine algae. Finally, no drug should be placed directly into a reef tank, as virtually all drugs can result in the death of invertebrates. Drugs should always be applied to the water or the afflicted fish in a bare hospital tank.

Stimulation of the immune system may aid the fish in clearing pathogenic bacteria without medication. The fish's immune system works at the physiological optimum when stress is reduced in the tank with vigorous aeration and with darkness or hiding places (PVC tubes, flower pots).

Important in the immune system of fish and invertebrates are special phagocytic white cells that engulf bacteria and kill them. One particular carbohydrate extracted from yeast, beta 1,3-D glucan, strongly activates white cells. Used as an immersion or a food additive, beta glucan protects larvae and juveniles from bacterial attack, effective at 0.5–1.0 ppt against *Vibrio vulnificus*. An aquaculture product not well known in the pet industry, beta glucan is available from Immustim of Laguna Vista, Texas, tel. 210-943-7189, or from Zeigler Brothers of Gardners, Pennsylvania, tel. 717-677-6181.

Fungal Diseases

Fungal diseases are uncommon in marine fish, usually occurring deep inside internal organs where they remain undetected and untreatable. These diseases should not be a cause of concern to marine aquarists. If you suspect a mycosis (fungus infection), provide specimens for necropsy to a veterinarian familiar with fish diseases, but keep in mind that fungal diseases are essentially untreatable. To prevent contagion, always remove dead or dying fish so that the healthy fish are not able to eat its tissues, a common route for spreading diseases.

Protozoal Diseases

Protozoa are common skin parasites of marine fish. The recommended treatments are heat (to speed up the life cycle of the parasite and enable the drug to hit it at a vulnerable stage) combined with up to 5 drops of formalin per gallon, 0.1 mg/L malachite green, or 0.2 mg/L chelated copper sulfate, always in a hospital tank, and always with a two-week quarantine after all signs of the disease have disappeared.

Parasitic Worms

Parasitic worms include the roundworms (in any internal organs), tapeworms and thorny-headed worms (in the intestine), digenetic trematodes (anywhere in the intestinal tract including blind pockets), and monogenetic trematodes (on the skin or gills). All of these worms usually reside in tropical marine fish without causing much harm except for the monogeneans. Many tropical marine monogeneans can multiply to large numbers capable of damaging gills, skin, and eyes. Monogeneans can sometimes be tentatively diagnosed by lifting the fish's gill cover with a flat toothpick and seeking minute black spots, which are clusters of opaque eggs of these otherwise translucent minute worms. A scraping of gill slime will confirm infection if the worm species can be wiped off. A gill clip may be necessary.

Monogeneans may drop off in response to a freshwater dip (five minutes or until the fish becomes stressed), treatment with 5 drops of formalin per gallon of seawater, or anesthesia (up to 3 drops per gallon of 10 percent quinaldine in absolute alcohol). Some monogeneans are refractory to these drugs. A new treatment, highly effective, is a 1–2 ppm praziquantel bath for 24 hours. Sold under the brand name Droncit, it is available through veterinarians, and is nor-mally used to treat tapeworms in dogs. Intestinal parasites (roundworms, tapeworms, digenetic trematodes, etc.) rarely do as much harm as a treatment, and are best ignored.

Parasitic Crustaceans

The most important parasitic crustaceans are large isopods, small copepods, and fish lice. Large isopods sometimes occur on the throat, head, or in the mouth or gill cavity of marine fish and can be removed with tweezers or forceps. Minute parasitic copepods can overwhelm gills of fish and cause major damage. Copepods respond to dylox or other organophosphates available for treating pond fish infected with anchor worms, which are specialized, giant parasitic copepods. Fish lice are unsightly and cause minor damage, but are easily removed with tweezers.

Noninfectious Diseases

Fish can be sickened by noxious chemicals, high ammonia or nitrite concentrations, cold temperatures, low dissolved oxygen levels, high concentrations of carbon dioxide in the water, and depressed water quality associated with bacterial blooms. Bacterial blooms (not always visible) often follow feedings with liquid or suspension food supplements, which I strongly discourage.

Eroding lateral line pores on the head and flank are usually due to poor water quality, high nitrates, low pH, and/or dietary deficiencies. Swollen bodies may be caused by bacterial infection of the kidneys or gills, or by kidney damage or intestinal blockage.

Cyanide

Cyanide has been used as an anesthetic in fishery studies (Wiley, 1984), but is tricky to use because its anesthetic dose is very close to its lethal dose. Cyanide is widely used in Asia to stun food fish and aquarium fishes for the live restaurant and aquarium markets. Because cyanide is dispensed at target fish with a squirt bottle, the dose is uncontrolled and many fish are killed for the few that recover from anesthesia. Cyanide is even more toxic to invertebrates, for which there is no anesthetic dose. Squirting cyanide over a reef indiscriminately destroys corals and coral reef communities.

Aside from the acute toxicity that causes asphyxiation, the other known pathologic effects of cyanide are associated with long-term, sublethal (chronic) exposure. Chronic exposure from mine drainage and other industrial pollution causes sublethal pathologic changes in liver and gonad. These changes are potentiated (increased) when combined with other stressors such as ammonia, hypoxia, and heavy metals.

In the laboratory, fishes that recover from a single anesthetic (acute) exposure to cyanide appear normal, with no pathologic changes in their tissues. Fish collected with an anesthetic dose of cyanide on reefs also have no visible pathology.

Unexplained delayed deaths are often blamed on cyanide. However, these deaths are more likely caused by various other forms of stress, leading possibly to irreversible, ammonia-induced gill damage, perhaps kidney damage, and/or starvation. Exposure to stress capable of inducing such damage and leading to delayed death might occur in dirty, hot, acidic, hypersaline, unaerated, or ammoniated holding facilities where water is added but never changed. Or severe damage may occur during shipping from overheating on the tarmac, or from oxygen deprivation and carbon dioxide buildup in a bag with too little water and air space. Perhaps the fish was starved between the time it was collected and the time it arrived at a retail store in the United States.

The so-called syndrome (group of clinical signs) of "cyanide poisoning" is said to be heavy feeding with continual wasting away and a mucoid exudate from the gut. An article by D. R. Bellwood in 1981 that discussed epithelial sloughing of the gut seemed to support cyanide as the culprit inducing those signs.

However, mucoid exudates can be caused by any number of intestinal infections or physiological imbalances that interfere with nutrient and water uptake. Voracious feeding is not a sign of any known disease condition. Wasting can be caused by microbial infections (of the gut, blood, or other organs), kidney and gill failure, or nutritional deficiencies.

Subsequently, the 1981 report of cyanide-induced sloughing of intestinal epithelium was recanted when more carefully controlled studies failed to cause the signs reported earlier (Hall and Bellwood, 1995).

A bibliography on cyanide is available for $5 from Ocean Voice International, P.O. Box 37026, 3332 McCarthy Road, Ottawa, ON K1V OWO Canada.

Appendix

Relationships

watts	=	volts × amps
amps	=	volts/watts
1 amp	=	120 watts at 120 volts
30 amp line capacity	=	3,600 watts (30 × 120)
20 amp line capacity	=	2,400 watts (20 × 120)
15 amp line capacity	=	1,800 watts (15 × 120)
1 gallon	=	3.785 L (liter)
	=	3,785 cc (cubic centimeter)
	=	3,785 ml (milliliter)
1 liter	=	1,000 ml
	=	1,000 cc
	=	0.264 gal
	=	35.28 oz (weight)
	=	33.8 fluid oz
	=	2.25 lb
	=	1 kg water
cc	=	ml
drop	=	1/20 ml
ml	=	20 drops
tsp	=	5 ml
tbsp	=	15 ml
fl.oz	=	30 ml
aquarium capacity (gal)	=	L × W × H (inches) /231
(liters)	=	L × W × H (cm) /1,000
(liters to gal)	=	× 0.264
parts per thousand (o/oo or ppt)	=	ml/L (liter)
	=	3.8 ml/gal
	=	3.8 gm/gal
	=	gm/1,000 gms
	=	gm/kilogram (Kg)
	=	gm/2.2 lbs
part per million (ppm)	=	mg/L
	=	3.8 mg/gal
	=	gm/cubic meter of water
	=	ml/1,000 L

1 percent solution	=	38 gm/gal
	=	38 ml/gal
	=	1 oz/3 quarts
	=	1.3 oz/gal
	=	10 gm/L
	=	1 gm/100 ml
	=	10 ml/L
1:1,000 solution	=	1 ml/L
	=	0.1 gm/100 ml
	=	3.8 gm/gal
	=	3.8 ml/gal
	=	0.13 oz/gal
Centigrade or Celsius	=	$(F - 32) \times 5/9$
Fahrenheit	=	$(C \times 9/5) + 32$
Oxygen in ppm x 0.7	=	O_2 in cc/L or ml/L
Oxygen in ml/L or cc/L $\times$ 1.429	=	O_2 in ppm
CO_2 in ppm $\times$ 0.509	=	CO_2 in ml/L or cc/L
CO_2 in cc/L or ml/L $\times$ 1.964	=	CO_2 in ppm

Logarithm to the base 10 prefix terms

billion	10^9	(G)	giga	1,000,000,000
million	10^6	(M)	mega	1,000,000
thousand	10^3	(k)	kilo	1,000
hundred	10^2	(h)	hecto	100
ten	10	(dk)	deka	10
(tenth)	10^{-1}	(d)	deci	0.1
(hundredth)	10^{-2}	(c)	centi	0.01
(thousandth)	10^{-3}	(m)	milli	0.001
(millionth)	10^{-6}	(µ)	micro	0.000001
(billionth)	10^{-9}	(n)	nano	0.000000001
(ten billionth)	10^{-10}	—		0.0000000001

Mixing Solutions

Normal and molar solutions are often expressed in percent because it's simpler to calculate and mix. Aquarists can use percent solutions for all their needs. You will also see the terms w/v, v/v, etc., referring to weight and volume.

A percent solution of a solid in a liquid is grams per 100 ml of liquid, or ten grams per liter (10 gms/L). A 40 percent aqueous salt solution would be 400 gms/L of water or 40 gm/100 ml.

A percent solution of a liquid in a liquid is ml/100 ml or ten ml/L. A 70 percent alcohol solution would be 700 ml of 100 percent alcohol per liter, the balance of the liter container (300 milliliters) made up with water.

100 percent alcohol is expensive, but 95 percent alcohol is cheap. Suppose we want to make up 70 percent alcohol and have lots of cheap 95 percent alcohol on hand. Fill a 1-liter graduated cylinder or graduated flask with 95 percent alcohol to the 700 ml line. Then add water up to the 950 ml line, and presto, you've got 70 percent alcohol. For smaller volumes, use a 100 ml graduate cylinder, fill to the 70 ml line and top off to the 95 ml line with water. Should you need 30 percent alcohol, you can add 95 percent alcohol to the 30 ml mark in a 100 ml graduated cylinder, and top with water to 95 ml. Or, you could fill to the 30 ml mark with 70 percent alcohol and top with water to the 70 ml mark. You can cut any percent solution to a more dilute solution using the same procedure.

Associations

Breeder's Registry
(Journal of Maquaculture)
P.O. Box 255373
Sacramento, CA 95865
breeders@kplace.monrou.com

Coral Reef Alliance
809 Delaware Street
Berkeley, CA 94710
CoralReefA@aol.com

International Center for Living
Aquatic Resource
Management
MCPO Box 2631
0718 Makati M.M.
Philippines
j.mcmanus@cgnet.com

International Coral Reef Initiative,
OES/ETC
Room 4325
2201 C Street NW
Washington, DC 20520
sdrake@state.gov

International Society for Reef
Studies
(Coral Reef, Reef Encounter)
Dr. John Ogden
Florida Institute of Oceanography
830 First Street S
St. Petersburg, FL 33701

Marine Aquarium Societies of
North America
(MACNA Conference)
P.O. Box 508
Penns Park, PA 18943

Periodicals

Aquarium Frontiers
P.O. Box 6050
Mission Viejo, CA 92690

Aquarium Fish Magazine
P.O. Box 6050
Mission Viejo, CA 92690

Journal of Maquaculture
Breeders Registry
P.O. Box 255373
Sacramento, CA 95865
tel. 1-916-487-3752

Makai.
University of Hawaii Sea Grant
College Program
1000 Pope Road
Room 200
Honolulu, HI 96822
tel. 1-808-956-8191

Marine Aquarist. Aquacraft, Inc.
P.O. Box 653
San Carlos, CA 94070
tel. 1-415-637-0322

Marine Fish Monthly
Publishing Concepts Corp.
3243 Highway 61
East, Luttrell, TN 37779
tel. 1-423-992-3892

Sea Grant in the Caribbean
Sea Grant College Program
P.O. Box 5000 UPR-RUM
Mayaguez, PR 00681
tel. 1-809-834-4726

SeaScope
Aquarium Systems, Inc.
8141 Tyler Blvd.
Mentor, OH 44060
tel. 1-800-822-1100

References

Abbott, R.T., and P.A. Morris. 1995. *Shells of the Atlantic and Gulf Coasts and the West Indies.* Peterson Field Guide 3. Houghton Mifflin Company, New York, 350 pp.

Adey, W.H., and K. Loveland. 1991. *Dynamic Aquaria, Building Living Ecosystems.* Academic Press, Inc., San Diego, 643 pp.

Agbayani, N. 1995. Beam sizes for aquarium stands. Freshwater and Marine Aquarium 18(8): 51.

Aho, G., and K. Sabolcik. 1996. Two approaches to building a fluidized bed reactor. Freshwater and Marine Aquarium Magazine 19(7): 128.

Albarado, R. 1990. Water current and the reef aquarium. Freshwater and Marine Aquarium 13(11): 172.

Allen, G.R. 1991. *Damselfishes of the World*. Mergus Publishers, Melle, Germany and Aquarium Systems, Mentor, Ohio, 271 pp.

Allen, G.R. 1996. The king of the cardinalfishes. Tropical Fish Hobbyist 44(9): 32.

Anderson, D.M. et al. 1994. Biogeography of toxic dinoflagellates in the genus *Alexandrium* from the northeastern United States and Canada. Marine Biology 120: 467.

Ankley, M. 1996. Jellies: phantoms of the deep. Sea Scope 13 (Spring): 1.

Antonius, A. 1985. Coral diseases in the Indo-Pacific: a first record. P.S.Z.N.I.: Marine Ecology 6(3): 197.

Ates, R. 1991. Fishes eating corals. Freshwater and Marine Aquarium 14(7): 179.

Ates, R. 1992. Cnidaria, or stinging animals. Freshwater and Marine Aquarium 15(4): 32.

Ates, R. 1992. Tube anemones. Freshwater and Marine Aquarium 15(5): 8.

Ates, R. 1992. Fighting tentacles in sea anemones. Freshwater and Marine Aquarium 15(6): 16.

Ates, R.M.L. 1991. Predation on cnidaria by vertebrates other than fishes. Hydrobiologia 216/217: 305.

Bailey, S. et al. 1996. Husbandry of one species of squid in captivity. Freshwater and Marine Aquarium 19(1): 196.

Bailey-Brock, J.H. 1987. The polychaetes of Fanga'uta Lagoon and coral reefs of Tongatapu, Tonga, with discussion of the Serpulidae and Spirorbidae. Biological Society of Washington 7: 280.

Baker, B.J. et al. 1985. Punaglandins: halogenated antitumor eicosanoids from the octocoral *Telesto riisei*. Journal of the American Chemical Society 107: 2976.

Baker, D.E., Jr. 1992. Live rock syndrome, USA. Tropical Fish Hobbyist 40(9): 58.

Bartley, D.M., and C.T. Turk. 1991. Nutrition and feeding in the marine environment. Part VI. Introduction to feeding live corals. Freshwater and Marine Aquarium 14(3): 35.

Bauchot, M.L., and A. Pras. 1980. Guide des Poissons Marins d'Europe. Delachaux & Niestle, Neuchatel, Switzerland, 427 pp.

Belliveau, R.J. 1994. Marine snail frenzy. Freshwater and Marine Aquarium 17(11): 197.

Bellwood, D.R. 1981. Cyanide—an investigation into the long term histological effects of sodium cyanide doses upon the gastrointestinal tract of Dascyllus trimaculatus. Freshwater and Marine Aquarium 4: 31.

Beuret, K., and J.O. Straub. 1992. Reproduction in cuttlefish. Freshwater and Marine Aquarium 15(7): 195.

Bingman, C. 1995. Limewater, Part I. Precipitation of phosphate in limewater and in the aquarium. AF 2(4): 6.

Blanchot, J., and R. Pourriot. 1982. Influence de trois facteurs de l'environnement, lumiere, temperature et salinite, sur l'eclosion des oeufs de duree d'un clone de *Brachionus plicatilis* (O.F. Muller) Rotifere. C.R. Academie des Sciences Paris 295 (3): 243.

Blasiola, G.C. 1996. Treating diseases in mixed-community reef aquariums. Pet Age 25(11): 27.

Bohlke, J.E. and C.C. Chaplin. 1968. *Fishes of the Bahamas and Adjacent Tropical Waters*. Livingston Publishing Co., Wynnewood, PA. 771 pp.

Booth, G. 1996. Nitrate reduction. Aquarium Fish Magazine 8(7): 40.

Bouchard, E.C. et al. 1992. Nitrate contamination of groundwater: sources and potential health effects. Journal American Water Works Association 84(9): 85.

Brockmann, D., and A.J. Nilsen. 1995. A critical comparison of the most commonly used methods for dosing calcium in seawater aquariums. Part 2: CO_2 and the calcium reactor. Aquarium Fish 2(4): 2.

Brons, R. 1996. Reproduction and captive breeding of two Red Sea dottybacks: *Pseudochromis fridmani* and *P. flavivertex*. Freshwater and Marine Aquarium 19(6): 48.

Burgess, W.E. 1996. New triplefins from Taiwan. Tropical Fish Hobbyist 44(8): 46.

Carcasson, R.H. 1977. *A Field Guide to the Coral Reef Fishes of the Indian and West Pacific Oceans*. Collins Publishers, London, 320 p.

Carlson, B.A. 1991. *Tridacna* clams: true giants in their field. Freshwater and Marine Aquarium 14(4): 24.

Carney, J.R. et al. 1992. Napalilactone, a new halogenated norsesquiterpenoid from the soft coral *Lemnalia africana*. Tetrahedron Letters 33(47): 7115.

Cassidy, E. 1995. Denitrification. Freshwater and Marine Aquarium 18(9): 68.

Chang, C.W.J. et al. 1987. Kalihinols, multifunctional diterpenoid antibiotics from marine sponges *Acanthella* spp. Journal of the American Chemical Society 109: 6119.

Chung, A.P.S. 1996. Survival tactic sustains coral-smothering bubble algae. Makai 18(3): 3.

Corley, D.G. et al. 1988. Laulimalides: new potent cytotoxic macrolides from a marine sponge and a nudibranch predator. Journal of Organic Chemistry 53: 3644.

Couch, J.A., and J.W. Fournie, Editors. 1993. Pathobiology of Marine and Estuarine Organisms. CRC Press, Boca Raton, 552 pp.

Couturier-Bhaud, Y. 1974. Cycle biologique de *Lysmata seticaudata* Risso (Crustace, Decapoda). I. Cycle biologique des animaux adultes. Vie Milieu 24(3): 413.

Couturier-Bhaud, Y. 1974. Cycle biologique de *Lysmata seticaudata* Risso (Crustace, Decapoda). II. Sexualite et reproduction. Vie Milieu 24(3): 423.

Couturier-Bhaud, Y. 1974. Cycle biologique de *Lysmata seticaudata* Risso (Crustace, Decapoda). III. Etude du developpement larvaire. Vie Milieu 24(3): 431.

Coval, S.J. et al. 1984. Two new xenicin diterpenoids from the octocoral *Anthelia edmondsi*. Tetrahedron 40(19): 3823.

Danilowicz, B.S. 1996. Choice of coral species by naive and field-caught damselfish. Copeia 1996(3): 735.

Danilowicz, B.S., and C.L. Brown. 1992. Rearing methods for two damselfish species: *Dascyllus albisella* (Gill) and *D. aruanus* (L.). Aquaculture 106: 141–149.

Delbeek, C. 1990. Reef aquariums: filtration. Aquarium Fish Magazine 2(3): 28.

Delbeek, C. 1992. Dutch minireefs: an update. Aquarium Fish Magazine 5(1): 52.

DeMarte, J. 1992. Pier to peer. Freshwater and Marine Aquarium 15(2): 176.

DeMartini, E.E., and T.J. Donaldson. 1996. Color morph-habitat relations in the arc-eye hawkfish *Paracirrhites arcatus*. Copeia 1996(2): 362.

DiGeronimo, A. 1994. Should it be glass or acrylic? Aquarium Fish Magazine 6(11): 52.

DiRoberto, K. 1995. Hydraulic cement for aquascaping. SS 12 (summer): 1.

Dixon, B.A., S.O. van Poucke, M Chair, M. Dehasque, HY.J. Nelis, P. Sorgeloos, and A.P. De Leenheer. 1995. Bioencapsulation of the antibacterial drug sarafloxacin in nauplii of the brine shrimp *Artemia franciscana*. Journal of Aquatic Animal Health 7: 42.

Donovan, P. 1995. A beginner's guide to the nitrogen cycle. Part 1. Ammonia. Freshwater and Marine Aquarium 18(6): 226.

Donovan, P. 1995. A beginner's guide to the nitrogen cycle. Part 2. Nitrite. Freshwater and Marine Aquarium 18(7): 152.

Donovan, P. 1995. A beginner's guide to pH. Freshwater and Marine Aquarium 18(10): 190.

Donovan, P. 1995. A beginner's guide to venomous marine invertebrates. Freshwater and Marine Aquarium 18(11): 160.

Doole, C. 1991. The complete ORP primer. Part 1. Freshwater and Marine Aquarium 14(7): 119.

Doole, C. 1991. The complete ORP primer. Part 2. Freshwater and Marine Aquarium 14(8): 102.

Eaton, A. 1995. Measuring UV-absorbing organics: a standard method. Journal American Water Works Association 87(2): 86.

Edmunds, P.J. 1991. Extent and effect of black-band disease on a Caribbean reef. Coral Reefs 10(3): 161.

Emmons, C.W. 1992. Coral reefs and miniature reefs. Freshwater and Marine Aquarium 15(2): 131.

Epps, J.E. 1994. Ultraviolet sterilization. Freshwater and Marine Aquarium 17(11): 168.

Escobal, P.R. 1991. The time required to sterilize a body of water with an ultraviolet sterilizer. Freshwater and Marine Aquarium 14(2): 46.

Escobal, P.R. 1995. Venturi! Freshwater and Marine Aquarium 18(6): 152.

Fairfield, T.F. 1991. Marine sudden death syndrome: *Vibrio anguillarum*. Freshwater and Marine Aquarium 14(1): 108.

Feddern, H.A. 1990. Live rock for the marine aquarium. Freshwater and Marine Aquarium 13(12): 102.

Feingold, J.S. 1988. Ecological studies of a cyanobacterial infection on the Caribbean sea plume *Pseudopterogorgia acerosa*. J.H. Choat et al., eds. Proc. Sixth International Coral Reef Symposium, Townsville, Australia, vol 3, pp. 157–162.

Fitt, W.K. et al. 1993. Utilization of dissolved inorganic nutrients in growth and mariculture of the tridacnid clam *Tridacna derasa*. Aquaculture 109: 27.

Fitt, W.K. et al. 1993. Recovery of the coral *Montastrea annularis* in the Florida Keys after the 1987 Caribbean "bleaching event." Coral Reefs 12(2): 57.

Fitzhardinge, R.C., and J.H. Bailey-Brock. 1989. Colonization of artificial reef materials by corals and other sessile organisms. Bulletin of Marine Science 44(2): 567.

Flood, A.C. 1992. Better by the bottle. Freshwater and Marine Aquarium 15(7): 166.

Flood, A.C. 1996. The lucious little loreto. Marine Fish Monthly 11(4): 31.

Fox, G.A. 1990. Venomous and potentially dangerous marine animals. Part II. Freshwater and Marine Aquarium 13(1): 82.

Fox, N. 1993. Berline school aquaria. Freshwater and Marine Aquarium 16(1): 8.

Frische, J. 1996. The brown rockhopper. Tropical Fish Hobbyist 44(8): 40.

Gant, W., Jr. 1996. The brine shrimp. Freshwater and Marine Aquarium 19(7): 186.

George, J.D., and J.J. George. 1979. *Marine Life, an Illustrated Enclyclopedia of Invertebrates in the Sea*. John Wiley & Sons, New York, 288 pp.

Giovanetti, T. 1991. The deepwater marine reef aquarium. Aquarium Fish Magazine 3(8): 26.

Giwojna, P. 1991. The acrobatic sex life of the arrow crab. Freshwater and Marine Aquarium 14(9): 190.

Gladstone, W. 1996. Unique annual aggregation of longnose parrotfish (*Hipposcarus harid*) at Farasan Island (Saudi Arabia, Red Sea). Copeia 1996(2): 483.

Gleeson, M.W., and A.E. Strong. 1995. Applying MCSST to coral reef bleaching. Advances in Space Research 16(10): 151.

Glodek, G. 1991. Ammonia in the closed system aquarium. Freshwater and Marine Aquarium 14(6): 22.

Glodek, G. 1992. Coldwater anemones. Part 1. Freshwater and Marine Aquarium 15(5): 32.

Glodek, G. 1993. Autotomy and regeneration in marine invertebrates. Freshwater and Marine Aquarium 16(1): 139.

Glodek, G. 1995. The biology of nudibranchs. Freshwater and Marine Aquarium 18(5): 72.

Glodek, G. 1996. Echinoderms for the cold water aquarium. Freshwater and Marine Aquarium 19(9): 8.

Goemans, B. 1995. Product review: Tsunami wavemaker. Marine Fish Monthly 10(5): 28.

Goemans, B. 1995. Living sand. Freshwater and Marine Aquarium 18(3): 136.

Goemans, B. 1995. Constructing a living sand filter. Freshwater and Marine Aquarium 18(8): 128.

Goemans, B. 1996. A report on MACNA VII. Freshwater and Marine Aquarium 19(1): 129.

Goldstein, R.J. 1990. Tomato clownfish: bred and raised in the home. Aquarium Fish Magazine 3(3): 56.

Goldstein, R.J. 1992. Spectacular serranids. Aquarium Fish Magazine 5(1): 18.

Goldstein, R.J. 1994. Do-it-yourself trickle filter. Aquarium Fish Magazine 6(4): 60.

Goldstein, R.J. 1994. All about powerheads. Aquarium Fish Magazine 6(11): 62.

Goldstein, R.J.1995. Air pumps. Aquarium Fish Magazine 7(14): 64.

Goldstein, R.J. 1996. Water pumps. Aquarium Fish Magazine 8(5): 68.

Gosliner, T.M., D.W. Behrens, and G.C. Williams. 1996. *Coral Reef Animals of the Indo-Pacific*. Sea Challengers, Monterey, CA, 314 pp.

Grigg, R.W. 1988. Recruitment limitation of a deep benthic hard-bottom octocoral population in the Hawaiian Islands. Marine Ecology Progress Series 45: 121.

Gutierrez, S. 1991. From a reef's point of view. Freshwater and Marine Aquarium 14(9): 16.

Guttierez, S., and J. Sprung. 1992. Still more on lighting. Freshwater and Marine Aquarium 15(4): 136.

Guzman, H.M., and J. Cortes. 1984. Mass death of *Gorgonia flabellum* on the Caribbean coast of Costa Rica (in Spanish). Revue Biologia Tropica 32(2): 305.

Hall, K.C., and D.R. Bellwood. 1995. Histological effects of cyanide, stress and starvation on the intestinal mucosa of *Pomacentrus coelestis*, a marine aquarium fish species. Journal of Fish Biology 47: 438.

Hamel, J.F., and A. Mercier. 1996. The secret of the giant clam. Freshwater and Marine Aquarium 19(5): 112.

Haywood, M., and S. Wells. 1989. *The Manual of Marine Invertebrates*. Tetra Press, Morris Plains, NJ, 208 pp.

Headlee, L., L. Read, and M. Barnes. 1996. Super Glue use in live rock culture. Sea Scope 13(Spring): 4.

Hellgren, M. 1996. Giant clams promise to revitalize Pacific island economy. Makai 18(2): 3.

Hemdahl, J.A. 1992. The use of calcium hydroxide to control *Aiptasia* anemones. Freshwater and Marine Aquarium 15(4): 122.

Hoff, F.H. 1996. *Conditioning, spawning and rearing of fish with emphasis on marine clownfish*. Aquaculture Consultants, Dade City, FL, 212 pp.

Hoover, J.P. 1995. Hawaii's wrasses. Freshwater and Marine Aquarium 18(6): 8.

Hovanec, T.A. 1992. Filtration on the march. Aquarium Fish Magazine 4(6): 50.

Hovanec, T.A. 1995. Central aquarium filtration. Aquarium Fish Magazine 7(12): 76.

Hovanec, T.A. 1995. DI or RO? Aquarium Fish Magazine 7(15): 72.

Hovanec, T.A. 1996. Water quality: freshwater. Aquarium Fish Magazine 8(6): 34.

Hovanec, T.A. 1996. Phosphorus explained. Aquarium Fish Magazine 8(7): 12.

Hovanec, T.A., and E. DeLong. 1996. Comparative analysis of nitrifying bacteria associated with freshwater marine aquaria. Applied and Environmental Microbiology 62(8): 2888.

James, D.M. et al. 1993. Metal binding by the trisoxazole portion of the marine natural product dihydrohalichondramide. Heterocycles 35(2): 675.

Jeffries, O.R. 1995. Automatic pH controllers for the aquarium. Freshwater and Marine Aquarium 18(4): 158.

Jeffries, O.R. 1995. Electronic measuring devices for the aquarium. Freshwater and Marine Aquarium 18(12): 203.

Jeong, H.J. 1994. Predation by the hereotrophic dinoflagellate *Protoperidinium* cf. *divergens* on copepod eggs and early naupliar stages. Marine Ecology Progress Series 114: 203.

Johannes, R.E., and M. Riepen. 1995. Environmental, economic, and social implications of the live reef fish trade in Asia and the western Pacific. The Nature Conservancy.

Jurek, J. and P.J. Scheuer. 1993. Sesquiterpenoids and norsesquiterpenoids from the soft coral *Lemnalia africana*. Journal of Natural Products 56(4): 508.

Kaden, J. 1992. Biological control of algae using crabs. Tropical Fish Hobbyist 40(9): 44.

Kalidindi, R.S. et al. 1994. Pokepola ester: a phosphate diester from a Maui sponge. Tetrahedron Letters 35(31): 5579.

Kaplan, E.H. 1982. *Coral Reefs*. Peterson Field Guide 27. Houghton Mifflin Company, New York, 289 pp.

Kerstich, A. 1991. Living molluscs. Freshwater and Marine Aquarium 14(12): 32.

Kerstich, A. 1992. Crabs in the aquarium. Freshwater and Marine Aquarium 15(2): 24.

Kerstich, A. 1995. Chemical warriors. Freshwater and Marine Aquarium 18(10): 206.

Kleppel, G.S. et al. 1989. Changes in pigmentation associated with the bleaching of stony corals. Limnology and Oceanography 34(7): 1331.

Klostermann, A.F. 1991. The calcium question. Part I. Freshwater and Marine Aquarium 14(4): 78.

Klostermann, A.F. 1991. The calcium question. Part II. Freshwater and Marine Aquarium 14(7): 104.

Kraul, S. 1989. Part 56. Production of live prey for marine fish larvae. In, Advances in Tropical Aquaculture, Tahiti, Aquacop. Infremer, Actes de Colloque 9: 567.

Lamberton, K. 1994. Some perfect marine echinoderms. Freshwater and Marine Aquarium 17(11): 109.

Lamberton, K. 1995. Some perfect marine crustaceans. Freshwater and Marine Aquarium 18(7): 206.

Lansdell, W., B. Dixon, N. Smith, and L. Benjamin. 1993. Isolation of several *Mycobacterium* species from fish. Journal of Aquatic Animal Health 5: 73.

Lee, K.J. et al. 1995. Molecular cloning of a cDNA encoding putative molt-inhibiting hormone from the blue crab, *Callinectes sapidus*. Biochemical and Biophysical Research Communications 209(3): 1126.

Leis, J.M., and T. Trnski. 1989. *The larvae of Indo-Pacific shore fishes*. University of Hawaii Press, Honolulu, HI, 371 pp.

Li, M,K.W., and P.J. Scheuer. 1984. Halogenated blue pigments of a deep sea gorgonian. Tetrahedron Letters 25(6): 587.

Li, M,K.W., and P.J. Scheuer. 1984. A guaianolide pigment from a deep sea gorgonian. Tetrahedron Letters 25(20): 2109.

Li, M,K.W., and P.J. Scheuer. 1984. N,N-dimethylamino-3-guaiazulenylmethane from a deep sea gorgonian. Tetrahedron Letters 25(42): 4707.

Littler, D.S., M.M. Littler, K.E. Bucher, and J.N. Norris. 1989. *Marine Plants of the Caribbean, A Field Guide from Florida to Brazil*. Smithsonian Institution Press, Washington, 263 pp.

Littler, M.M., and D.S. Littler. 1995. Impact of CLOD pathogen on Pacific coral reefs. Science 267: 1356.

Lutnesky, M.M.F. 1994. Density-dependent protogynous sex change in territorial-haremic fishes: models and evidence. Behavioral Ecology 5: 375.

Lutnesky, M.M.F. 1996. Size-dependent rate of protogynous sex change in the pomacanthid angelfish, *Centropyge potteri*. Copeia 1996(1): 209.

Mack, M.E. 1996. Using charcoal in the marine aquarium. Marine Fish Monthly 11(4): 3.

Mancini, A. 1992. Zoanthidae in tropical marine aquariums. Freshwater and Marine Aquarium 15(3): 74.

Mancini, A. 1995. Tropical algae of the genus *Caulerpa* Lamouroux, 1809. Freshwater and Marine Aquarium 18(6): 118.

Manem, J.A., and B.E. Rittmann. 1992. The effects of fluctuations in biodegradable organic matter on nitrification filters. Journal American Water Works Association 84(4): 147.

Mather, P., and I. Bennett. 1994. *A coral reef handbook*. Surrey Beatty & Sons Pty Limited, Chipping Norton, Australia, 262 pp.

McAllister, D.E. 1988. Environmental, economic and social costs of coral reef destruction in the Philippines. Galaxea 7: 161.

McGregor, G. 1996. Cyanobacteria. Freshwater and Marine Aquarium 19(7): 99.

Michael, S.W. 1990. An aquarist's guide to the dottybacks (Genus *Pseudochromis*). Part II. Freshwater and Marine Aquarium 13(11): 16.

Michael, S.W. 1996. Angels of the reef (Pomacanthidae). Aquarium USA (Aquarium Fish Magazine Annual): 22.

Michael, S.W. 1996. Choosing coral. Aquarium Fish Magazine 8(7): 86.

Michael, S.W. 1996. Fishes for the marine aquarium. The dartfishes. Aquarium Fish Magazine 8(12): 19.

Minor, K.I. 1993. Making (small) waves in reef keeping. Freshwater and Marine Aquarium 16(8): 184.

Minor, K.I. 1994. Florida gorgonians. Freshwater and Marine Aquarium 17(11): 152.

Minor, K.I. 1995. What is that? (bubble algae). Freshwater and Marine Aquarium 18(6): 126.

Minor, K.I. 1995. What is that? (sponges). Freshwater and Marine Aquarium 18(7): 112.

Minor, K.I. 1995. What is that? (calcareous algae). Freshwater and Marine Aquarium 18(10): 200.

Moe, M.A., Jr. 1989. *The Marine Aquarium Reference, Systems and Invertebrates*. Green Turtle Publications, Plantation, FL, 510 pp.

Moe, M.A., Jr. 1992. *The Marine Aquarium Handbook, Beginner to Breeder*. Green Turtle Publications, Plantation, FL, 318 pp.

Mohan, P. 1990. Ultraviolet light in the marine reef aquarium. Freshwater and Marine Aquarium 13(1): 4.

Montgomery, B. 1991. Plastic biomedia: myths and misconceptions. Aquarium Fish Magazine 3(12): 46.

Morse, D.E., and A.N.C. Morse. 1993. Marine biotechnology: control of larval metamorphosis, p. 206. In, W. Tien et al. eds., Biotechnology. Development Center for Biotechnology, Taipai.

Mosher, C. 1954. Observations on the spawning behavior and the early larval development of the sargassum fish, *Histrio histrio*. Zoologica 39:141–152.

Nagl, G. 1996. Eliminating H_2S from H_2O. Econ 11(6): 44.

Nilson, A.J. 1990. The successful coral reef aquarium. Freshwater and Marine Aquarium 13(11): 32.

Nilson, A.J. 1990. The successful coral reef aquarium. Freshwater and Marine Aquarium 13(12): 98.

Nilson, A.J. 1991. The successful coral reef aquarium. Freshwater and Marine Aquarium 14(1): 32.

Nilsen, A.J. 1991. The successful coral reef aquarium. Freshwater and Marine Aquarium 14(3): 114.

Nilson, A.J. 1991. Coral reefs and reef aquariums. Part I. Aquarium Fish Magazine 3(12): 18.

Nilson, A.J. 1991. Coral reef vs. reef aquarium. Part II. Aquarium Fish Magazine 4(1): 18.

Noga, E.J. 1995. *Fish Disease— Diagnosis and Treatment*. Mosby, St. Louis, 367 pp.

Nursall, J.R. 1974. Some territorial behavioral attributes of the surgeonfish *Acanthurus lineatus* at Heron Island, Queensland. Copeia 1974(4): 950.

O'Callaghan, M. 1995. Village farmed giant clams. Freshwater and Marine Aquarium 18(4): 8.

Okuda, R.K. et al. 1982. Marine natural products: the past twenty years and beyond. Pure and Applied Chemistry 54(10): 1907.

Paletta, M. 1995. Redox revisited. Aquarium Fish Magazine 7(14): 50.

Paletta, M. 1995. Live sand. Aquarium Fish Magazine 7(12): 60.

Pearl, H.W. 1995. Coastal eutrophication in relation to atmospheric nitrogen deposition: current perspectives. Ophelia 41: 237.

Peters, E.C. et al. 1986. Calicoblastic neoplasms in *Acropora palmata*, with a review of reports on anomalies of growth and form in corals. Journal of the National Cancer Institute 76(5): 895.

Peters, E.C. 1993. Chapter 15. Diseases of other invertebrate phyla: Porifera, Cnidaria, Ctenophora, Annelida, Echinodermata, pp. 393–449. In, J.A. Couch and J.W. Fournie, eds., *Pathobiology of marine and estuarine organisms*. Advances in Fisheries Science. CRC Press, Boca Raton, FL. 552 pp.

Peters, M.J., and J. Wilkerson. 1996. Scarlet cleaner shrimp larval development. Freshwater and Marine Aquarium 19(3): 48.

Pietsch, T.W. 1984. The genera of frogfishes (family Antennariidae). Copeia 1984(1):27–44.

Pietsch, T.W. 1984. A review of the frogfish genus *Rhycherus* with the description of a new species from western and south Australia. Copeia 1984(1):68–72.

Pietsch, T.W. and D.B. Grobecker. 1980. Parental care as an alternative reproductive mode in an antennariid anglerfish. Copeia 1980(3):551–553.

Pontius, F.W. 1996. Regulatory compliance using membrane processes. Journal American Water Works Association 88(5):12.

Rakness, K.L., L.D. DeMers, and B.D. Blank. 1996. Ozone fundamentals for drinking water treatment. Opflow 22(7):1.

Rasquin, P. 1958. Ovarian morphology and early embryology of the pediculate fishes *Antennarius* and *Histrio*. Bulletin of the American

Museum of Natural History 114(4):327–372.

Reed, J.K. 1992. Submersible studies of deep-water *Oculina* and *Lophelia* coral banks off southeastern U.S.A. Proceedings of the American Academy of Underwater Sciences Twelfth Annual Scientific Diving Symposium, UNC-Wilmington, Wilmington, NC, pp.143.

Riddle, D. 1995. Infrared radiation and the reef aquarium. Freshwater and Marine Aquarium 18(4): 176.

Riddle, D. 1995. Life, light and lipids. Part 1. Freshwater and Marine Aquarium 18(6): 194

Riddle, D. 1995. Life, light and lipids. Part 2. Freshwater and Marine Aquarium 18(7): 88.

Riddle, D. 1995. *The Captive Reef. Energy Savers Unlimited.* Harbor City, CA, 297 pp.

Riddle, D. 1996. A simple live sand tank. Marine Fish Monthly 11(3): 37.

Riddle, D. 1996. Opposite ends of the spectrum: ultraviolet and infrared radiation in the reef aquarium. Aquarium Frontiers 3(2): 32.

Ritchie, K.B., and G.W. Smith. 1994. Carbon source utilization patterns of coral associated marine heterotrophs. Third International Marine Biotechnology Conference, Tromsoe Norway: Program and Abstracts: 18.

Robertson, D.R. 1983. On the spawning behavior and spawning cycles of eight surgeonfishes (Acanthuridae) from the Indo-Pacific. Environmental Biology of Fishes 9(3/4): 193.

Roesener, J.A., and P.J. Scheuer. 1986. Ulapualide A and B, extraordinary antitumor macrolides from nudibranch eggmasses. Journal of the American Chemical Society 108: 846.

Ruppert, E.E., and R.D. Barnes. 1994. *Invertebrate Zoology, Sixth Edition.* Saunders College Publishing, Harcourt Brace Publishers, New York, 1,056 pp.

Sale, P.F. 1991. *The Ecology of Fishes on Coral Reefs.* Academic Press, New York, 754 pp.

Schettler, J. 1995. New treatment of gill flukes in marine fish. Freshwater and Marine Aquarium 18(9): 80.

Schiemer, G. 1996. Underwater epoxies for the aquarium. Aquarium Frontiers 3(2): 43.

Schroeder, H. 1991. Polychaetes: worms in the marine aquarium. Freshwater and Marine Aquarium 14(6): 160.

Schultz, L.P. 1964. Three new species of frogfishes from the Indian and Pacific Oceans with notes on other species (Family Antennariidae). Proceedings of the United States National Museum (Smithsonian Institution) 116(3500):171–182.

Shimek, R. 1996. Without a backbone. Aquarium Frontiers 3(1): 2.

Shimek, R. 1996. Without a backbone. Aquarium Frontiers 3(2): 2.

Shimek, R. 1996. Without a backbone. Aquarium Frontiers 3(3): 2.

Shtob, D. 1995. A practical guide to calcium use in a reef aquarium. Aquatica (Brooklyn Aquarium Society), March.

Siddiqui, M.S. and G.L.Amy. 1993. Factors affecting DBP formation during ozone-bromide reactions. Journal American Water Works Association 85(1): 63.

Siddiqui, M.S. et al. 1995. Bromate ion formation: a critical review. Journal American Water Works Association 87(10): 58.

Smith, T.W., and A. Shuman. 1991. The denitrator in the reef aquarium. Freshwater and Marine Aquarium 14(4): 66.

Sprung, J. 1991. Baby mandarin. Freshwater and Marine Aquarium 14(7): 20.

Sprung, J. 1995. Magnificent mangroves. Aquarium Fish Magazine 7(15): 50.

Sprung, J. 1996. Water quality: saltwater. Aquarium Fish Magazine 8(6): 42.

Steslow, F.A. 1991. Ozone kinetics in seawater. Freshwater and Marine Aquarium 14(11): 154.

Strathmann, M.F. 1987. *Reproduction and Development of Marine Invertebrates of the Northern Pacific Coast.* University of Washington Press, Seattle, 670 pp.

Symons, J.M. et al. 1994. Precursor control in waters containing bromide. Journal American Water Works Association 86(6): 48.

Tommasini, R. 1992. Fish math. Freshwater and Marine Aquarium 15(2): 20.

Tommasini, R. 1992. Fish math. Freshwater and Marine Aquarium 15(4): 164.

Tucker, J.W., Jr. 1992. Marine fish nutrition. In: G.L. Allan and W. Dall (Editors), Proceedings of Aquaculture Nutrition Workshop, Salamander Bay, 15–17 April 1991. NSW Fisheries, Brackish Water Fish Culture Research Station, Salamander Bay, Australia, pp. 25–40.

Tucker, J.W., Jr. 1992. Feeding intensively-cultured marine fish larvae. In: G.L. Allan and W. Dall (Editors), Proceedings of Aquaculture Nutrition Workshop, Salamander Bay, 15-17 April 1991. NSW Fisheries, Brackish Water Fish Culture Research Station, Salamander Bay, Australia, pp. 129–146.

Tullock, J. 1992. Successful saltwater aquariums. Part 3. Aquarium Fish Magazine 4(6): 18.

Tullock, J. 1992. Successful saltwater aquariums. Part 6. Aquarium Fish Magazine 4(9): 18.

Tullock, J. 1996. All about anemones, part I. Aquarium Fish Magazine 8(4): 48.

Turk, C., and D. Bartley. 1990. Marine fish and invertebrate nutrition. Part IV. Surgeonfish and damselfish. Freshwater and Marine Aquarium 13(1): 96.

UNEP/IUCN. 1988. *Coral Reefs of the World*. Volume 1: Atlantic and Eastern Pacific. United Nations Environment Programme, Regional Seas Directories and Bibiographies. IUCN, Gland, Switzerland and Cambridge, U.K./Nairobi, Kenya. 373 pp.

UNEP/IUCN. 1988. *Coral Reefs of the World*. Volume 2: Indian Ocean, Red Sea, and Gulf. United Nations Environment Programme, Regional Seas Directories and Bibiographies. IUCN, Gland, Switzerland and Cambridge, U.K./ Nairobi, Kenya. 389 pp.

UNEP/IUCN. 1988. *Coral Reefs of the World*. Volume 3: Central and Western Pacific. United Nations Environment Programme, Regional Seas Directories and Bibiographies. IUCN, Gland, Switzerland and Cambridge, U.K./Nairobi, Kenya. 329 pp.

US EPA. 1988. Short-term methods for estimating the chronic toxicity of effluents and receiving waters to marine and estuarine organisms. EPA 600 4–87 028.

Vallejo, B.M., Jr. 1996. Aquarium culture of giant clams. Journal of Maquaculture 4(3): 7.

Vargas, T. 1995. *Acropora*: the reef builder. Freshwater and Marine Aquarium 18(5): 144.

Verloop, R., and R. Ates. 1992. *Nephthea*. Freshwater and Marine Aquarium 15(7): 26.

Veron, J.E.N. 1993. *Corals of Australia and the Indo-Pacific*. University of Hawaii Press, 644 pp.

Veron, J.E.N. 1995. Corals in space and time. Comstock/Cornell, Ithaca and London, 321 pp.

Volkart, B. 1990. Disease control in marine aquaria. Freshwater and Marine Aquarium 13(11): 4.

Volkart, B. 1991. Controlling excess algae in reef aquaria. Freshwater and Marine Aquarium 14(6): 115.

Volkart, B. 1992. Shedding light on coral requirements. Tropical Fish Hobbyist 40(9): 34.

Voss, G.L. 1976. *Seashore Life of Florida and the Caribbean*. E.A. Seeman Publishing, Miami, 168 pp.

Walker, K.F. 1981. A synopsis of ecological information on the saline lake rotifer *Brachionus plicatilis* Muller 1786. Hydrobiologia 81: 159.

Warner, M., and W.K. Fitt. 1991. Mechanisms of bleaching of zooxanthellate symbioses. American Zoologist 31(5): 28A.

Watts, M. 1994. Live rock reborn. Freshwater and Marine Aquarium 17(11): 176.

Watts, M. 1995. Up to your neck in sand. Freshwater and Marine Aquarium 18(12): 96.

Weingarten, R.A. 1991. *Tridacna*, the giant clam. Freshwater and Marine Aquarium 14(2): 101.

Weingarten, R.A. 1991. Sexual/reproductive patterns in Caribbean wrasses (Labridae). Freshwater and Marine Aquarium 14(12): 123.

Wiley, R.W. 1984. A review of sodium cyanide for use in sampling stream fishes. North American Journal of Fisheries Management 4: 249.

Wilkins, P. 1989. Tropical shrimps in the marine aquarium. Tropical Fish Hobbyist 38(3): 54.

Wilkens, P. 1995. Sexual reproduction of a firecoral (*Millepora alcicornis*). Aquarium Fish Magazine 2(4): 10.

Wilkerson, J. 1996. Fish mariculture 1996. Marine Scene 7(1): 6.

Williams, E.H., Jr., and L. Bunkley-Williams. 1990. *The world-wide coral reef bleaching cycle and related sources of coral mortality*. Atoll Research Bulletin 335, National Museum of Natural History, Smithsonian Institution, Washington, D.C., 71 pp.

Wrobel, D. 1992. Native marine invertebrates in the home aquarium. Freshwater and Marine Aquarium 15(5): 136.

Young, F.A. 1995. Aquarium cultivation of *Cassiopeia*. Freshwater and Marine Aquarium 18(6): 62.

Zeiller, W. 1974. *Tropical Marine Invertebrates of Southern Florida and the Bahama Islands*. John Wiley & Sons, New York, 132 pp.

Glossary

Å Ångstrom, 10^{-10} meter

absorption removal by consumption

acid-fast staining characteristic of some bacteria

acontia fighting tentacles, extended digestive tract filaments

acrorhagi stinging sweeper tentacles

actinic blue wavelength of light used by actinarians (cnidarians or relatives of sea anemones)

activated carbon carbon treated with high temperatures

adsorption removal by adherance

aerobic living in an oxygen-rich atmosphere

ahermatypic coral without symbiotic algae in its tissues

alanine an amino acid

allelopathic toxic to related animals

anaerobic, anoxic devoid of oxygen

anion a negatively charged ion

anthropogenic of human origin

aragonite form of calcium carbonate containing strontium, found in hard corals

archaeocyte amoeboid feeding cell of a sponge

benthic living on the bottom

benthos life on the bottom

bifurcate branched

bioballs plastic cubes or spheres with extensive surfaces and open areas for colonization by aerobic bacteria

blue-green algae cyanobacteria

byssus silky filament secreted by mussels for attachment

calcareous containing calcium carbonate and calcium phosphate

calcite form of calcium carbonate in many shellfish

carbonate carbonic acid

cation a positively charged ion

cavitation effect when a water pump accidentally draws in air, and the propellers spin uselessly

cc cubic centimeter, same as milliliter

chelation ionic chemical bonding that can either be used to keep a substance in solution or to take it out of solution

chitin repeating, cross-linked mucopolysaccharide shell of crustaceans

choanocyte internal flagellated cell of a sponge

cnidarian coelenterate, phylum of corals

cnidocyte firing cell of a coral

commensal two species opportunistically living together with no harm to either

coprophagous feeding on feces

corallite aragonite cup holding a coral polyp

corallum stony skeleton of a colonial coral, connected corallites

CRI color rendering index

cyanobacteria algaelike life with characteristics of bacteria

deionization removal of minerals having two or three positive charges from tap water using chemicals having a negative charge

denitrification anaerobic or microaerophilic conversion of nitrate to nitrogen gas

deposit feeder a creature that feeds on detritus, mud or silt

detritus decomposing plant fragments

DH one of three terms (dH, GH, KH) used for the German scale of alkalinity

DHA dodecohexaenoic acid, the most important HUFA

DI deionized (water)

diatom fast-growing, nuisance golden-brown algae

diatomaceous earth powdered glasslike shells of fossil diatoms

diploid having a set of maternal and a set of paternal chromosomes in each cell

DOC dissolved organic compounds (secreted by animals and plants)

dolomite ancient form of calcium carbonate

echinoderm animals of the phylum Echinodermata, including sea stars, sea cucumbers, brittle stars, sea urchins, and sand dollars

EDTA ethylenediaminetetraacetic acid, a binder of cations

elasmobranchs the cartilagenous sharks, rays, and skates

El Nino year in which Pacific Ocean surface temperatures are altered from normal, resulting in widespread atmospheric disturbances that produce unusually heavy rains in some parts of the world and drought in others

enzyme a protein that catalyzes a specific reaction

EPA eicosapentaenoic acid, an important HUFA

epibenthic growing on the surface of the bottom

epiphytic growing on the surface of plants

errant actively roaming

eutrophic characterized by high levels of nitrates and phosphates

foam fractionater protein skimmer

GAC granular activated carbon

gametes eggs and sperm

gemmation type of coral asexual reproduction in which the polyp divides at the base

gph gallons per hour

GH one of three terms (dH, GH, KH) used for German scale of alkalinity

Gram-negative, Gram-positive staining characteristics of bacteria

H+ hydrogen ion or proton, the essence of acidity

haploid each cell having a single set of chromosomes from one parent only

head pressure pump output in pounds per square inch; for water pumps, an indicator of how high water can be pushed; for air pumps, an indicator of how deeply air can be pushed below water level

hermaphrodite having both male and female sex organs

hermatypic coral containing symbiotic algae in its tissues

HO high output (fluorescent lamp)

HUFA omega 3 highly unsaturated fatty acids

hydrometer instrument that measures the dissolved mineral content of a solution compared with the absence of minerals in distilled water

hypoxic deficient in oxygen

infauna minute animal community living within sand or gravel

IR infrared (radiation)

isoprene 2-methyl butadiene, a natural fat soluble hydrocarbon

isoyake edible coralline red algae

Kalkwasser German for limewater, or calcium hydroxide solution

KH one of three terms (dH, GH, KH) used for the German scale of alkalinity

limewater solution of calcium hydroxide; Kalkwasser

live sand submersed reef sand containing living meiofauna

lumens illuminence or instantaneous output of a light source

lux lumens per square meter reaching a target

lysine an amino acid

macroalgae plantlike attached algae

malacologist mollusc scientist

meandrine, meandroid with ridges meandering like a river

meiofauna infauna capable of passing through a 0.1 mm screen

meq/L milliequivalents per liter, a measure of the amount of alkali or base required to neutralize a specific level of acidity

mesohyl central mostly acellular layer in a sponge

mg/L milligrams (thousandths of a gram by weight) per liter of volume

microalgae microscopic algae in water or as surface scum

microaerophilic living in a very low oxygen atmosphere

milliliter thousandth of a liter, same as a cubic centimeter or cc

minor element occurring in micrograms per liter (μg/L)

monocentric with a single center

monotypic genus containing only one species

mucopolysaccharide a complex carbohydrate combined with a peptide

mulm aquarium term for layer of sediment composed of solid animal wastes

nanometer (nm) 10^{-9} meter; one billionth of a meter

nauplius early larval stage in some invertebrates (plural, nauplii)

nematocyst stinging cnidocyte

nematosome minute cnidarian internal organ containing a coiled filament

neurotransmitter chemical triggering impulses between nerve cells

nitrification aerobic conversion of ammonia to nitrite or nitrite to nitrate

⁻OH hydroxyl ion, the principal form of alkalinity

oolite type of calcium carbonate secreted by corals and algae

ophiopluteus larva of a basket star

organic containing carbon and hydrogen atoms

organophosphate class of agricultural pesticides

O-ring cylindrical rubberlike seal often shaped as a circle

orthophosphate inorganic phosphate, a plant nutrient

osculum discharge port of a sponge colony

PAC powdered activated carbon

PAR photosynthetically active radiation (part of spectrum) used by plants

parapodium side appendage of a polychaete worm

pelagic drifting or swimming in the water column of the ocean

peptide short chain of amino acids

percent parts per hundred (o/o)

Perciformes the largest group of modern (advanced) bony fishes (teleosts), containing typically fish-shaped families such as the perches, damsels, cichlids, sunfishes, and many others, but not containing the flounders, puffers, pipefishes, herrings, minnows, tetras, or eels

pH negative logarithm of the hydrogen ion concentration, used to distinguish acidic solutions (pH below 7.0) from alkaline solutions (pH above 7.0)

pheromone hormonal attractant emitted to air or water, detectable by the opposite sex in minute concentrations often at great distances

photic zone depth range within which algae can photosynthesize

phycology study of algae

phytoplankton minute drifting aquatic algae

piscivorous fish-eating

planktivorous plankton eater

planula swimming larval stage of a coral

polycentric with several centers

polyp the individual animal within a coral colony, or living alone rather than as a member of a colony

polysaccharide large carbohydrate molecule composed of sugars

polyvalent ionized with more than one charge, e.g., Ca^{++}

porocyte sponge cell with a hole to allow intake of water

powerhead small submersible water pump

ppm parts per million

ppt parts per thousand (o/oo)

protandrous hermaphrodite male first, changing to a female

protein a specific assemblage of peptides

protein skimmer foam fractionater

protogynous hermaphrodite female first, changing to a male

radula rasping band of teeth in gastropods

reef sand pulverized aragonite

RO reverse osmosis (water)

sessile immobile or attached on the bottom

setae bristles, as on polychaete worms

sintered fractured composite (glass)

speciose consisting of many species

spirocyst sticky cnidocyte

SPS small polyp stony (corals), a group requiring intense light

SRP soluble reactive phosphate = dissolved orthophosphate

substrate, substrates the substance(s) acted upon by an enzyme

substratum, substrata bottom(s), such as sand, gravel, or rock

sugar alcohol a nutrient derived from sugar

sump a spare aquarium or other container used as a reservoir beside or below the display aquarium

supermale in some fish groups like the wrasses, males and females of a population spawn mostly in groups, but a few very large and differently colored males (supermales) spawn as individuals with a single female at a time

symbiotic intimate biological dependency between unrelated species that may be obligatory or not, and benefit one or both species

Tc contact time (reaction time)

teleosts bony typical fish

terpene polymer of isoprene, e.g., diterpene, sesquiterpene, etc.

terpenoid terpene-derived, e.g, camphor, lemon oil, carotene, phytol (of chlorophyll), lanosterol, many marine toxins, etc.

titration drop-by-drop addition of a reagent, where the number of drops to the color change times a factor gives the value sought

trace element less than 1 microgram per liter (μg/L)

tridacnids family of Pacific clams that includes giant clams

trochophore early stage mollusc larva

UV ultraviolet light

UV-A 4,000–3,200 Å, low energy

UV-B 3,200–2,800 Å, moderate energy

UV-C 3,200–1,900 Å, high energy

venturi suction created by change in pressure

veliger late stage mollusc larva

VHO very high output (fluorescent lamp)

w/v weight to volume, as in ten percent or ten milligrams in 100 milliliters

zooplankton minute drifting aquatic animals

zooxanthellae symbiotic members of the dinoflagellate algae

zygote fertilized egg

Index